Women's Rights
DOCUMENTS DECODED

The ABC-CLIO series *Documents Decoded* guides readers on a hunt for new secrets through an expertly curated selection of primary sources. Each book pairs key documents with in-depth analysis, all in an original and visually engaging side-by-side format. But *Documents Decoded* authors do more than just explain each source's context and significance—they give readers a front-row seat to their own investigation and interpretation of each essential document line-by-line.

Women's Rights
DOCUMENTS DECODED

Aimee D. Shouse

Documents Decoded

 ABC-CLIO

Library of Congress Cataloging-in-Publication Data

Shouse, Aimee D.
  Women's rights : documents decoded / Aimee D. Shouse.
    pages cm. — (Documents decoded)
  ISBN 978-1-61069-199-4 (hardback) — ISBN 978-1-61069-200-7 (ebook)
 1. Women's rights—United States. I. Title.
  HQ1236.5.U6S55 2014
  305.420973—dc23   2013023941

ISBN: 978-1-61069-199-4
EISBN: 978-1-61069-200-7

18 17 16 15 14   1 2 3 4 5

This book is also available on the World Wide Web as an eBook.
Visit www.abc-clio.com for details.

ABC-CLIO, LLC
130 Cremona Drive, P.O. Box 1911
Santa Barbara, California 93116-1911

This book is printed on acid-free paper ♾
Manufactured in the United States of America

Contents

CHAPTER 5: WOMEN AND VIOLENCE 119

CHAPTER 6: WOMEN'S RIGHTS IN THE 21ST CENTURY 143

Debating Contraceptive Coverage in the Affordable Care Act, 163
Remarks of Representatives Darrell Issa and Carolyn Maloney at Hearings of the House
Committee on Oversight and Government Reform
February 16, 2012

A Mississippi Ballot Initiative to Change the Definition of Personhood, 167
Voters' Guide to Arguments for and against Mississippi's Initiative No. 26
Summer 2011

Senator Leahy Urges Reauthorization of the Violence Against Women Act, 170
Statements of Senator Pat Leahy
May 16 and December 20, 2012

Preface

MOST STUDENTS IN THE UNITED STATES TODAY HAVE GROWN UP in a country in which men and women are considered more or less equal. Women's rights have become the status quo, and the struggle for women's rights is considered to be merely one more facet of our country's history, something celebrated during March of each year for Women's History Month. What students may not perceive, however, is that our government still considers issues that directly relate to women's rights. The difficulty comes in allowing students to see that the historical aspects of women's struggle for equal rights are simply the early stages of a continuum that spans into current times. The struggle hasn't ended; it has simply changed. In *Women's Rights: Documents Decoded,* this history of women's rights is deciphered to make it relevant to contemporary times, illustrating that while many issues of rights have indeed been settled, the fundamental questions asked about women's rights are still being posed as new issues rise in importance.

In the Introduction to this book, students and readers are provided a framework for understanding women's rights in the context of men's rights and broader human rights. Theories about the source of rights are discussed, including how men were often assumed to simply have rights, while women were reliant on the government to give them these same rights. Additionally, the Introduction includes feminist critiques of women's accepted roles across history and how they have served to justify women's inferior positions relative to men. These frameworks will help students better grasp the arguments that are made by both supporters and detractors of women's rights as they read through the various issues of women's rights presented in *Women's Rights: Documents Decoded.* The Introduction also includes a current snapshot of women in American society today, reflecting the advances they have made in their fight for equality as well as where women's rights still fall short.

There are five broad themes addressed in *Women's Rights: Documents Decoded:* women and work, women and education, women and politics, women's health and reproduction, and women and violence. Within each theme, excerpts from original policy statements are included to illustrate not only the specific issues for which women fought but also how women and their access to rights were perceived and addressed by those in positions of power. The policy statements are taken from such sources as

U.S. Supreme Court opinions, witness testimony at congressional hearings, floor statements by members of both the U.S. House of Representatives and the U.S. Senate, and presidential statements. These issues are ordered chronologically within each theme, allowing the evolution in women's rights to be more easily perceived. Just as important as seeing how women's rights have changed, though, is seeing how some of the arguments about women and their rights have not changed all that much across time.

In fact, many of the same concerns about women's equality that are discussed today, such as on issues regarding equal pay or combating violence against women, are remarkably similar to the concerns raised more than a century ago. The context and the specific issues under consideration have changed, but the underlying questions remain the same. For instance, across many of the issues, readers will see speakers address the very nature of what it means to be a woman, and often this nature is defined by motherhood. If women are perpetually seen as mothers or even potential mothers, this can affect how women's rights are perceived in relation to men's rights. This issue was raised in some of the earliest policy statements included in *Women's Rights: Documents Decoded,* such as the concurrent opinion of Supreme Court associate justice Joseph P. Bradley in *Bradwell v. Illinois* (1872), in which he agrees that women could be prohibited from becoming lawyers, as well as in some of the most recent issues, such as the National Science Foundation's policy in 2011 to promote family and workplace balance for people, but particularly women, employed in the fields of science and technology. Similarly, another theme that is seen across time and the different issues is the behavior that is considered appropriate for women as compared to men. This was seen when John Dewey argued in 1885 that it was not detrimental to women for them to pursue a college degree as well as when the Supreme Court decided that universities could eliminate sports programs for men in order to provide equal sports opportunities for women in 1999, in *Neal v. Board of Trustees of the California State Universities.* In both cases, opponents questioned whether higher education or access to sports was appropriate or necessary for women.

Women's Rights: Documents Decoded provides a background to issues that are associated with women's rights, which will enable students and readers to understand some of the most important documents in the field, a skill that is useful to many disciplines. Given the range of years from which these policy statements are selected, *Women's Rights: Documents Decoded* will be of particular use to students of American history. Less evident, perhaps, is the benefit of this volume for people who study public policy, political science, and women's studies. Taken collectively, the five themes illustrate the common barriers that exist across policy areas hindering the attainment of women's equality. This would be useful for readers interested in applying feminist theories to the practical problems faced by women in society and the political arena. Taken individually, each theme gives a glimpse into the politics behind women's rights in a specific policy area. Students interested in an area of public policy such as education or law enforcement could benefit by honing in on a particular chapter that provides some depth into that policy area. More narrowly, the analysis of each individual policy statement provides rich context to the issue and also draws out the political strategies and rhetoric used by politicians and others with an interest in these issues. Students who are interested in the art of politics will be able to see how different political interests attempt to frame issues in ways that most benefit them. *Women's Rights: Documents Decoded* will provide a variety of students with useful resources for their own research.

Introduction

Women's Rights: A Brief Explanation of Difference

In 1949, French feminist and philosopher Simone de Beauvoir wrote what has become a classic in feminist theory. In *The Second Sex,* Beauvoir explores how men have been placed at the center of society throughout history, while women are peripheral to what is even considered the human experience. The male experience has shaped our perceptions of humanity itself, while women's experiences are seen as unique to women and not representative of the human experience as a whole. In short, humans are male, while females are the other, or second, sex. This observation is not unique to Beauvoir. In *Public Man, Private Woman: Women in Social and Political Thought* (1981), American scholar Jean Bethke Elshtain similarly asserts that men and women occupy different spheres of existence: the public sphere of political influence is the domain of men, while the private sphere of domestic life is the realm of women. Like Beauvoir, Elshtain claims that throughout history, the public sphere has been perceived as superior to the private sphere, defined as more important and even more interesting than the private sphere. Given men's position in the public sphere, they have generally held more power than women and have defined the very roles that are considered appropriate for women. The roles permitted for women have typically benefitted men and allowed them to maintain their relative positions of privilege over women.

Although there are clearly innate physical differences between males and females, it is less clear whether the social differences described by Beauvoir and Elshtain, among others, are also innate or if they have been created by human society. If women's and men's differing behaviors and roles occur naturally, referred to as essentialism, then men and women are simply playing out the roles that nature—or God—intended them to play. In fact, advocates for essentialism have argued, both historically and contemporarily, that men should occupy positions of power relative to women in politics, in business, and in the family if they are inherently more suited to those roles. In contrast, if differences in gender roles are social constructs, or dependent on the society in which they emerge, women's and men's behaviors would be able to change to reflect changes in society, and these changes could actually be changed intentionally. Thus, barriers that have kept women in inferior positions relative to men can be dismantled through laws or social movements for change.

It may be that the explanation for men's and women's relative positions in society is some combination of essentialism and social construction, but it is not always easy to identify why humans are the way they are. What can be done, however, is to examine what has changed and what has not changed. Exploring the changes in women's rights in the United States is an excellent way to see how women's and men's relative positions of power have changed over time and to witness the different arguments made for why women should or should not be granted certain rights. The issue of rights actually illustrates well the very phenomena discussed by Beauvoir and Elshtain. Whenever groups have sought their rights from government, the people in the government who make the decisions typically already have the rights being sought by a given group. Thus, when women have sought equal rights in the United States, it has most often been men, who already have the particular rights being sought, who get to decide if women get the same rights.

This raises a question of why Americans think they are entitled to rights. Do people have rights simply because they are human, or does the government give them their rights? The founders of the United States, exemplified for instance by Thomas Jefferson's Declaration of Independence, held that people had certain rights simply by virtue of being human. Rights such as "life, liberty, and the pursuit of happiness" were not granted to the people by the government but instead existed apart from government and were ultimately protected from government intrusion by the addition of the Bill of Rights to the U.S. Constitution. But it is clear from the country's history that these so-called God-given rights were assumed to exist only for some people, namely white men. As early as 1848, Elizabeth Cady Stanton wrote the Declaration of Sentiments and Resolutions at the first women's rights conference in Seneca Falls, New York. The document outlined the many ways that women were kept subordinate to men and was modeled on the Declaration of Independence, underscoring the many ways that Jefferson's vision had fallen short for women. The rights of slaves, African Americans, Native Americans, and women have all been approached differently than the rights assumed to exist for white men. History shows us that the rights of these groups were not simply assumed to exist but were instead dependent on the decisions of people in positions of power. The rights of marginalized people were in essence bestowed by others rather than seen as simply existing because they were human.

A complicating factor for women, however, has been the physiological differences between males and females. Can men and women be equal if they are not the same? Can the concept of equality accommodate differences, for instance, in the reproductive functions of women and men? Many of the differences in the rights accorded to men and women throughout the country's history have been justified by the fact that women can become pregnant and bear children. For instance, until the 1960s, government policies on women's rights to work were premised on the idea that women needed to be protected due to the physical demands of pregnancy and motherhood. These maternal roles were considered the primary functions of women, while working outside the home was the primary role for men. Consequently, it was acceptable to treat male and female employees differently in their pay and in the types of jobs they could hold because of this key difference between the sexes. In contrast, advocates for women's rights have generally argued that these protective policies provide a justification for discrimination against women. The only way to eliminate discrimination, it was argued, was to treat women and men largely the same under the law. Even now, there is no absolute consensus on how to reconcile women's and men's physical differences with the demand for equal rights. The dilemma is this: Does equality for men and women permit specific accommodations for pregnancy, childbirth, and the responsibilities of motherhood, or does equality require that men and women be treated the same? This dilemma has been considered time and again throughout the country's history, and the answers provided to this question have varied across time.

Women's Rights: Contemporary Challenges and Successes

It is this dilemma of how to accommodate women's and men's differences while still providing equal rights that continues to shape discussions of women's rights. In some cases, protecting the rights of women is addressed by simply requiring by law that sex is treated as an irrelevant factor. In short, equality for women is ensured by treating women and men the same. For instance, the policy that makes it illegal to discriminate based on sex in employment decisions is relatively straightforward. Title VII of the Civil Rights Act of 1964 states in short that sex cannot be used as a determinant in employment decisions; in other words, men and women should be treated the same. However, rights become more difficult to identify and protect when circumstances apply solely, or primarily, to only one sex. In the case of reproductive rights, for instance, it may not be clear what actually constitutes equality, since only women can become pregnant. The situations that women face as a result of their reproductive abilities are not comparable to situations faced by men. Thus, it may be difficult to determine what a woman's rights are in some circumstances because equality has to be conceptualized differently. Rather than understanding equal rights as women being treated the same as men, the relevant measure of equality would be fairness. Fairness would result when the attributes that women and men each bring to humanity are equally valued. This approach to equal rights would allow men's and women's differences to be accommodated under the law without giving one sex supremacy over the other.

This change in how equality is conceptualized may in part explain the political conflict that surrounds women's reproductive rights. The assertion that women have a right to control their reproduction is susceptible to challenge, in part because these are not rights that apply to men and women equally. Since 1973 when the U.S. Supreme Court overturned state laws prohibiting abortions, women's reproductive rights have been one of the most contentious, divisive issues on the American political landscape. Those who support women's reproductive rights have made the more traditional comparison to men's rights, claiming that until women can control their own reproduction, they will never have the same access to rights that men have. Thus, advocates would argue that reproductive rights are foundational to all other rights that women have obtained. Opponents of abortion, on the other hand, have contrasted women's rights not with men's rights but instead with the rights of the unborn. The extent to which the unborn have rights in the same way that women have rights is a debatable issue, but antiabortion groups reject that women can be the same as men on issues of reproduction without infringing on the rights of the fetus. Thus, such groups would argue that women do not actually have the right to an abortion because it illegitimately infringes on the rights of others. Although abortion remains legal in the United States, opponents have won victories in the states that limit women's access to the procedure, and the highly charged political environment surrounding the issue has resulted in fewer physicians deciding to provide abortions. The result of these changes has been a decrease in the number of abortions performed. Between 2000 and 2009, the number of abortions declined by 6 percent.

Similarly, violence against women has raised some new questions regarding women's rights that are as challenging to address as those regarding reproductive rights. Although men are much more likely to be victims of violence than women, women are significantly more likely to be victims of certain types of violence, namely sexual violence and violence committed by an intimate partner. For instance, the Centers for Disease Control and Prevention reports that 18.1 percent of all women in the United States have been raped. Half of those women have been raped by an intimate partner, and more than three-fourths of these women were first raped before the age of 25. The Violence Against Women Act, passed originally in 1994 and reauthorized most recently in 2013, specifically addresses the gendered nature of these types of crimes. But for many women's rights groups, the issue of violence against women brings to light a new type of problem regarding women's rights: the prevailing culture of the United States objectifies women's bodies and portrays women as existing for the pleasure of men. This has contributed to a culture that is not only plagued by sexual violence but also often blames the victim for the violence that was committed against her. This is not a problem that can easily be addressed by legislation in the way that Title VII addressed employment discrimination. While the Violence Against Women Act attempts to provide resources to law enforcement and social service agencies to combat sexual violence and its effects on victims, advocates for women's rights have taken steps to counter the prevailing attitudes toward women that contribute to the country's so-called rape culture. Events such as "Take Back the Night" held on college campuses and the more controversial "Slut Walks" taking place around the world have challenged the notion that women can have equality in a culture that victimizes them and then subsequently blames them.

Despite these continued challenges, women in the United States have made tremendous inroads toward achieving equal rights. Looking at women in the workforce, 58.6 percent of women over the age of 16 are in the workforce, up from about 35 percent in 1950. Despite the relatively high unemployment rates in the United States in the early 2010s, women's unemployment rate was virtually the same as men's, with women experiencing a 7.3 percent rate of unemployment, compared to men's unemployment rate of 7.2 percent. Thus, women as a whole are not more likely to be unemployed than men even when the economy is suffering. Similarly, women have made amazing advances in education, graduating with more degrees than men at every level of higher education. During the 2009–2010 academic year, 57 percent of bachelor's degrees were awarded to women; for master's and doctorate degrees, the rate of women graduating was 63 percent and 53 percent, respectively. These general trends in higher education apply to white, black, and Hispanic women. One measure of success for high school girls is their access to varsity sports opportunities. In 1972, only 1 in 27 girls participated in high school varsity sports; by 2012, 2 out of 5 girls were participating in high school varsity sports. This has translated into more women playing sports at the collegiate level, where there has been a 500 percent increase in the number of sports opportunities open to women. One striking consequence of this increase in girls' and women's participation in sports was seen at the 2012 Olympic Games, where the majority of athletes on Team American were women and 58 percent of American gold medal winners were women.

Yet given the continued discussions of women's rights, it is clear that success has not been absolute. As discussed above, two of the most prominent current issues related to women's rights are also two of the most difficult to address, either because the issue is so politically charged, as in the case of reproductive rights, or because the issue is so pervasive in our culture that it is difficult to change, as in the case of violence against women. One explanation for these continued challenges to women's rights is the scarcity in the number of women who serve in elective office in the United States. With so few women in political office, it may be harder for women's unique perspectives to be represented among policy makers. For instance, in 2013, women in the U.S. Congress are a small minority of members, with only 18 percent of the House of Representatives and 20 percent of the Senate being women. Looking at state legislatures, the numbers are not much better. While the percentage of women serving in state legislatures varies from state to state, on average only 24 percent of these positions are held by women. Lower still, only 10 percent of the states' governors are women.

This book considers some of the major issues of women's rights in the United States. In Chapters 1–5, women's rights in five policy areas are considered, including rights in regard to women's employment, education, politics, health and reproduction, and violence. Each chapter considers several major issues for women's rights, including original policy statements and commentary to explain the context of the particular question of rights. Consistent with Beauvoir's and Elshtain's assertions, it can be seen that questions of how women differ from men are relevant in the vast majority of the issues considered. These differences have often defined women, especially in regard to what rights they are granted. As will be seen in the first five chapters, it has been difficult for women to define themselves in ways that do not simply contrast them to men. Chapter 6, which looks at more current issues in the five different policy areas, makes apparent that questions regarding the rights of women have not been resolved but simply have changed to reflect new problems and situations faced by women.

Note that primary sources have been printed here as the originals, without attempt to "clean-up" typos or other rough text.

Chapter 1

Women and Work

Introduction

With the exception of the right to vote, it could be argued that gaining access to work outside the home was one of the most important rights that women secured in the United States. Not only does paid employment provide a means of financial independence, but it can also provide a sense of fulfillment and the realization of one's abilities. Although women have always worked, their access to work for wages has historically been denied or severely constrained in the United States. Even in current times, women and men still largely work in sex-segregated jobs, with women more likely to work in traditionally female, or pink-collar, occupations. Women also continue to earn on average 20 percent less than men. These limitations are due in large part to society's perception of the appropriate roles and tasks for women and men. Traditional gender role expectations provide a clear division between work that is done outside the home for pay, largely the domain of men, and domestic work done inside the home, typically the responsibility of women. Most specifically, the role of mother has dominated all other roles expected of women, which is often seen in government and employer policies related to female employees. Policy makers often equate mothers' interests with women's interests, although not all women are mothers.

Prior to the Industrial Revolution, the unpaid labor of working at home was crucially important to the survival of the family. Even though certain household tasks were seen as women's jobs, providing food, maintaining a household, and caring for children were often physically demanding jobs that required skill and knowledge to accomplish. The Industrial Revolution brought about changes both in the types of paid labor that were available and the type of work required in a household. Mass production provided employment in urban areas to more people, including women, but the work was long, poorly paid, and often dangerous. Yet even when poor and immigrant women worked in factories for wages, as many of them did, they still had traditional responsibilities at home, and the fact that these women were working outside the home was seen as an unfortunate circumstance that poor women had to endure in order to survive. Even as women started moving into the workforce in greater numbers during the 20th century out of either necessity or desire, the so-called ideal image of the feminine woman was still centered squarely on her place within the home. As such, many of the early government policies regarding the working conditions of female employees considered how to best protect women's most important roles, which were those of motherhood and domestic life.

After the American Civil War, as more women moved into the labor force, state governments became concerned with the working conditions of women and passed what is referred to as protective legislation, such as limiting women's working hours to no more than 10 hours a day, proscribing how long they could stand on the job in a day, and limiting the types of jobs that women could do. These policies were ostensibly designed to protect women's health and morals, but policy makers were also mindful of protecting women's abilities to bear and care for children. The perceptions of a proper feminine woman and her ultimate domestic responsibilities clearly shaped lawmakers' perceptions of women as employees as well.

While these protective policies were met with support from early women's rights organizations who recognized that female employees had greater responsibilities at home once they left work, employers were less supportive of these laws, arguing that they infringed upon employers' rights to determine their own business practices. Because these laws required employers to treat their female and male employees differently and give greater protections to women, hiring women was more costly. Several state laws were challenged as unconstitutional violations of the Fourteenth Amendment, but in 1908 the U.S. Supreme Court ruled in *Muller v. Oregon* that women's inherently weaker physical structure and their proper reliance on men for their well-being justified the intrusion of the state into employers' business practices. It was this perception of women's different needs as employees that prompted Congress to create the Women's Bureau in 1920 to oversee labor practices from the perspective of women employees and to make sure that their unique needs were accommodated.

By the mid-20th century, women's rights groups recognized that there were negative consequences to these protective policies, such as an unwillingness of employers to hire women into more highly paid positions or even hire women at all. As such, some women's rights advocates moved from supporting policies that claimed to protect women to supporting equal rights for women. This change in perspective, from protecting women to protecting women's rights, reflected other monumental changes that were also taking place in American society during the mid-20th century. First, more women were continuing with their education after high school by going to college. Thus, there was an increase in the number of women graduating with college degrees who were finding few or no jobs available to them that were commensurate with their level of education. Second, domestic life had changed with the advent of time-saving devices, such as washing machines and vacuum cleaners. Consequently, women had considerably more time on their hands than they did in the years where cleaning clothes and floors required a great deal of time and strenuous physical labor. Third, the Civil Rights Movement was gaining momentum in American society, highlighting racial discrimination in employment and education and consequently drawing attention to other forms of discrimination.

The 1963 publication of *The Feminine Mystique* by Betty Friedan seemed to punctuate this shift in perspectives among women. Friedan was the first to articulate "the problem that has no name," the fact that many women, especially educated women, found the traditional roles of staying home and focusing on children and housework to be unfulfilling. Obviously, having to stay home and take care of children had not been a problem for poor women, who had been in the workforce for nearly a century by the time Friedan published her book. However, Friedan touched a nerve among women who on the surface met society's expectations of women in their proper domestic roles but felt held back from their full potential as a result of these roles. The realization that the inequality between men's and women's employment opportunities was something imposed on women by traditional gender roles and was not due to any inherent limitations of their sex prompted the women's movement that has continued to shape women's work opportunities in the United States.

The women's rights movement of the 1960s and 1970s, often referred to as the second wave of feminism, focused on two key rights: equality between women and men in employment and equality in education. But it was the focus on women's rights to employment that really initiated this social movement toward greater women's rights. In particular, women wanted equality on the job, such as equal pay when they were doing the same jobs as men, and they wanted equality in gaining access to jobs for which they met the qualifications. More precisely, they did not want their sex to be a consideration in determining whether or not they were qualified for a position. The women's rights movement was ultimately able to get equality written into the laws. However, as straightforward as this sounds, equality can be a difficult standard to measure. Is equality being treated identically, or can the differences between men and women be accommodated, with men and women still being considered equal? For instance, in 1963 Congress passed the Equal Pay Act, which requires that men and women receive equal pay for equal work. But even in current times, men and women often work in largely sex-segregated jobs, with so-called men's jobs generally drawing a higher income than women's jobs. Thus, equality is difficult to achieve even under the law if men and women are employed in different types of positions.

Similarly, in 1964 Congress passed the Civil Rights Act, which made it illegal to use sex as a criterion for employment-related decisions, such as hiring and promotions. This was a tremendous advance in women's employment rights, but it also required the government, through court cases and later laws, to clarify how equality is to actually be achieved in various situations, such as in the cases of pregnancy and sexual harassment. For instance, in 1978 Congress amended the Civil Rights Act of 1964 by passing the Pregnancy Discrimination Act, specifying that discrimination due to pregnancy or potential for pregnancy is a form of sex discrimination and thus is a violation of the Civil Rights Act. The Civil Rights Act was further strengthened by President Lyndon Johnson, who signed two executive orders outlining how the federal government would operate in order to comply with the law. As head of the executive branch, the president has the discretion to require units of the federal government to operate in specific ways as long as his orders are not in violation of the law. In the case of the Civil Rights Act of 1964, President Johnson required the federal government to practice affirmative action, or employment decisions that prevent discrimination from occurring against people due to their race, sex, national origin, and creed. The first executive order in this regard, Executive

Order 11246 signed in 1965, omitted sex from the requirements, but Executive Order 11375 broadened the original order to include consideration of sex in affirmative action policies.

Similarly, the Civil Rights Act of 1964 became the basis of a pivotal Supreme Court case, *United Auto Workers v. Johnson Controls* (1991), which considered whether it was a violation of the law to prevent all fertile women of childbearing age from working jobs on which they would be exposed to substances that could be hazardous to the health of the fetus. That same year, the application of the law to workplace sexual harassment gained national attention when President George H. W. Bush's Supreme Court nominee Clarence Thomas was accused of sexually harassing Anita Hill, who had worked for him in several government offices. While it was already illegal to engage in sexual harassment by 1991, the nomination hearings drew heightened attention to a problem that is predominantly experienced by women.

Finally, the difficulty with defining what is meant by equal rights in employment arises when there are actual physical differences between women and men. Specifically, how does the law accommodate the physical demands of pregnancy, childbirth, and lactation experienced by women? For many women's groups, this raises a dilemma. On one hand, there is the acknowledgment that pregnancy, childbirth, and lactation are natural and normal experiences of women that sometimes need accommodation but should not be used to hinder a woman's occupational aspirations. On the other hand is the concern that different accommodations for men and women, even when those accommodations reflect significant physical differences between them, hark back to protectionist legislation and can be used by employers as a rationale for not hiring women. The balance of these two concerns can be seen in the Family and Medical Leave Act of 1993, when Congress required that both men and women be allowed to take unpaid leave from their employer due to family needs without fear of losing their jobs.

The following seven issues are related to the attainment of women's rights to work. The most common theme running across these issues is the consideration of women's maternal role and how that role can best be accommodated as women move into the workforce. The answer to this question varies across time, ranging from providing different protections to women because of their ability to be mothers to providing women complete equality with men.

The U.S. Supreme Court Limits Women's Employment Rights

Supreme Court Ruling in *Muller v. Oregon*

1908

In 1903, the State of Oregon passed a law limiting the amount of time a woman could work in factories and laundries to no more than 10 hours a day. If found to be in violation of this law, an employer could be fined between $10 and $25. This law, along with many others passed during the Progressive Era (1896–1916) were designed to protect women's health from harsh working conditions but were met with opposition from employers and several women's rights organizations, who argued that the law violated the rights of employees and employers to enter into contracts with each other without interference from the government. In 1905 the owner of a laundry in Portland, Oregon, was found guilty of violating this law and was fined $10. His case came before the Oregon Supreme Court, which considered whether the law was in violation of the state constitution. When the state court upheld the owner's conviction, he eventually took his case to the U.S. Supreme Court, which considered the constitutionality of the law under the U.S. Constitution. By taking the case, the Supreme Court ruling would apply to all states that had laws mandating different working standards for male and female employees. The Court eventually upheld the laundry owner's conviction, ruling that these laws designed to protect women did not violate the U.S. Constitution.

Unlike members of Congress or the president who are elected to office, federal judges are appointed by the president and confirmed by the Senate. The hope of the framers of the U.S. Constitution was that judges would be able to make fair and reasoned rulings on legal and constitutional decisions without the undue and ever-changing influence of public opinion. Instead, judges would be able to make decision in an unbiased fashion, using only the words of the laws or the U.S. Constitution as a guide for their decisions. Clearly judges have their own political and ideological perspectives, but as Justice David J. Brewer states in the opinion of the Court, their intent is to consider constitutional questions separate from the outside influence of public opinion. In this case, however, the Court softens this stance, arguing that when there is not a clear answer to a question, such as in regard to women's physical abilities to work long hours, then the public's perspective does have some merit in the Court's consideration.

It is the law of Oregon that women, whether married or single, have equal contractual and personal rights with men.

As said by Chief Justice Wolverton in *First National Bank v. Leonard,* 36 Oregon 390, 396, after a review of the various statutes of the State upon the subject: "We may therefore say with perfect confidence that, with these three sections [of the law] upon the statute book, the wife can deal not only with her separate property, acquired from whatever source, in the same manner as her husband can with property belonging to him, but that she may make contracts and incur liabilities, and the same may be enforced against her, the same as if she were a *femme sole.* There is now no residuum of civil disability resting upon her which is not recognized as existing against the husband. The current runs steadily and strongly in the direction of the emancipation of the wife, and the policy, as disclosed by all recent legislation upon the subject in this State, is to place her upon the same footing as if she were a *femme sole* not only with respect to her separate property, but as it affects her right to make binding contracts; and the most natural corollary to the situation is that the remedies for the enforcement of liabilities incurred are made coextensive and coequal with such enlarged conditions."

It thus appears that, putting to one side the elective franchise, in the matter of personal and contractual rights, they stand on the same plane as the other sex. Their rights in these respects can no more be infringed than the equal rights of their brothers. . . .

The legislation and opinions referred to... may not be, technically speaking, authorities, and in them is little or no discussion of the constitutional question presented to us for determination, yet they are significant of a widespread belief that woman's physical structure, and the functions she performs in consequence thereof, justify special legislation restricting or qualifying the conditions under which she should be permitted to toil.

Constitutional questions, it is true, are not settled by even a consensus of present public opinion, for it is the peculiar value of a written constitution that it places in unchanging

form limitations upon legislative action, and thus gives a permanence and stability to popular government which otherwise would be lacking. At the same time, when a question of fact is debated and debatable, and the extent to which a special constitutional limitation goes is affected by the truth in respect to that fact, a widespread and long-continued belief concerning it is worthy of consideration. We take judicial cognizance of all matters of general knowledge.

It is undoubtedly true, as more than once declared by this Court, that the general right to contract in relation to one's business is part of the liberty of the individual, protected by the Fourteenth Amendment to the Federal Constitution; yet it is equally well settled that this liberty is not absolute, and extending to all contracts, and that a State may, without conflicting with the provisions of the Fourteenth Amendment, restrict in many respects the individual's power of contract. . . .

That woman's physical structure and the performance of maternal functions place her at a disadvantage in the struggle for subsistence is obvious. This is especially true when the burdens of motherhood are upon her. Even when they are not, by abundant testimony of the medical fraternity, continuance for a long time on her feet at work, repeating this from day to day, tends to injurious effects upon the body, and, as healthy mothers are essential to vigorous offspring, the physical wellbeing of woman becomes an object of public interest and care in order to preserve the strength and vigor of the race.

A great deal of research at the time supported the idea that women's health and the ability of women to bear and care for children were negatively affected by standing on their feet and being on the job for too long. The Court concluded that the maternal roles of women were so important to society that their protection took precedence over a woman's individual right to enter into contracts with an employer regarding her working hours. Furthermore, the court concluded that while women did have some rights, the state was within its right to place limits on these rights if doing so was deemed to be in the best interests of society.

Still again, history discloses the fact that woman has always been dependent upon man. He established his control at the outset by superior physical strength, and this control in various forms, with diminishing intensity, has continued to the present. As minors, though not to the same extent, she has been looked upon in the courts as needing especial care that her rights may be preserved. Education was long denied her, and while now the doors of the schoolroom are opened and her opportunities for acquiring knowledge are great, yet, even with that and the consequent increase of capacity for business affairs, it is still true that, in the struggle for subsistence, she is not an equal competitor with her brother.

The *Muller* decision was eventually nullified when Congress passed the Fair Labor Standards Act in 1938, but the cultural standard detailed in *Muller*, of prioritizing the role of motherhood for women over all other roles they may play, is still evident in today's political and social environments.

Though limitations upon personal and contractual rights may be removed by legislation, there is that in her disposition and habits of life which will operate against a full assertion of those rights.

She will still be where some legislation to protect her seems necessary to secure a real equality of right. Doubtless there are individual exceptions, and there are many respects in which she has an advantage over him; but, looking at it from the viewpoint of the effort to maintain an independent position in life, she is not upon an equality. Differentiated by these matters from the other sex, she is properly placed in a class by herself, and legislation designed for her protection may be sustained even when like legislation is not necessary for men, and could not be sustained. It is impossible to close one's eyes to the fact that she still looks to her brother, and depends upon him. Even though all restrictions on political, personal, and contractual rights were taken away, and she stood, so far as statutes are concerned, upon an absolutely equal plane with him, it would still be true that she is so constituted that she will rest upon and look to him for protection; that her physical structure and a proper discharge of her maternal functions—having in view not merely her own health, but the wellbeing of the race—justify legislation to protect her from the greed, as well as the passion, of man. The limitations which this statute places upon her contractual powers, upon her right to agree with her employer as to the time she shall labor, are not imposed solely for her benefit, but also largely for the benefit of all. Many words cannot make this plainer. The two sexes differ in structure of body, in the functions to be performed by each, in the amount of physical strength, in the capacity for long-continued labor, particularly when done standing, the influence of vigorous health upon the future wellbeing of the race, the self-reliance which enables one to assert full rights, and in the capacity to maintain the struggle for subsistence. This difference justifies a difference in legislation, and upholds that which is designed to compensate for some of the burdens which rest upon her.

Source: *Muller v. Oregon,* 208 U.S. 412 (1908): 421–423, http://caselaw .lp.findlaw.com/scripts/getcase.pl?court=US&vol=208&invol=412.

Women's Rights Advocates Lobby for a Women's Bureau

Testimony from the Women's Bureau Hearings before the Joint Committees on Labor

March 4, 1920

Statement of Agnes Nestor, Chairman of the National Legislative Committee of the Women's Trade Union League

My name is Miss Agnes Nestor, and I am chairman of the national legislative committee of the Women's Trades Union League. . . .

Mr. Chairman and gentlemen of the committee, I want to say that the Women's Trade Union League was the first to make a move for such a bureau as has been considered here this morning.

Away back in 1909, in our national convention of the Women's Trade Union League, a resolution was passed urging the creation of a division in the Department of Labor and Commerce. . . .

We were very much concerned that the country should know something about conditions under which women are working, that there should be a particular division whose duty it would be to concern itself about such investigations, and for that reason we urged that provision. . . .

In 1913 Congress created the Department of Labor to oversee the welfare of workers in the United States. Three years later, in response to the number of women filling industrial jobs during World War I and the often harsh working conditions that they faced, the Department of Labor created a separate office to look specifically at the needs of working women. However, by 1920 the call was being made for a more permanent and formal branch within the department to oversee women's working conditions. This hearing included testimony from numerous witnesses who advocated for a new office whose sole function would be to study and monitor women's experiences in the workplace.

I want you to know that the working woman has from the very beginning advocated and worked for this principle, and they are looking to you here now to enact this law. They feel that it carries a very meager appropriation for what they have to do, taking into consideration what is being appropriated for other divisions. One hundred and fifty thousand dollars is a small amount to appropriate for a bureau that has got to concern itself with the wage earning women of this country. We do feel that the country does not know at all the conditions under which women are working, and the changes which have been made due to the speeding up and the whole plan upon which industry is conducted to-day and we do not want to sap the vitality of the Nation, the vitality of the women of the Nation, and we want to be informed so that we will be able to give the facts to the country, and then if they don't act, if the industries don't act, they will at least be standing back knowing that the conditions exist and that it ought to be their concern to remedy them. . . .

I know the problems of the wage earners of my own clay, and there was some speeding up and changes while I was in the factory, and I can remember from the time when we made a glove all the way through and at that time there was some rest because of the break between the operations, because of changing from one operation to another, but I have seen that changed so that a girl is set at one machine, and given the monotony of one work, and that change has come about by the speeding up, and I do not think that the legislators in the State are keeping posted, because they are not concerned, and they do not understand the strain that is placed upon the women workers and how that strain saps the vitality of the women.

Statement of Miss Mary Stewart . . . Executive Secretary of the Women's Committee of the National Republican Congressional Committee

I am the executive secretary of the women's committee of the national Republican congressional committee. . . . I am working with the national committee; and I was asked to come here by the national committee to represent the Republican women. . . . The point is this: I suppose you want to know whether the women think this is a bill that ought to be passed; and if they do, why do they think so?

The fact is that you have heard from representatives of so many bodies of women here, regardless of religion or politics, which I think conclusively shows to the committee that all of the women, regardless of whom they represent, think that this bill is a good thing. . . .

The bill has been in existence for some time, and it probably contains the wisdom of that experience. The chief of the reasons for wanting a woman's bureau in the Department of Labor is our present state of social evolution. I think someone said very wisely this morning that while we might evolve toward a time when there should not be and need not be a differentiation between men and women, we are a very long ways from that, and that is the reason for a women's bureau in the Department of Labor.

The question that so puzzled Dr. Meeker a few moments ago was answered in the question itself; that is, the point of view. That is why Dr. Meeker could not do better work, because the women bring to these problems a peculiar point

While every woman who testified at the hearing supported the creation of the Women's Bureau, it is not accurate that all women supported the bill. Alice Paul, a prominent advocate of women's rights and head of the National Women's Party, did not support the Women's Bureau. Opponents such as Paul were concerned that the bureau would promote protective policies that treated female employees differently because of their ability to have children and that this preferential treatment would itself become the basis for discrimination against women in the workforce. Paul preferred that women and men employees be treated exactly the same, although this particular perspective on women's rights did not triumph until Congress passed the Civil Rights Act of 1964, effectively ending the practice of employment laws that treated male and female employees differently.

of view that is very much needed in the adjustment of all these problems. They see things in a different way. That is best answered by propounding another question, and that is, Can you conceive of a Department of Labor manned entirely by women studying the conditions that affect the men of the country? If it had to, could it? So, can you conceive of a Department of Labor entirely manned by men understanding all of the points of view which affect the welfare of women?

Now, women are comparatively new in industry and in many places they have been almost overlooked, and in order to bring intelligence and conscientious consideration of the product of women it is necessary that we shall have women on the job who can bring in their points of view, and the psychology of the thing makes it necessary that there should be a recognition of the women on the job in the Department of Labor. That is why I like the idea of having the appointment made by the President. It gives a clear conception of her responsibility and shows that the women are responsible to the country.

The first director of the Labor Department's Women's Bureau was Mary Anderson, who served in that capacity from 1920 to 1944. All 16 of her successors have been women, including Latifa Lyles, who in May 2012 was named the bureau's acting director. The mission of the bureau, meanwhile, remains the same as at its founding: to safeguard the interests of working women and advocate for their fair treatment and economic security.

Now, we know that the women of the country who have taken into consideration this important subject agree, as viewed by the women who represent the various groups here, that this bill should be passed, and I think that Mrs. Whitney told you that the Republican women who have been in conference have indorsed this particular measure. . . .

. . . [Women] are just about politically where we think we are in the labor business; that is, we have the right to vote, and now we are trying earnestly and conscientiously and honestly to demonstrate our interest and show our right to vote. Somebody said that up in New England the women take their politics as they do their marriage vows. Some of them, it would seem, take their politics more seriously.

We are trying to get our point of view into the political world, and we are going to be factors politically, we are going to be factors in the political and labor world, and we can not be unless we are recognized in this coordinate way.

It is perhaps not a coincidence that the question of creating a permanent Women's Bureau was considered by Congress the very year that women were granted the right to vote. At the time of this hearing, the Nineteenth Amendment granting women the right to vote had not yet been ratified by the necessary 36 states. However, there was little doubt that women would get the right to vote before the November election of 1920, and no one, including politicians, knew exactly what to expect when women started heading to the polling booths. Members of Congress undoubtedly wanted to be seen by these newly enfranchised voters as representing the interests of women.

I think that the women do see progressively in all the parties, because they see practically. It is their job to feed and clothe and care for the children and for the men.

Source: *Women's Bureau Hearings before the Joint Committees on Labor, Congress of the United States, 66th Congress, 2nd Session* (Washington, DC: U.S. Government Printing Office, 1920), 21–22, 48–50.

Kennedy Signs the Equal Pay Act

President John F. Kennedy's Remarks upon Signing the Equal Pay Act

June 10, 1963

During his first year as president, John F. Kennedy created the President's Commission on the Status of Women to study issues and make recommendations related to women in the workplace. The Equal Pay Act was the first recommendation to come out of the commission and to be considered by Congress. The act was relatively uncontroversial, making it illegal to pay men and women different wages for doing jobs requiring "equal skill, effort and responsibility" and that "are performed under similar working conditions." The Equal Pay Act was a first step in acknowledging that women and men should be considered on an equal basis in employment decisions and that one's sex should not be a determinant in employment decisions. What the law did not take into account, however, is that men and women are largely employed in different fields. Sex-segregated occupations, jobs that are predominantly held by men or women, are still common in current times, but it was especially the case in 1963 that men and women held different jobs. In those cases, the Equal Pay Act would have little effect on women's pay relative to men's pay.

It is interesting to note that President Kennedy consistently discusses the benefit of the new law in regard to mothers without noting that unmarried women and women without children would also benefit from it. This is a common tactic, one employed as recently as 2013 when President Barack Obama was criticized for the same sort of focus on mothers when he expressed his support for legislation promoting fair pay between men and women. Perhaps President Kennedy thought that using the imagery of mothers working to care for their children would elicit greater support for the law. The president also uses the fanfare of this signing to promote additional ideas that he thought would be of assistance to mothers in the workplace, such as day care assistance and tax exemptions.

I am delighted today to approve the Equal Pay Act of 1963, which prohibits arbitrary discrimination against women in the payment of wages. The act represents many years of effort by labor, management and several private organizations unassociated with labor or management, to call attention to the unconscionable practice of paying female employees less wages than male employees for the same job.

This measure adds to our laws another structure basic to democracy. It will add protection at the working place to the women, the same rights at the working place in a sense that they have enjoyed at the polling place.

While much remains to be done to achieve full equality of economic opportunity—for the average woman worker earns only 60 percent of the average wage for men—this legislation is a significant step forward.

Our economy today depends upon women in the labor force. One out of three workers is a woman. Today, there are almost 25 million women employed, and their number is rising faster than the number of men in the labor force.

It is extremely important that adequate provision be made for reasonable levels of income to them, for the care of the children which they must leave at home or in school, and for protection of the family unit. One of the prime objectives of the Commission on the Status of Women, which I appointed 18 months ago, is to develop a program to accomplish these purposes.

The lower the family income, the higher the probability that the mother must work. Today, 1 out of 5 of these working mothers has children under 3. Two of 5 have children of school age. Among the remainder, about 50 percent have husbands who earn less than $5,000 a year—many of them much less. I believe they bear the heaviest burden of any group in our Nation. Where the mother is the sole supporter of the family, she often must face the hard choice of either accepting public assistance or taking a position at a pay rate which averages less than two-thirds of the pay rate for men.

It is for these reasons that I believe we must expand day-care centers and provide other assistance which I have recommended to the Congress. At present, the total facilities of all the licensed day-care centers in the Nation can take care of only 185,000 children. Nearly 500,000 children under 12 must take care of themselves while their mothers work. This, it seems to me, is a formula for disaster.

I am glad that Congress has recently authorized $800,000 to State welfare agencies to expand their day-care services during the remainder of this fiscal year. But we need much more. We need the $8 million in the 1965 budget for the Department of Health, Education, and Welfare allocated to this purpose.

We also need the provisions in the tax bill that will permit working mothers to increase the deduction from income tax liability for costs incurred in providing care for their children while the mothers are working. In October the Commission on the Status of Women will report to me. This problem should have a high priority, and I think that whatever we leave undone this year we must move on this in January.

I am grateful to those Members of Congress who worked so diligently to guide the Equal Pay Act through. It is a first step. It affirms our determination that when women enter the labor force they will find equality in their pay envelopes.

President Kennedy had received significant support from women voters but was criticized by women's organizations for appointing so few women to cabinet-level offices. Some political analysts have proposed that he created the Commission on the Status of Women and offered his support of the Equal Pay Act in the hope of appeasing his female supporters. At the same time, he was aware that there was still a rift between the women's groups that favored the continuation of protective legislation and those that desired equality between men and women, and his comments were made to minimize the division between these two groups. This legislation appeared to be a good compromise between the perspectives of women in the workplace in that it provided for a measure of equality without eliminating any protective legislation that was still in place.

We have some of the most influential Members of Congress here today, and I do hope that we can get this appropriation for these day-care centers, which seems to me to be money very wisely spent, and also under consideration of the tax bill, that we can consider the needs of the working mothers, and both of these will be very helpful, and I would like to lobby in their behalf.

Source: John F. Kennedy, "Remarks upon Signing the Equal Pay Act," June 10, 1963, The American Presidency Project, http://www.presidency.ucsb.edu/ws/?pid=9267.

Congress Debates Sex Discrimination Provisions in the Civil Rights Act

Statements Supporting and Opposing an Amendment to Prohibit Sexual Discrimination in Title VII of the Civil Rights Act of 1964

February 8, 1964

In 1964 Congress passed an expansive civil rights bill, including numerous prohibitions of employment and education discrimination based on race, color, religion, and national origin. As originally proposed in the House of Representatives, the bill did not include any provision for sex discrimination. In fact, the inclusion of sex discrimination came very late in the legislative process, being added as an amendment to the bill's original wording a mere two days before the House voted to approve the bill. The inclusion of the one word, "sex," to Title VII of the Civil Rights Act created considerable controversy, as this represented a momentous change in public policy. Not only did it give women equal rights in employment practices, it also effectively eliminated the prospect of additional protective legislation as supported by the Women's Bureau. The amendment represents an interesting story of political strategy and includes some intrigue as to the motivation behind the addition.

Statement of Representative Howard W. Smith (VA)

Mr. Chairman, this amendment is offered to the fair employment practices title of this bill to include within our desire to prevent discrimination against another minority group, the women, but a very substantial minority group, in the absence of which the majority group would not be here today.

Now, I am very serious about this amendment. It has been offered several times before, but it was offered at inappropriate places in the bill. Now this is the appropriate place for this amendment to come in. I do not think it can do any harm to this legislation; maybe it can do some good. I think it will do some good for the minority sex.

I think we all recognize and it is indisputable fact that all throughout industry women are discriminated against in that just generally speaking they do not get as high compensation for their work as do the majority sex. Now, if that is true, I hope that the committee chairman will accept my amendment.

That is about all I have to say about it except, to get off of this subject for just a moment but to show you how some of the ladies feel about discrimination against them, I want to read you an extract from a letter that I received the other day. This lady has a real grievance on behalf of the minority sex. She said that she had seen that I was going to present an amendment to protect the most important sex, and she says:

> I suggest that you might also favor an amendment or a bill to correct the present "imbalance" which exists between males and females in the United States.

Then she goes on to say—and she has her statistics, which is the reason why I am reading it to you, because this is serious—

> The census of 1960 shows that we had 88,331,000 males living in this country, and 90,992,000 females, which leaves the country with an "imbalance" of 2,661,000 females. . . . Just

why the Creator would set up such an imbalance of spinsters, shutting off the "right" of every female to have a husband of her own, is, of course, known only to nature. . . .

But I am sure you will agree that this is a grave injustice to womankind and something the Congress and President Johnson should take immediate steps to correct . . . especially in this election year.

Now, I just want to remind you here that in this election year it is pretty nearly half of the voters in this country that are affected, so you had better sit up and take notice. . . .

I read that letter just to illustrate that women have some real grievances and some real rights to be protected. I am serious about this thing. I just hope that the committee will accept it. Now, what harm can you do this bill that was so perfect yesterday and is so imperfect today—what harm will this do to the condition of the bill?

The motivation behind Representative Smith's amendment to add the term "sex" to Title VII has been the subject of speculation for years. Because he had originally opposed the Civil Rights Act, some scholars assume that Smith proposed this so-called radical amendment as a last-ditch effort to kill the entire bill. His inclusion of a rather frivolous suggestion from one of his constituents about the imbalance between men and women and the need for husbands for the country's spinsters lends some support to the idea that the amendment was added in jest. However, given Smith's association with some advocates of the Civil Rights Act, there is some evidence that his motivations were sincere and that he thought that women's employment rights should be protected if the bill was going to be passed anyway, which by early February of 1964 seemed likely.

Statement by Representative Emanuel Celler (NY)

Mr. Chairman, I rise in opposition to the amendment. . . . [W]e have an expression of opinion from the Department of Labor to the effect that it will be ill advised to append to this bill the word "sex" and provide for discrimination on the basis of race, color, creed, national origin, and sex as well. Of course, there has been before us for a considerable length of time, before the Judiciary Committee, an equal rights amendment. At first blush it seems fair, just, and equitable to grant these equal rights. But when you examine carefully what the import and repercussions are concerning equal rights throughout American life, and all facets of American life you run into considerable amount of difficulty. . . .

Imagine the upheaval that would result from adoption of blanket language requiring total equality. Would male citizens be justified in insisting that women share with them the burdens of compulsory military service? What would become of traditional family relationships? What about alimony? Who would have the obligation of supporting whom? Would fathers rank equally with mothers in the right of custody to children? What would become of the crimes of rape and statutory rape? . . .

You know the biological differences between the sexes. In many States we have laws favorable to women. Are you going to strike those laws down? This is the entering wedge, an amendment of this sort. The list of foreseeable consequences, I will say to the committee, is unlimited.

Because the amendment was added late in the legislative process and had not seemed to be a major priority for Congress when it considered and ultimately passed the Civil Rights Act, the actual implementation of the law faced some challenges. The law created the Equal Employment Opportunity Commission to carry out the provisions of the law, but this commission did not initially enforce the prohibition of sex discrimination, focusing instead on claims of racial discrimination. Ultimately Congress passed additional laws to clarify and reassert the significance of women's place in the Civil Rights Act, passing the Equal Employment and Opportunity Act in 1972 and the Pregnancy Discrimination Act of 1978. Regardless of Smith's motivation, the addition of this one word—"sex"—has had a tremendous effect on women's experiences in the workforce, shaping business practices as well as girls' and women's expectations and opportunities for their careers.

Statement of Representative Frances P. Bolton (OH)

Mr. Chairman, it is always perfectly delightful when some enchanting gentleman, from the South particularly, calls us the minority group. We used to be but we are not any more. I have just had the figures sent me. You males, as you seem to like to call yourselves, are 88,331,494. We females, as you like to call us, are 90,991,681. So I regret to state that we can no longer be the minority; indeed, we have not been for some time.

Source: *Congressional Record,* 88th Congress, Vol. 110 (1964), 2577–2584, 2718, 2720–2721.

Johnson and Nondiscrimination in Government Employment

Text of President Lyndon B. Johnson's
Executive Order 11246

September 24, 1965

EQUAL EMPLOYMENT OPPORTUNITY

Under and by virtue of the authority vested in me as President of the United States by the Constitution and statutes of the United States, it is ordered as follows:

PART I—NONDISCRIMINATION IN GOVERNMENT EMPLOYMENT

Section 101. It is the policy of the Government of the United States to provide equal opportunity in Federal employment for all qualified persons, to prohibit discrimination in employment because of race, creed, color, or national origin, and to promote the full realization of equal employment opportunity through a positive, continuing program in each executive department and agency. The policy of equal opportunity applies to every aspect of Federal employment policy and practice.

Sec. 102. The head of each executive department and agency shall establish and maintain a positive program of equal employment opportunity for all civilian employees and applicants for employment within his jurisdiction in accordance with the policy set forth in Section 101.

Sec. 103. The Civil Service Commission shall supervise and provide leadership and guidance in the conduct of equal employment opportunity programs for the civilian employees of and applications for employment within the executive departments and agencies and shall review agency program accomplishments periodically. In order to facilitate the achievement of a model program for equal employment opportunity in the Federal service, the Commission may consult from time to time with such individuals, groups, or organizations as may be of assistance in improving the Federal program and realizing the objectives of this Part.

Sec. 104. The Civil Service Commission shall provide for the prompt, fair, and impartial consideration of all complaints of discrimination in Federal employment on the basis of race, creed, color, or national origin. Procedures for the

President Lyndon Johnson is probably best remembered for his Great Society, a series of government programs designed to create a more equitable society. The main facet of these initiatives was to eliminate poverty in the United States and better address civil rights on issues related to race and color. While Johnson's predecessor, John F. Kennedy, was also an advocate for civil rights legislation, his proposals were not as extensive as those attempted by Johnson. Some suspect that Johnson was able to translate the national grief after Kennedy's assassination into these more far-reaching policies addressing economic and racial inequality, such as the Civil Rights Act of 1964. A year after this law was passed, Johnson signed an executive order specifying how the federal government would approach the implementation of nondiscrimination policies within the federal government, at least in regard to race, color, national origin, and religion. While Title VII of the Civil Rights Act had included the term "sex" among the characteristics subject to nondiscrimination, Johnson's executive order omitted the term, focusing only on the other factors. This omission was not addressed until 1967 in Executive Order 11375.

consideration of complaints shall include at least one impartial review within the executive department or agency and shall provide for appeal to the Civil Service Commission.

Sec. 105. The Civil Service Commission shall issue such regulations, orders, and instructions as it deems necessary and appropriate to carry out its responsibilities under this Part, and the head of each executive department and agency shall comply with the regulations, orders, and instructions issued by the Commission under this Part.

Lyndon B. Johnson
The White House
September 24, 1965

Source: 30 Federal Register 12319, September 28, 1965.

Johnson Bans Sex Discrimination in Federal Hiring Policies

Text of President Lyndon B. Johnson's Executive Order 11375

October 13, 1967

It is the policy of the United States Government to provide equal opportunity in Federal employment and in employment by Federal contractors on the basis of merit and without discrimination because of race, color, religion, sex or national origin.

The Congress, by enacting Title VII of the Civil Rights Act of 1964, enunciated a national policy of equal employment opportunity in private employment, without discrimination because of race, color, religion, sex or national origin.

Executive Order No. 11246 of September 24, 1965, carried forward a program of equal employment opportunity in Government employment, employment by Federal contractors and subcontractors and employment under Federally assisted construction contracts regardless of race, creed, color or national origin.

It is desirable that the equal employment opportunity programs provided for in Executive Order No. 11246 expressly embrace discrimination on account of sex.

Executive Order 11246 required the federal government to be proactive in its employment decisions to prevent discrimination from occurring, a process referred to as affirmative action. While laws such as the Civil Rights Act forbid certain behaviors by making them illegal, affirmative action requires that certain actions be taken in order to prevent a violation of the law from occurring. Requiring affirmative action to be taken to prevent employment discrimination by the federal government was momentous in that the number of civilians employed by the federal government in 1965 was just under 2.5 million. The executive order also required the secretary of labor to ensure nondiscrimination in the award of government contracts to companies that provide products or services to the government. This broadened the reach of the executive order even further. In 1967 President Johnson amended Executive Order 11246 by signing Executive Order 11375. This kept most of the provisions from Executive Order 11246 in place but broadened its application to include sex discrimination in the government's affirmative action policies.

NOW, THEREFORE, by virtue of the authority vested in me as President of the United States by the Constitution and statutes of the United States, it is ordered that Executive Order No. 11246 of September 24, 1965, be amended as follows:

(1) Section 101 of Part I, concerning nondiscrimination in Government employment, is revised to read as follows:

'SEC. 101. It is the policy of the Government of the United States to provide equal opportunity in Federal employment for all qualified persons, to prohibit discrimination in employment because of race, color, religion, sex or national origin, and to promote the full realization of equal employment opportunity through a positive, continuing program in each executive department and agency. The policy of equal opportunity applies to every aspect of Federal employment policy and practice.'

(2) Section 104 of Part I is revised to read as follows:

'SEC. 104. The Civil Service Commission shall provide for the prompt, fair, and impartial consideration of all complaints of discrimination in Federal employment on the basis of race, color, religion, sex or national origin. Procedures for the consideration of complaints shall include at least one impartial review within the executive department or agency and shall provide for appeal to the Civil Service Commission.'

(3) Paragraphs (1) and (2) of the quoted required contract provisions in section 202 of Part II, concerning nondiscrimination in employment by Government contractors and subcontractors, are revised to read as follows:

(1) The contractor will not discriminate against any employee or applicant for employment because of race, color, religion, sex, or national origin. The contractor will take affirmative action to ensure that applicants are employed, and that employees are treated during employment, without regard to their race, color, religion, sex or national origin. Such action shall include, but not be limited to the following: employment, upgrading, demotion, or transfer; recruitment or recruitment advertising; layoff or termination; rates of pay or other forms of compensation; and selection for training, including apprenticeship. The contractor agrees to post in conspicuous places, available to employees and applicants for employment, notices to be provided by the contracting officer setting forth the provisions of this nondiscrimination clause.

(2) The contractor will, in all solicitations or advertisements for employees placed by or on behalf of the contractor, state that all qualified applicants will receive consideration for employment without regard to race, color, religion, sex or national origin.' (4) Section 203(d) of Part II is revised to read as follows:

(d) The contracting agency or the Secretary of Labor may direct that any bidder or prospective contractor or subcontractor shall submit, as part of his Compliance Report, a statement in writing, signed by an authorized officer or agent on behalf of any labor union or any agency referring workers or providing or supervising apprenticeship or other training, with which the bidder or prospective contractor deals, with supporting information, to the effect that the signer's practices and policies do not discriminate on the grounds of race, color, religion, sex or national origin, and that the signer either will affirmatively cooperate in the implementation of the policy and provisions of this order or that it consents and agrees that recruitment, employment, and the terms and conditions of employment under the proposed contract shall be in accordance with the purposes and provisions of the order.

The practice of affirmative action was not without controversy. The intent of the policy was twofold: first, to prevent future discrimination of protected-class citizens from taking place, and second, to remedy historical discrimination against these groups. In addressing previous discrimination, an employer could take into account an applicant's or employee's protected classification, such as race or sex, in making employee decisions if such decisions would result in more diversity in the workplace. The idea behind this form of affirmative action was that the workplace would have included more women and minorities had there never been discrimination against them to begin with. Affirmative action was seen as remedying past wrongs against people in these groups. However, this approach was perceived by some as reverse discrimination in that white males, who had historically been privileged in employment decisions, would now suffer the same disadvantages that women and minorities had experienced throughout history. Also, some people incorrectly perceived affirmative action as a quota system in which employers were required to hire a certain number of women. These perceptions of affirmative action have led to numerous lawsuits, but for the most part affirmative action policies were upheld by the courts and are still in place in an effort to prevent employers from violating the law.

In the event that the union, or the agency shall refuse to execute such a statement, the Compliance Report shall so certify and set forth what efforts have been made to secure such a statement and such additional factual material as the contracting agency or the Secretary of Labor may require.

The amendments to Part I shall be effective 30 days after the date of this order. The amendments to Part II shall be effective one year after the date of this order.

Lyndon B. Johnson
THE WHITE HOUSE,
October 13, 1967.

Source: 32 Federal Register 14303, October 17, 1967.

The U.S. Supreme Court Strikes Down Gender-Based Fetal Protection Policies

Supreme Court Ruling in *United Automobile Workers v. Johnson Controls*

1991

In this case, the U.S. Supreme Court had to determine whether sex discrimination took place when employers adopted policies limiting access to certain jobs out of a concern for an employee's fertility and for fetal health if those policies applied only to women and not also to men. In the case of Johnson Controls, the battery manufacturer prohibited some women from holding jobs that required them to come into contact with lead, an element that can cause problems in the neural and bone development of fetuses and can cause fertility problems in both men and women. The policy only applied to women, but in order to dispel concerns that their policy was a violation of sex discrimination laws, the company allowed women to work in these positions as long as they could demonstrate that they were infertile due to either their age or sterilization. The Court noted some inconsistencies in the company's policy in that it was unclear whether the policy was to protect employees' fertility, since men's fertility did not seem to be of concern, or whether the policy was to protect the fetus of a pregnant woman. At the heart of the matter, however, the concern was most likely to protect the company from lawsuits by employees whose fertility or babies were adversely affected by lead exposure.

In this case, we are concerned with an employer's gender-based fetal-protection policy. May an employer exclude a fertile female employee from certain jobs because of its concern for the health of the fetus the woman might conceive?

Respondent Johnson Controls, Inc., manufactures batteries. In the manufacturing process, the element lead is a primary ingredient. Occupational exposure to lead entails health risks, including the risk of harm to any fetus carried by a female employee.

Before the Civil Rights Act of 1964... became law, Johnson Controls did not employ any woman in a battery-manufacturing job. In June, 1977, however, it announced its first official policy concerning its employment of women in lead-exposure work....

Johnson Controls "stopped short of excluding women capable of bearing children from lead exposure," but emphasized that a woman who expected to have a child should not choose a job in which she would have such exposure. The company also required a woman who wished to be considered for employment to sign a statement that she had been advised of the risk of having a child while she was exposed to lead. The statement informed the woman that, although there was evidence "that women exposed to lead have a higher rate of abortion," this evidence was "not as clear... as the relationship between cigarette smoking and cancer," but that it was, "medically speaking, just good sense not to run that risk if you want children and do not want to expose the unborn child to risk, however small...."

Five years later, in 1982, Johnson Controls shifted from a policy of warning to a policy of exclusion.... The company responded by announcing a broad exclusion of women from jobs that exposed them to lead: ". . . [I]t is [Johnson Controls'] policy that women who are pregnant or who are capable of bearing children will not be placed into jobs involving lead exposure or which could expose them to lead through the exercise of job bidding, bumping, transfer or promotion rights." The policy defined "women... capable of bearing

21

children" as "[a]ll women except those whose inability to bear children is medically documented...."

In April 1984, petitioners filed in the United States District Court for the Eastern District of Wisconsin a class action challenging Johnson Controls' fetal-protection policy as sex discrimination that violated Title VII of the Civil Rights Act of 1964, as amended.... Among the individual plaintiffs were petitioners Mary Craig, who had chosen to be sterilized in order to avoid losing her job, Elsie Nason, a 50-year-old divorcee, who had suffered a loss in compensation when she was transferred out of a job where she was exposed to lead, and Donald Penney, who had been denied a request for a leave of absence for the purpose of lowering his lead level because he intended to become a father.

The bias in Johnson Controls' policy is obvious. Fertile men, but not fertile women, are given a choice as to whether they wish to risk their reproductive health for a particular job. Section 703(a) of the Civil Rights Act of 1964 ... prohibits sex-based classifications in terms and conditions of employment, in hiring and discharging decisions, and in other employment decisions that adversely affect an employee's status. Respondent's fetal-protection policy explicitly discriminates against women on the basis of their sex. The policy excludes women with childbearing capacity from lead-exposed jobs, and so creates a facial classification based on gender....

Johnson Controls' policy classifies on the basis of gender and childbearing capacity, rather than fertility alone. Respondent does not seek to protect the unconceived children of all its employees. Despite evidence in the record about the debilitating effect of lead exposure on the male reproductive system, Johnson Controls is concerned only with the harms that may befall the unborn offspring of its female employees.... Johnson Controls' policy is facially discriminatory because it requires only a female employee to produce proof that she is not capable of reproducing.

Our conclusion is bolstered by the Pregnancy Discrimination Act of 1978 (PDA)... in which Congress explicitly provided that, for purposes of Title VII, discrimination "on the basis of sex" includes discrimination "because of or on the basis of pregnancy, childbirth, or related medical conditions."...

The PDA's amendment to Title VII contains a BFOQ standard... : unless pregnant employees differ from others "in their ability or inability to work," they must be "treated

While exposure to lead can have adverse effects on both men and women, the individuals bringing the suit argued that the company focused exclusively on the potential effects on women's fertility, which, they argued, made the company's policy illegal sex discrimination. The policy is illegal because it limits women from holding certain jobs for which they may be qualified and does not offer fertile men the same protections as fertile women. The company asserted that the prohibition on women's employment in these jobs was not due to their sex per se but instead was intended to protect fetuses. In the Court's opinion, Justice Harry Blackmun notes that fetal protection does not justify employment discrimination when the burden of the policy is placed only on women. He cites the Pregnancy Discrimination Act, which makes the use of pregnancy as a basis for employment decisions illegal. More significant perhaps is that this case marks an important shift that was taking place in the United States in regard to the perception of the fetus. Blackmun's opinion in essence separates the interests of a woman from the interests of her children, including her unborn children. This becomes a relevant point when groups opposed to abortion begin advocating for fetal rights after the year 2000.

the same" as other employees "for all employment-related purposes." 42 U.S.C. § 2000e(k). This language clearly sets forth Congress' remedy for discrimination on the basis of pregnancy and potential pregnancy. Women who are either pregnant or potentially pregnant must be treated like others "similar in their ability... to work." *Ibid.* In other words, women as capable of doing their jobs as their male counterparts may not be forced to choose between having a child and having a job.

We have no difficulty concluding that Johnson Controls cannot establish a BFOQ.

Fertile women, as far as appears in the record, participate in the manufacture of batteries as efficiently as anyone else. Johnson Controls' professed moral and ethical concerns about the welfare of the next generation do not suffice to establish a BFOQ of female sterility.

Although the Civil Rights Act of 1964 had prohibited employment discrimination on the basis of sex, the law allows for exceptions when a person's sex is considered a bona fide occupational qualification (BFOQ) for a particular job. The language outlining the legal standard for exceptions states that sex as well as religion and national origin could only be used as criterion in employment decisions when a person's sex was "reasonably necessary to the normal operation of that particular business or enterprise." In this particular case, the Supreme Court ruled that the policy prohibiting fertile women from working in certain jobs did not fall under BFOQ guidelines.

Decisions about the welfare of future children must be left to the parents who conceive, bear, support, and raise them, rather than to the employers who hire those parents. Congress has mandated this choice through Title VII, as amended by the PDA [Pregnancy Discrimination Act]. Johnson Controls has attempted to exclude women because of their reproductive capacity. Title VII and the PDA simply do not allow a woman's dismissal because of her failure to submit to sterilization....

Our holding today that Title VII, as so amended, forbids sex-specific fetal-protection policies is neither remarkable nor unprecedented. Concern for a woman's existing or potential offspring historically has been the excuse for denying women equal employment opportunities. *See, e.g., Muller v. Oregon,* 208 U.S. 412 (1908). Congress in the PDA prohibited discrimination on the basis of a woman's ability to become pregnant. We do no more than hold that the Pregnancy Discrimination Act means what it says.

It is no more appropriate for the courts than it is for individual employers to decide whether a woman's reproductive role is more important to herself and her family than her economic role. Congress has left this choice to the woman as hers to make.

Source: *United Automobile Workers v. Johnson Controls,* 499 U.S. 187 (1991), Legal Information Institute, Cornell University Law School, http://www.law.cornell.edu/supct/html/89-1215.ZO.html.

Anita Hill Testifies against Clarence Thomas

Testimony at Senate Hearings for Supreme Court Nominee Clarence Thomas

October 11, 1991

During this period at the Department of Education, my working relationship with Judge Thomas was positive. I had a good deal of responsibility as well as independence. I thought that he respected my work and that he trusted my judgment. After approximately three months of working together, he asked me to go out with him socially. I declined and explained to him that I thought that it would only jeopardize what, at the time, I considered to be a very good working relationship. I had a normal social life with other men outside of the office and, I believed then, as now, that having a social relationship with a person who was supervising my work would be ill-advised. I was very uncomfortable with the idea and told him so.

I thought that by saying "no" and explaining my reasons, my employer would abandon his social suggestions. However, to my regret, in the following few weeks he continued to ask me out on several occasions. He pressed me to justify my reasons for saying "no" to him. These incidents took place in his office or mine. They were in the form of private conversations which would not have been overheard by anyone else.

My working relationship became even more strained when Judge Thomas began to use work situations to discuss sex. On these occasions he would call me into his office for reports on education issues and projects or he might suggest that because of time pressures we go to lunch at a government cafeteria. After a brief discussion of work, he would turn the conversation to discussion of sexual matters. His conversations were very vivid. He spoke about acts that he had seen in pornographic films involving such matters as women having sex with animals and films showing group sex or rape scenes. He talked about pornographic materials depicting individuals with large penises or large breasts involved in various sex acts. On several occasions Thomas told me graphically of his own sexual prowess.

Because I was extremely uncomfortable talking about sex with him at all and particularly in such a graphic way, I told him that I did not want to talk about those subjects. I would

Under certain circumstances, when a person directs unwanted sexual behavior toward another, it is considered to be a violation of Title VII of the Civil Rights Act, since the sexual harassment is seen as being related to the victim's sex. Although the problem of sexual harassment had gained some national attention by the 1990s, the real groundswell of interest came when Supreme Court nominee Clarence Thomas was accused of sexual harassment by law professor Anita Hill, who had worked for Thomas at both the Department of Education's Office of Civil Rights and the Equal Employment Opportunity Commission (EEOC). Nominated by President George H. W. Bush, Thomas had nearly completed the confirmation process in the Senate when the media broke the story of Hill's claims of sexual harassment. The Senate Judiciary Committee, responsible for holding confirmation hearings for judicial nominees, reopened its hearings to consider testimony specifically related to Professor Hill's allegations.

In most early sex discrimination cases, there was a clear economic consequence to the victim whereby the ability to get a job or be promoted was adversely affected. Certainly some forms of sexual harassment may have an economic consequence, such as when an employee loses a position because she or he did not submit to the sexual demands of a superior, but that is not the only consequence of harassment. Sexual harassment can also have emotional and psychological effects in that one's workplace becomes a hostile environment, leading to stress and emotional strain. This form of sexual harassment is also illegal, even when the consequences are not directly economic in nature.

also try to change the subject to education matters or to non-sexual personal matters such as his background or beliefs. My efforts to change the subject were rarely successful.

Throughout the period of these conversations, he also from time-to-time asked me for social engagements. My reactions to these conversations was to avoid having them by eliminating opportunities for us to engage in extended conversations. This was difficult because I was his only assistant at the Office for Civil Rights. During the latter part of my time at the Department of Education, the social pressures and any conversation of this offensive kind ended. I began both to believe and hope that our working relationship could be on a proper, cordial and professional base.

When Judge Thomas was made Chairman of the EEOC, I needed to face the question of whether to go with him. I was asked to do so. I did. The work itself was interesting and at that time it appeared that the sexual overtures which had so troubled me had ended. I also faced the realistic fact that I had no alternative job. While I might have gone back to private practice, perhaps in my old firm or at another, I was dedicated to civil rights work and my first choice was to be in that field....

For my first months at the EEOC, where I continued as an assistant to Judge Thomas, there were no sexual conversations or overtures. However, during the Fall and Winter of 1982, these began again. The comments were random and ranged from pressing me about why I didn't go out with him to remarks about my personal appearance. I remember his saying that someday I would have to give him the real reason that I wouldn't go out with him. He began to show real displeasure in his tone of voice, his demeanor and his continued pressure for an explanation. He commented on what I was wearing in terms of whether it made me more or less sexually attractive. The incidents occurred in his inner office at the EEOC.

One of the oddest episodes I remember was an occasion in which Thomas was drinking a Coke in his office. He got up from the table at which we were working, went over to his desk to get the Coke, looked at the can, and said, "Who has put a pubic hair on my Coke?" On other occasions he referred to the size of his own penis as being larger than normal and he also spoke on some occasions of the pleasures he had given to women with oral sex.

The fact that Anita Hill had followed Clarence Thomas from the Department of Education to the EEOC after these alleged incidents of harassment raised questions among the members of the Senate Judiciary Committee as to why she would follow a man she claimed had harassed her. This line of questioning, among others, prompted considerable criticism by women's organizations, who argued that women should not have to make life-long career decisions simply to avoid being sexually harassed. This criticism was further fueled by the fact that no women or people of color served on the committee. The all-white all-male members of the committee at times appeared insensitive as they questioned and commented on the very personal testimony of Hill, an African American woman.

At this point, late 1982, I began to feel severe stress on the job. I began to be concerned that Clarence Thomas might take it out on me by downgrading me or not giving me important assignments. I also thought that he might find an excuse for dismissing me....

In January of 1983, I began looking for another job.... In February, 1983, I was hospitalized for five days on an emergency basis for an acute stomach pain which I attributed to stress on the job. Once out of the hospital, I became more committed to find other employment and sought further to minimize my contact with Thomas.

In the Spring of 1983, an opportunity to teach law at Oral Roberts University opened up. I agreed to take the job in large part because of my desire to escape the pressures I felt at the EEOC due to Thomas. When I informed him that I was leaving in July, I recall that his response was that now I "would no longer have an excuse for not going out with" him. I told him that I still preferred not to do so....

At some time after that meeting, he asked if he could take me to dinner at the end of my term. When I declined, he assured me that the dinner was a professional courtesy only and not a social invitation. I reluctantly agreed to accept that invitation but only if it was at the very end of a workday. On, as I recall, the last day of my employment at the EEOC in the summer of 1983, I did have dinner with Clarence Thomas. We went directly from work to a restaurant near the office. We talked about the work I had done both at Education and at EEOC. He told me that he was pleased with all of it except for an article and speech that I had done for him when we were at the Office of Civil Rights.

Finally, he made a comment which I vividly remember. He said that if I ever told anyone about his behavior toward me it could ruin his career. This was not an apology nor was there any explanation. That was his last remark about the possibility of our going out or reference to his behavior.

Source: *Nomination of Judge Clarence Thomas to Be Associate Justice of the Supreme Court of the United States: Hearings before the Committee on the Judiciary,* United States Senate, 102nd Congress, 1st Session, J–102–40 (Washington, DC: U.S. Government Printing Office, 1993), 36–39, http://www.gpoaccess.gov/congress/senate/judiciary/sh102-1084pt4/36-40.pdf.

Clarence Thomas's confirmation hearings received extensive media coverage, undoubtedly due in part to the salacious nature of some of the testimony. However, this heightened attention to the problem of sexual harassment had some significant consequences. Anita Hill's testimony and the committee's handling of some of the more sensitive issues that she raised are credited with both a surge in the number of sexual harassment cases filed after 1991 and an increase in the number of women running and being elected to office in 1992. In fact, 1992 was referred to as the "Year of the Woman" because of the increased number of women elected to office. It is important to note, however, that Thomas consistently denied all of Hill's charges and ultimately was confirmed by the Senate and seated on the Supreme Court. Thomas himself criticized the hearings for being racially motivated.

Clinton Signs the Family and Medical Leave Act

President Bill Clinton's Remarks upon Signing the Family and Medical Leave Act

February 5, 1993

As more women entered the workforce, new problems were identified for working parents. By the late 1980s, Congress was dealing with the issue that parents sometimes had to choose between taking care of their children and keeping their jobs, since extended leaves could result in the loss of a job. In 1990 and 1992, Congress passed different versions of the Family and Medical Leave Act (FMLA), but in both cases the bill was vetoed by President George H. W. Bush, who argued that the bill created an unnecessary intrusion by government into companies' business practices. In order to build broad support for the bill, advocates for the FMLA included many groups into their coalition to lobby for its passage, including labor unions, organizations representing certain disabilities, medical organizations, and organizations for elderly people. While early versions of the bill focused primarily on maternity leave for women, by the time it passed, it had been broadened to family leave, to include men as well as women. It wasn't until 1993, when President Bill Clinton had taken office, that the bill was passed and finally signed into law.

Today, I am pleased to sign into law H.R. 1, the "Family and Medical Leave Act of 1993." I believe that this legislation is a response to a compelling need—the need of the American family for flexibility in the workplace. American workers will no longer have to choose between the job they need and the family they love.

This legislation mandates that public and private employers with at least fifty workers provide their employees with family and medical leave. At its core is the provision for employees to take up to 12 weeks of unpaid leave for the care of a newborn or newly adopted child, for the care of a family member with a serious medical condition, or for their own illness. It also requires employers to maintain health insurance coverage and job protection for the duration of the leave. It sets minimum length of service and hours of work requirements before employees become eligible.

The need for this legislation is clear. The American work force has changed dramatically in recent years. These changes have created a substantial and growing need for family and medical leave for working Americans.

Although President Clinton emphasized the benefit that the law would provide to all employees, there was the recognition that it would disproportionately benefit women. Almost all of the personal stories of being fired for taking leave to care for a family member that were recounted during Congress's consideration of the bill were from female witnesses. Supporters of the law, however, recognized that restricting this benefit to women would put both female and male employees at a disadvantage, not to mention being a likely violation of Title VII. Had the law applied only to women, women would once again be saddled with the stigma of needing additional protections in their jobs due to their maternal and nurturing roles, and men would not be given the opportunity to take leave even if they needed it.

In 1965, about 35 percent of mothers with children under 18 were labor force participants. By 1992, that figure had reached 67 percent. By the year 2005, one of every two people entering the work force will be women.

The rising cost of living has also made two incomes a necessity in many areas of this country, with both parents working or looking for work in 48 percent, or nearly half, of all two parent families with children in the United States.

Single parent families have also grown rapidly, from 16 percent of all families with children in 1975 to 27 percent in 1992. Finally, with America's population aging, more working Americans have to take time off from work to attend to the medical needs of elderly parents.

As a rising number of American workers must deal with the dual pressures of family and job, the failure to accommodate these workers with adequate family and medical leave policies has forced too many Americans to choose between their job security and family emergencies. It has also resulted in inadequate job protection for working parents and other employees who have serious health conditions that temporarily prevent them from working.

As originally drafted, the legislation primarily supported parental leave for the birth, adoption, or care of a child. However, as proponents of the bill recognized the need for additional support, they broadened the scope of the legislation to include leave to care for elderly family members. This not only encouraged support from people who had aging family members in their care but also garnered the significant political support of the American Association of Retired Persons (AARP), the largest and most influential interest groups in the country on issues related to aging.

It is neither fair nor necessary to ask working Americans to choose between their jobs and their families—between continuing their employment and tending to their own health or to vital needs at home.

Although many enlightened companies have recognized the benefits to be realized from a system providing for family and medical leave, not all do. We all as a nation must join hands and extend the ethic of long-term workplace relationships and reciprocal commitment between employer and employee. It is only when workers can count on a commitment from their employer that they can make their own full commitments to their jobs. We must extend the success of those forward-looking workplaces where high-performance teamwork has already begun to take root and where family and medical leave already is accepted.

Data from the Bureau of Labor Statistics support the conclusion that American business has been fully responsive to the need of workers for family and medical leave. This data showed that, in 1991, for private business establishments with 100 workers or more, 37 percent of all full-time employees (and 19 percent of all part-time employees) had unpaid maternity leave available to them, and only 26 percent of all full-time employees in such establishments had unpaid paternity leave available. The most recently available data for smaller business establishments (those with fewer than 100 workers) are for 1990, and show that only 14 percent of all these employees had unpaid maternity leave available, and only 6 percent had unpaid paternity leave available.

The insufficient response to the family and medical leave needs of workers has come at a high cost to both the American family and to American business. There is a direct correlation between health and job security in the family home and productivity in the workplace. When businesses do not give workers leave for family needs, they fail to establish a working environment that can promote heightened productivity, lessened job turnover, and reduced absenteeism.

We all bear the cost when workers are forced to choose between keeping their jobs and meeting their personal and family obligations. When they must sacrifice their jobs, we all have to pay more for the essential but costly safety net. When they ignore their own health needs or their family obligations in order to keep their jobs, we all have to pay more for social services and medical care as neglected problems worsen.

American workers used the Family and Medical Leave Act to take unpaid leave from work more than 100 million times from 1993 to 2012, according to the U.S. Department of Labor. The agency asserts, however, that this assistance to employees and their families has not caused undue hardship to employers. According to a 2012 survey conducted by the Department of Labor, 91 percent of employers indicated that compliance with the act has had no noticeable detrimental effects on employee absenteeism, turnover, morale, or other aspects of their business operations.

The time has come for Federal legislation to bring fair and sensible family and medical leave policies to the American workplace. Currently, the United States is virtually the only advanced industrialized country without a national family and medical leave policy. Now, with the signing of this bill, American workers in all 50 States will enjoy the same rights as workers in other nations. This legislation balances the demands of the workplace with the needs of families. In supporting families, it promotes job stability and efficiency in the American workplace.

The Family and Medical Leave Act of 1993 sets a standard that is long overdue in working America. I am very pleased to sign this legislation into law.

Source: "Statement by the President," February 5, 1993, William J. Clinton Presidential Library, http://clinton6.nara.gov/1993/02/1993-02-05-family-and -medical-leave-act-statement-by-the-president.html.

Chapter 2

Women and Education

Introduction

In her 1977 address to students at Douglass College, poet Adrienne Rich articulated the importance of education, and in particular the importance of education for women. She stated that *"Responsibility* to yourself means refusing to let others do your thinking, talking, and naming for you; it means learning to respect and use your own brains and instincts" (Rich 1995, 233). Education, in short, provides a measure of independence to its recipients and gives individuals the tools to think for themselves, continue learning independently, and lessen one's dependence on others. This liberating nature of education is what makes it so powerful to the individual receiving the education. However, it is education's liberating nature that has long made the education of women and girls a subject of debate.

Although girls have been taught to read and write for much of the United States' history the type of education and the subjects they were taught have often differed considerably from the education received by boys. Until the middle of the 20th century, teachers and administrators in secondary schools encouraged girls to take classes that pertained to their traditional roles, such as home economics, or provided skills that contributed to professions that were open to women, such as nursing and teaching. Girls were often deterred, both directly and indirectly, from taking courses in mathematics and the sciences, while boys were encouraged to take courses that were more demanding academically and that better prepared them to take standardized tests for college admission.

There were numerous factors that contributed to the differing views of the value of education for males and females. First, because women were expected to marry and take on domestic duties as their primary responsibilities, it was thought that a woman's education should prepare her for the roles of wife and mother rather than for a career, as men were expected to do. Second, if women were expected to be dependent on men, as they have been for much of American history, the need for an education for women and girls that promoted independent thought and critical thinking was minimal. In fact, an education that promoted independence was actually seen as a barrier to a woman fulfilling her primary domestic roles. Finally, as a holdover from debates that began during the European Renaissance, many early Americans believed that an overly educated woman was unnatural, more like a man than a woman. While the strength of this view waned as the country moved into the 19th century, girls' and women's educational opportunities were still constrained by society's expectations of women's roles well into the 20th century.

The earliest universities in the United States were open only to men. In 1848, women's rights advocates at a convention in Seneca Falls, New York, listed among their grievances women's lack of access to higher education. Although there were some all-women's colleges at the time, the activists at the Seneca Falls Convention wanted greater coeducational opportunities for women and men. The activists believed that all women's colleges would continue to limit women's access to subjects considered gender-appropriate for them and that only coeducational opportunities would lead to true equality. By 1848, the only college that was open to both men and women was Oberlin College in Ohio, and it was not until 1870 that the University of Iowa became the first public university to open its doors to women. After the Civil War, additional women's colleges were opened in the Northeast and the South, such as Vassar and Wellesley, but coeducational opportunities were more likely to occur in state institutions opening west of the Mississippi River.

Once women had greater access to higher education, new issues related to women's equality emerged. For instance, would women have access to all programs offered at a university or only some? How could an institution best accommodate what was thought to be a woman's more fragile and moral nature? What actions could the government take to ensure that women were being treated equally in their quest for an education?

This chapter will consider six issues that emerged once women gained access to higher education. While most of these issues dealt with women's experiences with inequality at colleges and universities, some of the government's decisions about women's equality in education had implications for girls' opportunities in elementary and secondary schools as well.

One of the biggest hurdles to women gaining access to all aspects of an education was the societal belief that women's natures precluded them from certain roles in society. The belief that women naturally had more fragile bodies and emotional dispositions than men was the rationale for excluding women from certain programs at educational institutions. In the 1873 Supreme Court case *Bradwell v. Illinois,* this belief in women's and men's essential differences was used as the explanation for why women could not expect to reap the same benefits from their educations as could men. In 1969 Myra Bradwell passed the law exam in Chicago, Illinois. Prior to taking the exam, she had apprenticed with her husband's law practice and was encouraged by two prominent local judges to apply to the Illinois bar so that she could practice law. When her application was denied because she was a married woman, she ultimately took the case to the Supreme Court, arguing that her rights under the Fourteenth Amendment's Privileges and Immunities Clause had been violated. The Supreme Court disagreed, arguing that the right to hold a particular career was not based on the privileges of citizenship, at least not for women. Justice Joseph P. Bradley wrote the court's opinion, infamously stating that the "natural and proper timidity and delicacy which belongs to the female sex evidently unfits it for many of the occupations of civil life."

This concern for women's delicacy was the impetus of early social science research by John Dewey, who was interested in whether higher education was harmful to women's health. As with many of the limits placed on women in regard to working outside the home, there was a concern for women's reproductive functions in regard to their education, that either women's reproductive organs would somehow be harmed by too much education or that their reproductive abilities would themselves limit women's academic performance. Dewey used early survey research conducted by the State of Massachusetts to explore any evidence that higher education was harmful to women's health. While there is now much to criticize in terms of the research methods used and the questions asked of participant female college students, Dewey was one of the first to attempt to address the question of women's health and education in a relatively scientific manner that did not rely solely on people's preconceived notions of women's social and academic roles.

By the late 1960s and early 1970s, the link that had been made between women's academic abilities and their reproductive capabilities had lessened significantly, but there was still evidence of society's expectations of appropriate women's and girls' behavior in education. The fact that girls and women were clearly steered toward certain subjects, disciplines, and career choices and away from others was becoming a public policy issue, with the effect of this most easily measured in the relative salaries and wages of women and men. In 1972 Congress passed Title IX as part of the Education Amendments to the Higher Education Act to address issues of sex discrimination at any educational institution receiving federal funds. This momentous act for women's and girls' education was shepherded through Congress by Representative Edith Green, chair of the Subcommittee on Education of the Committee on Education and Labor, who was instrumental in many of the laws passed for women's rights during the 1960s and 1970s.

Like any law, once Title IX was passed, it had to be implemented. The law's general prohibition against sex discrimination in education had to be applied to the actual practices and policies of schools and universities. It was from the implementation of Title IX that numerous conflicts emerged. One of the first controversies that arose considered the law's language that it applied only to programs that received funds from the federal government. In *Grove City College v. Bell* (1984), the Supreme Court addressed whether the law prohibited sex discrimination only in the programs that actually received federal assistance or whether the prohibition applied to an entire institution if any of its programs received federal funds. In this case, the Court ruled that only the program receiving funds was affected by the law. Members of Congress claimed that this had not been their intent and clarified two years later that an entire institution must follow the law if any of its programs receive federal funds.

In 1996, a much more prominent case regarding sex discrimination in higher education emerged on the national scene. *United States v. Virginia* involved the all-male admissions policy of the Virginia Military Institute. The Department of Justice filed suit against Virginia on behalf of female students who had been rejected for admission due to their sex. While the argument could be made that this admissions policy was illegal under Title IX, the Department of Justice opted for a broader strategy, arguing that the discrimination was not only illegal but unconstitutional due to the Equal Protection Clause of the Fourteenth Amendment.

While Title IX applies to all areas of education, including admissions and access to all disciplines of study, its effect has been most visible in regard to athletic opportunities for women and girls. Because sports and athleticism have long been associated with men and masculinity, girls and women were not offered the same opportunities for athletics in school as boys and men until Title IX was passed. This adjustment did not come easily. In order to provide equal opportunities, schools often had to adjust their athletic budgets to accommodate these new sports opportunities for female students. These adjustments typically came in the form of redirecting existing athletic funding to newly created girls' and women's programs, which meant that some of the boys' and men's sports lost some funding. In some cases, less popular men's sports were cut altogether. Rather than framing Title IX as providing women with the opportunities that men had always had, opponents cast the law as taking opportunities away from men. This became the source of numerous lawsuits, including a 1999 case, *Neal v. Board of Trustees of the California State Universities,* in which the Supreme Court clarified that schools could engage in a variety of tactics to comply with the law, including the elimination of some men's sports.

The task of securing equality for women and girls in their educational pursuits has seen significant advances since Justice Bradley justified sex discrimination due to what he perceived was the inherent nature of females. While the most flagrant cases of discrimination have largely been addressed since Title IX was passed, there is still evidence that the experiences of male and female students differ. More recent cases involving women's rights in education will be addressed in Chapter 7.

The U.S. Supreme Court Sanctions Sex Discrimination in American Society

Justice Joseph P. Bradley's Concurrent Opinion in *Bradwell v. State of Illinois*

1872

By 1869, Mrs. Myra Bradwell had successfully completed her legal training and passed the Illinois law exam and had been recommended for admission to the Chicago bar by an Illinois judge. The Illinois Supreme Court, however, refused to admit her to the bar because she was a married woman and would be unable to adequately fulfill her duties as a lawyer while also fulfilling her role as a wife. The state court's decision was ultimately broadened to include all women, both married and unmarried. Bradwell appealed to the U.S. Supreme Court, claiming that the state's decision was a violation of the Fourteenth Amendment's Privileges and Immunities Clause, which prohibits states from passing laws that violate a person's rights of citizenship. Although the Court's opinion noted that there was a concern that the legal profession was unseemly for a woman, it noted that this was not the rationale for its decision allowing Illinois to deny women admission to the bar. Instead, the Supreme Court claimed that access to a particular profession was not guaranteed under the Fourteenth Amendment. Justice Bradley concurred with the Court's decision but not with the rationale for its decision. He focused almost exclusively on women's appropriate societal roles, which he found sufficient to limit women's access to certain professions.

I concur in the judgment of the court in this case, by which the judgment of the Supreme Court of Illinois is affirmed, but not for the reasons specified in the opinion just read.

The claim of the plaintiff, who is a married woman, to be admitted to practice as an attorney and counsellor-at-law, is based upon the supposed right of every person, man or woman, to engage in any lawful employment for a livelihood.

The Supreme Court of Illinois denied the application on the ground that, by the common law, which is the basis of the laws of Illinois, only men were admitted to the bar, and the legislature had not made any change in this respect, but had simply provided that no person should be admitted to practice as attorney or counsellor without having previously obtained a license for that purpose from two justices of the Supreme Court, and that no person should receive a license without first obtaining a certificate from the court of some county of his good moral character. In other respects it was left to the discretion of the court to establish the rules by which admission to the profession should be determined. The court, however, regarded itself as bound by at least two limitations. One was that it should establish such terms of admission as would promote the proper administration of justice, and the other that it should not admit any persons, or class of persons, not intended by the legislature to be admitted, even though not expressly excluded by statute. In view of this latter limitation the court felt compelled to deny the application of females to be admitted as members of the bar. Being contrary to the rules of the common law and the usages of Westminster Hall from time immemorial, it could not be supposed that the legislature had intended to adopt any different rule.

The claim that, under the fourteenth amendment of the Constitution, which declares that no State shall make or enforce any law which shall abridge the privileges and immunities of citizens of the United States, the statute law of Illinois, or the common law prevailing in that State, can no longer be set up as a barrier against the right of females to pursue any lawful employment for a livelihood (the practice of law included), assumes that it is one of the privileges and immunities of women as citizens to engage in any and every profession, occupation, or employment in civil life [83 U.S. 130, 141]. It certainly cannot be affirmed, as an historical fact, that this has ever been established as one of the fundamental privileges and immunities of the sex.

On the contrary, the civil law, as well as nature herself, has always recognized a wide difference in the respective spheres and destinies of man and woman. Man is, or should be, woman's protector and defender. The natural and proper timidity and delicacy which belongs to the female sex evidently unfits it for many of the occupations of civil life.

The constitution of the family organization, which is founded in the divine ordinance, as well as in the nature of things, indicates the domestic sphere as that which properly belongs to the domain and functions of womanhood. The harmony, not to say identity, of interest and views which belong, or should belong, to the family institution is repugnant to the idea of a woman adopting a distinct and independent career from that of her husband. So firmly fixed was this sentiment in the founders of the common law that it became a maxim of that system of jurisprudence that a woman had no legal existence separate from her husband, who was regarded as her head and representative in the social state; and, notwithstanding some recent modifications of this civil status, many of the special rules of law flowing from and dependent upon this cardinal principle still exist in full force in most States. One of these is, that a married woman is incapable, without her husband's consent, of making contracts which shall be binding on her or him. This very incapacity was one circumstance which the Supreme Court of Illinois deemed important in rendering a married woman incompetent fully to perform the duties and trusts that belong to the office of an attorney and counsellor.

It is true that many women are unmarried and not affected by any of the duties, complications, and incapacities arising out of the married state, but these are exceptions to the general rule.

The paramount destiny and mission of women are to fulfill the noble and benign offices of wife and mother. This is the law of the Creator. And the rules of civil society must be adapted to the general constitution of things, and cannot be based upon exceptional cases.

Justice Bradley's argument was consistent with a fundamental feature of the common law concept of coverture, which claimed that a woman's legal existence and rights cease to exist upon marriage. It was thought that a husband's legal rights essentially provided an adequate coverage of rights for both him and his wife, and thus a wife no longer needed any separate, individual rights. The notion that a man and woman became one person when married resulted in a legal sense with that one person being the husband. Having no rights of her own, a married woman's rights were similar to those of a child in that she had no ability to sign contracts, testify against her husband in court, or even have access to any wealth she brought into the marriage. This was justified on sentiments similar to Bradley's regarding the nature of women and their proper roles of wife and mother.

It is important to note how strongly gender role expectations influence people's behavior, including people who are in positions of authority. It is clear from his written opinion that Justice Bradley defined women largely by their family and reproductive roles. It was this societal definition of women rather than their individual abilities and talents that prevented women from undertaking occupations that were considered inconsistent with women's family roles. These ideas were not limited to Bradley, of course. In fact, in most cases of women fighting for their rights, such as the rights to the vote, to education, and to employment, they have had to fight against some version of these very sentiments.

". . . it is within the province of the legislature to ordain what offices, positions, and callings shall be filled and discharged by men, and shall receive the benefit of those energies and responsibilities, and that decision and firmness which are presumed to predominate in the sterner sex."

The humane movements of modern society, which have for their object the multiplication of avenues for woman's advancement, and of occupations adapted to her condition and sex, have my heartiest concurrence. But I am not prepared to say that it is one of her fundamental rights and privileges to be admitted into every office and position, including those which require highly special qualifications and demanding special responsibilities. In the nature of things it is not every citizen of every age, sex, and condition that is qualified for every calling and position. It is the prerogative of the legislator to prescribe regulations founded on nature, reason, and experience for the due admission of qualified persons to professions and callings demanding special skill and confidence. This fairly belongs to the police power of the State; and, in my opinion, in view of the peculiar characteristics, destiny, and mission of woman, it is within the province of the legislature to ordain what offices, positions, and callings shall be filled and discharged by men, and shall receive the benefit of those energies and responsibilities, and that decision and firmness which are presumed to predominate in the sterner sex.

For these reasons I think that the laws of Illinois now complained of are not obnoxious to the charge of abridging any of the privileges and immunities of citizens of the United States.

Source: *Bradwell v. Illinois,* 16 Wall, 83 U.S. 130 (1873), http://caselaw.lp.findlaw.com/scripts/getcase.pl?court=US&vol=83&invol=130.

A Scholar Studies the Impact of Higher Education on Women

John Dewey's "Education and the Health of Women"

1885

The tendency to apply the exact methods of science to problems of education, is one of the most hopeful signs of present pedagogy.

One of the more fruitful lines of application will be found, doubtless, in the consideration of the educational question in relation to the wider sphere of social science, and the application of the statistical method.

As one of the first fruits of this application, we hail the returns collected by the Association of college alumnae, wisely embodied in the current report of the Massachusetts labor bureau. These are directed especially to ascertaining the effect of education upon the health of women, but there are incidentally discussed a number of other very interesting problems.

The returns include 12 institutions, which had (1882) graduated 1,290 women, from 705 or 54.65 per cent of whom returns have been received. Of these the average age at beginning study was 5.6 years; at beginning of menstrual period, 13.6 years; at entering college, 18.3 years; and at the present time, 28.5 years. This gives about six years as the average time since graduation, certainly ample for the determination of the general effects upon health of their collegiate training. Of the 705 (women in the study), 19.5 per cent report a deterioration in health during college life; 59.3 per cent, no change; 21.1 per cent, an improvement. The corresponding figures for working girls of Boston show a deterioration of 16 per cent, a favorable balance of 3.5 per cent in favor of working girls. The total number of disorders reported by the 705 is 865. . . . One hundred thirty five consider constitutional weakness [the] cause of disorders; 81 bad sanitary conditions; 81 intellectual overwork; 73 emotional strain, and 47 physical accident, while the others report no cause. Defective as this report is in detail, it is remarkably suggestive. The general conclusion stated in the report is that the health of women engaged in the pursuit of a college education, does not suffer more than that of a corresponding number of other women in other occupations, or without occupation.

This general conclusion may be allowed to stand. But the figures are not "worked for all they are worth." A more

In 1885 John Dewey had recently received his doctorate and was a faculty member in the Philosophy Department at the University of Michigan. He had also recently met, to be married the next year, Alice Chipman, who was very active on issues of women's equality at the University of Michigan. In 1885 the University of Michigan was celebrating its 15th year of admitting women to college, and Dewey used the newly emerging field of statistics to ascertain whether education was harmful to women, an idea that was still widely believed by many in higher education at the time. Later in his life, Dewey became a supporter of women's suffrage and argued that democracy was dependent on an educated populace. Thus, it is not surprising that he favored giving women and girls access to education. This article considered whether education had any ill effects on women's and girls' health.

detailed examination of them brings out the following points which the report fails to explicitly notice.

Of those who entered college one or two years after the commencement of the menstrual function 20.5 per cent had poor health during the four years of college life, while of those entering three to five years after its establishment 17.7 per cent, and more than five years 15.4 per cent had poor health. The following figures tell the same story with slight variation: of those who entered at the age of 16, or under, 28.1 per cent deteriorated, 17.2 per cent improved in health; of those seventeen to nineteen 17.3 per cent deteriorated and 19.7 per cent improved; while of those who were twenty or over 17.9 per cent deteriorated, while 28.4 per cent improved—almost exactly reversing the figures for the youngest class.

When comparing the general state of health for women who went to college to those who did not, Dewey offered a preliminary conclusion that there was little reason to believe that education caused health problems for women. However, delving more deeply into the statistics, he looked specifically at the potential effect of education on women's reproductive health at various stages in their lives: adolescence, or what he calls "development"; the time while in college; and the years following college. Although he does not draw any substantive conclusions from the data, Dewey noted that higher education might have a diminishing effect on the number of children married women had. This observation is consistent with what is seen worldwide today; there is a correlation between the years of education women receive and the number of children they have. More educated women typically results in lower fertility rates in a country. While Dewey thought that this data raised some interesting questions about women's health while in college, he appeared to see this more as an opportunity for further research rather than as a rationale for limited women's access to higher education.

The fact that of the married [college women] 37 per cent are without children, although the average number of years spent in married life is 6.2, must be included in any discussion that wishes to reach complete results. There were, moreover, to those bearing children but an average of two children to every seven years of married life, while, if all married couples are included, the average falls to 1.2 for five years.

With such statistics, however, there must be borne in mind the general falling off in fertility of all women occupying about the same social rank. Of the children born, 12 per cent have died, and of these the unusually large percent of 25 is due to causes occurring contemporary with birth, still [birth], premature birth, etc. . . .

During the period of development 53 per cent were troubled during the menstrual period with disorders, including irregularities, uterine and reflex pain, one, two, or all three. During college life the per cent was 66; since graduation 64. If mere irregularities be isolated, and they and the more organic disturbances treated separately we find: Irregularities alone—development, 16 per cent; college life, 9 per cent; graduate life, 7 per cent. Uterine and reflex pain—development 24 per cent; college life, 36 per cent; graduate life 36 per cent. Of the disorders reported 7 per cent are brain troubles, 33 per cent nervousness, in addition to which 15 per cent report neuralgia; 26 per cent disorders of generative organs.

We give only figures, and these only such as bear directly upon the central question of the health of woman in reference to her education. They certainly show that the time for optimistic congratulations is not yet reached.

The other general conclusion of the report that such falling off in health during college life, as did appear, is due rather to predisposing causes, than directly attributable to college life itself, brings out some very interesting contributions to the scanty generalizations we already possess, concerning the relations between health and social environment. . . .

Dewey believed that it was important to know whether university life itself caused irregularities in women's health or whether there were other factors associated with university life that might be the cause of any discrepancies in the health of women in college and those who were not in college. He suggested additional questions that must be asked in future research in order to get a more complete picture of the effect of higher education on women's health. Dewey also thought that the information had to be more precise and thorough than what was gleaned from this first study in order to make any definitive conclusions about women and higher education.

First as to hereditary: A total of 35 per cent report a tendency to disease inherited from one or both parents. Those inheriting tendency from one parent only present some slight falling off in good health when compared with the entire average; while for those inheriting from both 58.3 per cent are in good health; 41.7 in poor. . . .

The report upon the whole is surprisingly full. For the social student, however, it presents certain notable deficiencies. The physical, social, and moral environment of the students during college requires infinitely more investigation. The details concerning intellectual surroundings are comparatively full, though the number of hours of study should be given instead of the indefinite terms, "moderate," "severe." The inquiries concerning social surroundings are virtually confined to the inquiry as to whether the person "entered society," a little, a good deal, or none. Such vague expressions are worse than none. The question is as to how the student spent the hours of social recreation, and how many were so spent. The complete answer of this question, it is hardly too much to say, would throw more light on the hygienic problem than almost all else. It should include information as to whether the institution is female only or co-education; what its social relations are to the town, the nature of the town; whether the young women live in dormitories, in cottages, in selected homes, or in ordinary boarding-houses; what regulations, if any, the faculty have made concerning study hours, and the hours not spent in study; whether the institution has a matron; whether her duties extend to moral and social matters, or to physical only; whether the institution has a gymnasium, etc. . . . If the association will study the conditions of the problem along this line, and frame questions accordingly, they will deserve still more at the hands of both the scientific educator, and the social student. Meanwhile we will be thankful for what we have.

Source: John Dewey, "Education and the Health of Women," *Science* 6 (151) (October 16, 1885): 341–342.

A Congresswoman's Statement on Sex Discrimination in Colleges and Universities

Representative Edith Green's Statement at House "Discrimination against Women" Subcommittee Hearings

June 17, 1970

Opening Statement of Representative Edith Green, Subcommittee Chair

Edith Green, Democratic representative from Oregon, was a member of the House of Representatives from 1955 until 1974. Prior to her election to Congress, she was active in the Democratic Party of Oregon, serving as a delegate to four Democratic National Conventions. She was also appointed by President John F. Kennedy to serve on the President's Commission on the Status of Women and was an advocate for the Equal Pay Act, the first policy that emerged from a commission recommendation. A former schoolteacher and public relations director for the Oregon Educational Association, she was considered an expert on education policy. In Congress, she chaired the Subcommittee on Education of the Committee on Education and Labor and helped promote equality for women by holding several days of hearings on legislation that would ultimately make it illegal for any educational institution receiving federal funds to discriminate on the basis of sex. The proposal ultimately became part of the 1972 Higher Education Act and is more commonly referred to as Title IX, which references the relevant section of the law.

It is with a great sense of personal pleasure that I welcome to the subcommittee today witnesses who will offer testimony on section 805 of H.R. 16098.

Section 805 would amend the Civil Rights Act to prohibit discrimination on the basis of sex in federally financed programs and would remove the exemption presently existing in Title VII of the Civil Rights Act with respect to those in education. It would authorize the Civil Rights Commission to study discrimination against women and lastly would remove the exemption of executive, administrative, and professional employees from the equal pay for equal work provision of the Fair Labor Standards Act.

It is to be hoped that the enactment of the provisions would be of some help in eliminating the discrimination against women which still permeates our society.

It seems ironic that in a period when we are more concerned with civil rights and liberties than ever before in our history—when minorities have vigorously asserted themselves—that discrimination against a very important majority—women—has been given little attention.

Increasingly women are constituting a greater proportion of our labor force. As of April of this year there were 31,293,000 women in the labor market constituting nearly 40 percent of the total.

However, despite the growth in the number of women working today, the proportion of women in the professions is lower in this country than in most countries throughout the world.

While the United States prides itself in being a leader of nations, it has been backward in its treatment of its working women.

Professionally, women in the United States constitute only 9 percent of all full professors, 8 percent of all scientists, 6.7 percent of all physicians, 3.5 percent of all lawyers, and 1 percent of all engineers.

Despite the fact that the Federal Government through Democratic and Republican administrations has given lip service to the equal opportunities for employment of women, the very large majority are in the lower grades of Civil Service and only a small portion in policy-making or administrative positions.

Despite increases in earnings, income and wage statistics illustrate dramatically a deep discrimination against women. The average median income for women working full-time year around is $4,457. The comparable figure for men is $7,664.

We have been concerned, and rightly so, about discrimination against the Negro in our society—about the Negro man who averages $5,603—only 69.9 percent of the average earnings for a white man.

But I hear little concern expressed for women who average only 58 percent in comparison. The average wage in the United States is: Negro women, $3,677; white women, 4,700; Negro men, $5,603; white men, $8,014.

The sorry fact is that the gap in earning power is widening. In 1956, for example, women's median income of $2,827 was 64 percent of the $4,466 received by men.

Women's median wage or salary income rose to $3,973 in 1966 while men's rose to $6,848. So, although both groups experienced increases, women's income increased at a slower rate and their median income in 1966 was only 58 percent of that of men—a 6-percent drop in the 10-year period.

Many of us would like to think of educational institutions as being far from the maddening crowd, where fair play is the rule of the game and everyone, including women, gets a fair roll of the dice.

Let us not deceive ourselves—our educational institutions have proven to be no bastions of democracy.

Initially many women are required to meet higher admission standards than men. While the Federal Government and the Office of Education, in effect, through their policies, encourage college admission standards to be waived for certain individuals, they have shown absolutely no concern over the higher admission requirements set for women in many institutions.

Our colleague from Michigan, Representative Martha Griffiths, cited instances recently where at the University of North Carolina admission of women on the freshman level is restricted to those who are especially well qualified. There is no similar restriction for male students.

In the State of Virginia, I am advised, during a 3-year period, 21,000 women were turned down for college entrance, while not one male student was rejected.

The requirement for educational equality between men and women included both academic and nonacademic educational opportunities. Academically the law applied broadly, including admissions policies, financial aid and scholarship decisions, curricular opportunities, and treatment within the classroom, which included a prohibition on sexual harassment. However, Title IX is best known for its application to girls' and women's athletic opportunities. Prior to the law's passage, few schools provided opportunities or resources for women's sports. Girls and college women might play intramural sports but rarely had access to competitive interschool sports. When schools and universities made sports available to female students, their facilities and equipment were often of lower quality than boys' and men's teams. Title IX required that girls and women be given the same opportunities to compete in sports as men and that these opportunities be funded at similar levels.

On the graduate level, not too surprisingly, the situation worsens.

Salary disparities by gender continue to be evident in the U.S. higher education system. Although gender gaps in faculty pay at some colleges and universities have vanished or become negligible, studies indicate that the gap persists at the national level and that this disparity cannot be fully explained away by the high seniority levels of male faculty members, the higher pay scales at four-year universities and research institutions (where men account for a higher percentage of total faculty), or the academic disciplines that draw heavily from one sex for their scholars. In fact, a 2010 report of faculty salaries issued by the American Association of University Professors (AAUP) indicated that institutions of higher learning have made virtually no headway in erasing this gap in the years since the NEA published its 1966 study. According to the AAUP, the overall average salary for women faculty members was 81 percent of that for male faculty members in 2009–2010—exactly the same gap that the association found in 1975–1976. The 2010 AAUP report found that women had nearly reached salary parity with men at community colleges but that they lagged far behind their male colleagues at all professorial ranks and in each institutional category, from doctoral to associate.

Sex differences in rank and salary at colleges and universities have also been reported by the Women's Bureau of the Department of Labor. A recent report by the Bureau pointed out that "in institutions of higher education women are much less likely than men to be associate or full professors." And citing a 1966 study by the [National Education Association] the report states that in 1965–66, "women full professors had a median salary of only $11,649 compared with $12,758 for men."

Total Federal support to institutions of higher education amounted to $3,367 million in fiscal year 1968. Over 2,100 universities and colleges participated in that support. The President's Executive Order 11246, as amended by Executive Order 11375, specifically forbids sex discrimination by Federal contractors. However, colleges and universities are still receiving Federal contracts and although forbidden by Executive order from discriminating against women, nevertheless continue in this course. I think this warrants our attention and the attention of the administration.

In Federal civil service, as well as in political appointments, there has been lip service in regard to equal opportunities for women but in reality there has been no change through Democratic or Republican administrations.

The National Congress and State legislatures have always been the best proof that this indeed is a man's world—and too often discrimination against women has been either systematically or subconsciously carried out.

In hearings I expect this to be well documented in our tax laws, in social security benefits, in labor unions which through the years negotiated contracts paying women less than men for identical work. Of course, invariably the negotiators for both management and labor have been men. . . .

As I said before, this seems to me to be ample evidence of the discrimination which does exist throughout our Government. As I said, during the next several days I hope that the various kinds of discrimination against women in our society will be discussed and will be fully documented, and that this can be made available to the men who run the world.

Source: Excerpt from "Discrimination against Women," Hearings before the Special Subcommittee on Education of the Committee on Education and Labor, House of Representatives, 91st Congress, 2nd Session, June 17, 1970, 1–4.

The U.S. Supreme Court Clarifies the Reach of Title IX

Supreme Court Ruling in *Grove City College v. Bell*

1984

Section 901(a) of Title IX of the Education Amendments of 1972 . . . prohibits sex discrimination in "any education program or activity receiving Federal financial assistance," and [Section] 902 directs agencies awarding most types of assistance to promulgate regulations to ensure that recipients adhere to that prohibition. Compliance with departmental regulations may be secured by termination of assistance "to the particular program, or part thereof, in which . . . noncompliance has been . . . found" or by "any other means authorized by law."

This case presents several questions concerning the scope and operation of these provisions and the regulations established by the Department of Education. We must decide, first, whether Title IX applies at all to Grove City College, which accepts no direct assistance but enrolls students who receive federal grants that must be used for educational purposes.

If so, we must identify the "education program or activity" at Grove City that is "receiving Federal financial assistance" and determine whether federal assistance to that program may be terminated solely because the College violates the Department's regulations by refusing to execute an Assurance of Compliance with Title IX. Finally, we must consider whether the application of Title IX to Grove City infringes the First Amendment rights of the College or its students.

Petitioner Grove City College is a private, coeducational, liberal arts college that has sought to preserve its institutional autonomy by consistently refusing state and federal financial assistance.

Grove City's desire to avoid federal oversight has led it to decline to participate, not only in direct institutional aid programs, but also in federal student assistance programs under which the College would be required to assess students' eligibility and to determine the amounts of loans, work-study funds, or grants they should receive.

Grove City has, however, enrolled a large number of students who receive Basic Educational Opportunity Grants (BEOG's). . . .

This particular case provides an excellent example of how the language of legislation must often be interpreted before it can be applied to actual situations. Title IX, passed in 1972, seems to clearly state that an educational program or activity that receives federal funds must not discriminate on the basis of sex. But this case raises the question of how widely the prohibition of sex discrimination applies and what actually constitutes the receipt of federal funds. Does the prohibition apply only to the particular program that receives aid, or does it apply to the institution as a whole? Furthermore, what kinds of aid from the federal government trigger this provision of the laws? It often falls to the Supreme Court to give the laws meaning by interpreting and applying them to real situations that come before the Court. In this case, Grove City College had refused to sign an Assurance of Compliance sent to it by the Department of Health, Education, and Welfare that stated that the college would comply with all federal regulations, including those included in Title IX. The Supreme Court had to decide whether the type of aid received by students at Grove City College made the college bound by the provisions of the law.

By refusing to receive any direct governmental funds, officials at Grove City College believed that the college was exempt from Title IX's prohibition against sex discrimination. While some of its students did receive grants from the federal government, Grove City College officials did not think that the college was obliged to follow the law regarding sex discrimination because these grants went directly to the students rather than to the college. Because these funds did not go directly to the college, administrators refused to sign an Assurance of Compliance, as required by the federal government for institutions that received federal funds. Thus, the first issue facing the Supreme Court was whether the student grants obligated the college to comply with the law. The court decided that Grove City College must comply with Title IX even though the aid was provided indirectly through federally funded student grants.

The Department concluded that Grove City was a "recipient" of "Federal financial assistance" as those terms are defined in the regulations implementing Title IX and, in July, 1977, it requested that the College execute the Assurance of Compliance required by [Title IX]. If Grove City had signed the Assurance, it would have agreed to "[c]omply, to the extent applicable to it, with Title IX . . . and all applicable requirements imposed by or pursuant to the Department's regulation . . . to the end that . . . no person in the United States shall, on the basis of sex, be . . . subjected to discrimination under any education program or activity for which [it] receives or benefits from Federal financial assistance from the Department." . . .

When Grove City persisted in refusing to execute an Assurance, the Department initiated proceedings to declare the College and its students ineligible to receive BEOG's. The Administrative Law Judge held that the federal financial assistance received by Grove City obligated it to execute an Assurance of Compliance and entered an order terminating assistance until Grove City "corrects its noncompliance with Title IX and satisfies the Department that it is in compliance" with the applicable regulations.

Grove City and four of its students then commenced this action in the District Court for the Western District of Pennsylvania, which concluded that the students' BEOG's constituted "Federal financial assistance" to Grove City but held, on several grounds, that the Department could not terminate the students' aid because of the College's refusal to execute an Assurance of Compliance. . . .

Finally, the Court of Appeals concluded that the Department could condition financial aid upon the execution of an Assurance of Compliance, and that the Department had acted properly in terminating federal financial assistance to the students and Grove City despite the lack of evidence of actual discrimination.

We granted certiorari . . . and we now affirm the Court of Appeals' judgment that the Department could terminate BEOG's received by Grove City's students to force the College to execute an Assurance of Compliance. . . .

It is not surprising to find . . . that the language of 901(a) contains no hint that Congress perceived a substantive difference between direct institutional assistance and aid received by a school through its students. The linchpin of Grove City's argument that none of its programs receives any federal assistance is a perceived distinction between direct and indirect aid, a distinction that finds no support in the text of 901(a). Nothing in 901(a) suggests that Congress elevated form over substance by making the application of the nondiscrimination

". . . the Court of Appeals concluded . . . that the Department [of Education] had acted properly in terminating federal financial assistance to the students and Grove City despite the lack of evidence of actual discrimination."

principle dependent on the manner in which a program or activity receives federal assistance. There is no basis in the statute for the view that only institutions that themselves apply for federal aid or receive checks directly from the Federal Government are subject to regulation.

With the benefit of clear statutory language, powerful evidence of Congress' intent, and a longstanding and coherent administrative construction of the phrase "receiving Federal financial assistance," we have little trouble concluding that Title IX coverage is not foreclosed because federal funds are . . . granted to Grove City's students rather than directly to one of the College's educational programs.

There remains the question, however, of identifying the "education program or activity" of the College that can properly be characterized as "receiving" federal assistance through grants to some of the students attending the College. . . .

Student financial aid programs, we believe, are sui generis. In neither purpose nor effect can BEOG's be fairly characterized as unrestricted grants that institutions may use for whatever purpose they desire. The BEOG program was designed, not merely to increase the total resources available to educational institutions, but to enable them to offer their services to students who had previously been unable to afford higher education. It is true, of course, that substantial portions of the BEOG's received by Grove City's students ultimately find their way into the College's general operating budget and are used to provide a variety of services to the students through whom the funds pass. However, we have found no persuasive evidence suggesting that Congress intended that the Department's regulatory authority follow federally aided students from classroom to classroom, building to building, or activity to activity.

We conclude that the receipt of BEOG's by some of Grove City's students does not trigger institutionwide coverage under Title IX. In purpose and effect, BEOG's represent [465 U.S. 555, 574] federal financial assistance to the College's own financial aid program, and it is that program that may properly be regulated under Title IX. . . .

The Supreme Court next addressed whether an entire institution had to follow the law when one of its programs received federal funds or whether only those programs that actually received the funds were subject to compliance. The Court ruled that only those programs receiving federal funds were required to follow Title IX and noted that since financial aid programs were sui generis, or unique in and of themselves, Title IX's prohibition against sex discrimination in regard to the receipt of student grant money as payment for tuition applied only to the financial aid program, not to the entire institution. This severely narrowed the effect of Title IX by allowing any program not receiving federal funds to continue discriminating on the basis of sex. Two years later Congress overruled the Supreme Court's decision by passing the Civil Rights Restoration Act of 1987, clarifying that an educational institution in its entirety must follow Title IX if any of its programs receives federal funds. It should also be noted that Grove City College eventually stopped accepting any student aid funds from the federal government, establishing its own loan programs to students in order to avoid government regulation of the college.

Source: *Grove City College v. Bell,* 465 U.S. 555 (1984), http://caselaw .lp.findlaw.com/cgi-bin/getcase.pl?court=us&vol=465&invol=555.

The U.S. Supreme Court Opens VMI to Women

Supreme Court Ruling in *United States v. Virginia et al.*

1996

VMI was the first state-supported military university in the United States, and since its establishment in 1839 it had been an all-male university. This policy was challenged in 1990 by the U.S. Department of Justice as illegally discriminating against women. Rather than rely on Title IX to counter VMI's all-male admissions policy, the Department of Justice argued that Virginia violated the Fourteenth Amendment's Equal Protection Clause, which prohibits states from denying citizens' equal protection of the law. Because the Fourteenth Amendment was ratified in 1868 following the Civil War, the Supreme Court had not historically interpreted the clause to apply to questions of sex discrimination, and not until 1971, in *Reed v. Reed,* did the Court apply the Fourteenth Amendment to women and cases of sex discrimination. In the case of VMI, Associate Justice Ruth Bader Ginsburg addressed in the Court opinion whether educational opportunities for both sexes were protected by the Fourteenth Amendment.

Unlike Grove City College, VMI is a public university in that it receives a significant portion of its budget from the state's tax revenues. VMI also receives considerable contributions from its alumni, providing the university with a large endowment and additional sources of funding. Because of the loyalty of its alumni, all of whom had attended VMI as a single-sex institution, there was a lot of pressure to maintain the traditions of VMI. As the case moved through the federal court system from the district court to the court of appeals to the U.S. Supreme Court, the courts had to weigh the various practical and emotional reasons for excluding women against the language of the Fourteenth Amendment, which requires states to provide equal protection under the law.

Virginia's public institutions of higher learning include an incomparable military college, Virginia Military Institute (VMI). The United States maintains that the Constitution's equal protection guarantee precludes Virginia from reserving exclusively to men the unique educational opportunities VMI affords. We agree.

Founded in 1839, VMI is today the sole single-sex school among Virginia's 15 public institutions of higher learning. VMI's distinctive mission is to produce "citizen-soldiers," men prepared for leadership in civilian life and in military service. VMI pursues this mission through pervasive training of a kind not available anywhere else in Virginia. Assigning prime place to character development, VMI uses an "adversative method" modeled on English public schools and once characteristic of military instruction. VMI constantly endeavors to instill physical and mental discipline in its cadets and impart to them a strong moral code. The school's graduates leave VMI with heightened comprehension of their capacity to deal with duress and stress, and a large sense of accomplishment for completing the hazardous course.

VMI has notably succeeded in its mission to produce leaders; among its alumni are military generals, Members of Congress, and business executives. The school's alumni overwhelmingly perceive that their VMI training helped them to realize their personal goals. VMI's endowment reflects the loyalty of its graduates; VMI has the largest per-student endowment of all public undergraduate institutions in the Nation.

Neither the goal of producing citizen-soldiers nor VMI's implementing methodology is inherently unsuitable to women. And the school's impressive record in producing leaders has made admission desirable to some women. Nevertheless, Virginia has elected to preserve exclusively for men the advantages and opportunities a VMI education affords. . . .

VMI today enrolls about 1,300 men as cadets. Its academic offerings in the liberal arts, sciences, and engineering are also available at other public colleges and universities in Virginia. But VMI's mission is special. It is the mission of the school "'to produce educated and honorable men, prepared for the varied work of civil life, imbued with love of learning, confident in the functions and attitudes of leadership, possessing a high sense of public service, advocates of the American democracy and free enterprise system, and ready as citizen soldiers to defend their country in time of national peril'" . . . (quoting Mission Study Committee of the VMI Board of Visitors, Report, May 16, 1986). . . .

In 1990, prompted by a complaint filed with the Attorney General by a female high-school student seeking admission to VMI, the United States sued the Commonwealth of Virginia and VMI, alleging that VMI's exclusively male admission policy violated the Equal Protection Clause of the Fourteenth Amendment. Trial of the action consumed six days and involved an array of expert witnesses on each side.

In the two years preceding the lawsuit the District Court noted, VMI had received inquiries from 347 women, but had responded to none of them. "[S]ome women, at least," the court said, "would want to attend the school if they had the opportunity." The court further recognized that, with recruitment, VMI could "achieve at least 10% female enrollment"—"a sufficient 'critical mass' to provide the female cadets with a positive educational experiences." And it was also established that "some women are capable of all of the individual activities required of VMI cadets." In addition, experts agreed that if VMI admitted women, "the VMI ROTC experience would become a better training program from the perspective of the armed forces, because it would provide training in dealing with a mixed-gender army."

The District Court ruled in favor of VMI, however, and rejected the equal protection challenge pressed by the United States. . . .

The District Court reasoned that education in "a single-gender environment, be it male or female," yields substantial benefits. . . . If single-gender education for males ranks as an important governmental objective, it becomes obvious, the District Court concluded, that the *only* means of achieving the objective "is to exclude women from the all-male institution. . . ."

The Court of Appeals for the Fourth Circuit disagreed and vacated the District Court's judgment. The appellate court held: "The Commonwealth of Virginia has not . . . advanced any state policy by which it can justify its determination, under

"In the two years preceding the lawsuit . . . VMI had received [enrollment] inquiries from 347 women, but had responded to none of them."

an announced policy of diversity, to afford VMI's unique type of program to men and not to women."

The appeals court greeted with skepticism Virginia's assertion that it offers single-sex education at VMI as a facet of the Commonwealth's overarching and undisputed policy to advance "autonomy and diversity." The court underscored Virginia's nondiscrimination commitment: "'[I]t is extremely important that [colleges and universities] deal with faculty, staff, and students *without regard to sex, race, or ethnic origin.*'" . . .

[T]he appeals court assigned to Virginia . . . responsibility for selecting a remedial course. The court suggested these options for the Commonwealth: Admit women to VMI; establish parallel institutions or programs; or abandon state support, leaving VMI free to pursue its policies as a private institution. . . .

[T]his suit present[s] two ultimate issues. First, does Virginia's exclusion of women from the educational opportunities provided by VMI—extraordinary opportunities for military training and civilian leadership development—deny to women "capable of all of the individual activities required of VMI cadets," the equal protection of the laws guaranteed by the Fourteenth Amendment? Second, if VMI's "unique" situation, as Virginia's sole single-sex public institution of higher education—offends the Constitutions' equal protection principle, what is the remedial requirement? . . .

The United States does not challenge any expert witness estimation on average capacities or preferences of men and women. Instead, the United States emphasizes that time and again since this Court's turning point decision in *Reed* v. *Reed,* (1971), we have cautioned reviewing courts to take a "hard look" at generalizations or "tendencies" of the kind pressed by Virginia, and relied upon by the District Court. . . . State actors controlling gates to opportunity, we have instructed, may not exclude qualified individuals based on "fixed notions concerning the roles and abilities of males and females." . . .

It may be assumed, for purposes of this decision, that most women would not choose VMI's adversative method. As Fourth Circuit Judge Motz observed, however, in her dissent from the Court of Appeals' denial . . . it is also probable the "many men would not want to be educated in such an environment." . . . Education, to be sure, is not a "one size fits all" business. The issue, however, is not whether "women—or

Given these three choices by the Fourth Circuit Court of Appeals, VMI opted to create a similar, parallel women's academy at the nearby Mary Baldwin College rather than admit women or sacrifice all state financial support. The Supreme Court ultimately acknowledged that this so-called comparable program was not in fact comparable in that it did not provide women with the same opportunities or experiences they would receive as cadets at VMI. As such, this approach to correcting the discrimination was rejected by the Supreme Court. Instead, the Court ruled that VMI must admit women to the university as long as it received state funds. It should be noted that although the Fourteenth Amendment has now been interpreted as applying to sex discrimination, the classification of sex still does not receive the same constitutional protections as does the classification of race in cases of racial discrimination.

men—should be forced to attend VMI"; rather, the question is whether the Commonwealth can constitutionally deny to women who have the will and capacity, the training and attendant opportunities that VMI uniquely affords.

The notion that admission of women would downgrade VMI's stature, destroy the adversative system and, with it, even the school, is a judgment hardly proved, a prediction hardly different from other "self-fulfilling prophec[ies] . . ." once routinely used to deny rights or opportunities. . . .

Women's successful entry into the federal military academics, and their participation in the nations' military forces, indicate that Virginia's fears for the future of VMI may not be solidly grounded. The Commonwealth's justification for excluding all women from "citizen-soldier" training for which some are qualified, in any event, cannot rank as "exceedingly persuasive," as we have explained and applied that standard. . . .

[G]eneralizations about "the way women are," estimates of what is appropriate for *most women,* no longer justify denying opportunity to women whose talent and capacity place them outside the average description. . . .

It is on behalf of these women that the United States has instituted this suit, and it is for them that a remedy must be crafted, a remedy that will end their exclusion from a state-supplied educational opportunity for which they are fit, a decree that will "bar like discrimination in the future."

In the wake of the Supreme Court's *United States v. Virginia* decision, VMI's board of directors voted 9 to 8 to accept women cadets rather than become a private institution and retain its all-male status. VMI reluctantly opened its doors to female cadets in August 1997. The institute's first coed class included 31 women, including a number of female students who were allowed to transfer to VMI from select junior colleges. In 1999, these female transfers became the first women cadets to earn their diplomas from VMI. In 2001, 14 female cadets became the first to graduate from VMI after spending all four years on campus. Since that time, women have generally accounted for about 10 percent of the total student body at VMI.

Source: *United States v. Virginia et al.* (94-1941), 518 U.S. 515 (1996), http://supreme.justia.com/cases/federal/us/518/515/case.html.

A Circuit Court Rules on Proportionality in Intercollegiate Sports

Ninth Circuit Court Ruling in *Neal v. Board of Trustees of California State Universities*

1999

The application of Title IX to sports opportunities for girls and women has probably fostered more controversy than any other aspect of the law. Before Title IX could be implemented, the Department of Health, Education, and Welfare was required to develop guidelines for schools and universities to help them follow the intent of the law. These guidelines, published in 1975, made it clear that colleges and universities would have to make substantial changes to their athletic programs. Colleges and universities were given three years to be in compliance with the guidelines. These efforts to comply with the law in regard to women's and men's access to sports have often resulted in adjustments made to the existing men's sports opportunities in order to provide equal opportunities to girls and women. Schools must provide equality in numerous aspects of athletics, including scholarships, facilities, equipment, funding, and the number of sports offered. In this case, California State University in Bakersfield, California, opted to decrease the number of roster spots on men's teams in order to create greater parity with the roster numbers on women's teams. The university was sued for allegedly violating Title IX and the Fourteenth Amendment by decreasing men's access to certain sports.

After Title IX's passage, the number of women attending college increased dramatically, and in fact women outnumber men in many universities. This posed a challenge for universities to meet the Department of Education's guidelines, which provided three methods by which a university could comply with Title IX. First, a school is in compliance if the ratio of male to female sports opportunities is consistent with the ratio of the student body as a whole. Second, the school can comply by illustrating a history of expanding opportunities to meet the interests in sports among the underrepresented group. Third, the university has complied if it is fully accommodating the interests of the underrepresented group. However, as in CSUB's case, women's access to athletics often did not reflect the ratio of women to men at the university. It was only after CSUB was sued by the California National Organization for Women that the university took steps to alleviate this disparity. One of the arguments made against decreasing men's opportunities to reach parity is that although they are often the minority of students, men tend to have more interest in sports than do women. This has not been determined to be a legitimate rationale for limiting access for women, however.

The instant case requires us to consider whether Title IX prevents a university in which male students occupy a disproportionately high percentage of athletic roster spots from making gender-conscious decisions to reduce the proportion of roster spots assigned to men. We hold that Title IX does not bar such remedial actions....

Neal's suit alleged that the decision of California State University, Bakersfield ("CSUB") to reduce the number of spots on its men's wrestling team, undertaken as part of a university-wide program to achieve "substantial proportionality" between each gender's participation in varsity sports and its composition in the campus's student body, violated Title IX and the Equal Protection Clause of the United States Constitution. The district court determined that regulations promulgated pursuant to Title IX, and CSUB's program, which was modeled after those regulations, violated Title IX.... We reverse, and vacate the injunction.

Defendant/Appellant CSUB is a large public university where female students outnumbered male students by roughly 64% to 36% in 1996. The composition of CSUB's varsity athletic rosters, however, was quite different. In the 1992–93 academic year, male students took 61% of the university's spots on athletic rosters and received 68% of CSUB's available athletic scholarship money.

This imbalance helped prompt a lawsuit by the California chapter of the National Organization for Women, alleging that the California State University system was violating a state law that is similar to the federal government's Title IX. That lawsuit eventually settled, resulting in a consent decree mandating ... that each Cal State campus have a proportion of female athletes that was within five percentage points of the proportion of female undergraduate students at that school.

This portion of the consent decree was patterned after the first part of the three-part Title IX compliance test promulgated by the Department of Education's Office for Civil Rights ("OCR").

When the university agreed to the consent decree, California was slowly emerging from a recession, and state funding for higher education was declining. As a result, CSUB administrators were seriously constrained in what they could spend on athletic programs. The university chose to adopt squad size targets, which would encourage the expansion of the women's teams while limiting the size of the men's teams. In order to comply with the consent decree, CSUB opted for smaller men's teams across the board, rejecting the alternative of eliminating some men's teams entirely. CSUB's plan was designed to bring it into compliance with the consent decree by the 1997–98 academic year, meaning that female students would fill at least 55% of the spaces on the school's athletic teams.

As part of this across-the-board reduction in the number of slots available to men's athletic teams, the size of the men's wrestling team was capped at 27. Although the reduction was protested vigorously by wrestling coach Terry Kerr, and team captain Stephen Neal expressed concerns that a smaller squad would prove less competitive, the smaller CSUB team performed exceptionally well, winning the Pac-10 Conference title and finishing third in the nation in 1996. In 1996–97, the men's wrestling roster was capped at 25, and four of these spots went unused. Nevertheless, in response to the rumored elimination of the men's wrestling team, on January 10, 1997, the team filed the instant lawsuit, alleging that the university's policy capping the size of the men's team constituted discrimination on the basis of gender in violation of Title IX and the Equal Protection Clause of the Federal Constitution. . . .

This case has its origins in Congress's passage of Title IX in 1972. Title IX was Congress's response to significant concerns about discrimination against women in education. . . . In the words of the legislation's primary sponsor, Senator Birch Bayh, Title IX was enacted to "provide for the women of America something that is rightfully theirs—an equal chance to attend the schools of their choice, to develop the skills they want, and to apply those skills with the knowledge that they will have a fair chance to secure the jobs of their choice with equal pay for equal work." . . .

The regulations promulgated pursuant to Title IX require schools receiving federal funding to "provide equal athletic opportunity for members of both sexes." In evaluating

"As part of this across-the-board reduction in the number of slots available to men's athletic teams, the size of the men's wrestling team was capped at 27. Although the reduction was protested vigorously by wrestling coach Terry Kerr, and team captain Stephen Neal expressed concerns that a smaller squad would prove less competitive, the smaller CSUB team performed exceptionally well, winning the Pac-10 Conference title and finishing third in the nation in 1996."

schools' compliance with that provision, one factor that will be considered is "whether the selection of sports and levels of competition effectively accommodate the interests and abilities of members of both sexes." At the same time, "it would require blinders to ignore that the motivation for promulgation of the regulation on athletics was the historic emphasis on boys' athletic programs to the exclusion of girls' athletic programs in colleges." . . . The drafters of these regulations recognized a situation that Congress well understood: Male athletes had been given an enormous head start in the race against their female counterparts for athletic resources, and Title IX would prompt universities to level the proverbial playing field.

Appellees recognize that, given this backdrop, it would be imprudent to argue that Title IX prohibits the use of all gender-conscious remedies. Appellees therefore suggest that gender-conscious remedies are appropriate only when necessary to ensure that schools provide opportunities to males and females in proportion to their relative levels of interest in sports participation. By contrast, Appellants contend that schools may make gender-conscious decisions about sports-funding levels to correct for an imbalance between the composition of the undergraduate student body and the composition of the undergraduate student athletic participants pool. This disagreement has real significance: Men's expressed interest in participating in varsity sports is apparently higher than women's at the present time—although the "interest gap" continues to narrow—so permitting gender-conscious remedies until the proportions of students and athletes are roughly proportional gives universities more remedial freedom than permitting remedies only until expressed interest and varsity roster spots correspond. . . .

Title IX is a dynamic statute, not a static one. It envisions continuing progress toward the goal of equal opportunity for all athletes and recognizes that, where society has conditioned women to expect less than their fair share of the athletic opportunities, women's interest in participating in sports will not rise to a par with men's overnight. The percentage of college athletes who are women rose from 15% in 1972 to 37% in 1998, and Title IX is at least partially responsible for this trend of increased participation by women. . . .

An extensive survey of Title IX's legislative history and the regulations promulgated to apply its provisions to college athletics concluded that boosters of male sports argued vociferously before Congress that the proposed regulations would require schools to shift resources from men's programs to women's programs, but that Congress nevertheless

"Title IX is a dynamic statute, not a static one. It envisions continuing progress toward the goal of equal opportunity for all athletes and recognizes that, where society has conditioned women to expect less than their fair share of the athletic opportunities, women's interest in participating in sports will not rise to a par with men's overnight."

sided "with women's advocates" by deciding not to repeal the [Health, Education, and Welfare Department]'s athletics-related Title IX regulations. . . . Congress thus appears to have believed that Title IX would result in funding reductions to male athletic programs. If a university wishes to comply with Title IX by leveling down programs instead of ratcheting them up, as Appellant has done here, Title IX is not offended. . . .

Title IX has enhanced, and will continue to enhance, women's opportunities to enjoy the thrill of victory, the agony of defeat, and the many tangible benefits that flow from just being given a chance to participate in intercollegiate athletics. Today we join our sister circuits in holding that Title IX does not bar universities from taking steps to ensure that women are approximately as well represented in sports programs as they are in student bodies. We REVERSE, and VACATE the preliminary injunction.

In 1971, the year before Title IX was enacted, approximately 294,000 girls played organized high school sports, and another 30,000 women participated in organized collegiate sports. That year, only about 1 in 27 girls participated in high school sports. Title IX, however, quickly transformed the landscape of women's athletics across America. In 2012, more than 3.1 million high school girls—about 2 out of every 5 female students—competed in school athletic programs, and women's intercollegiate programs included about 200,000 athletes.

Source: *Neal v. Board of Trustees of the California State Universities,* No. 99-15316 (1999), http://caselaw .findlaw.com/us-9th-circuit/1136450.html.

Chapter 3
Women and Politics

Introduction

In the United States, the concept of citizens' rights is broad, encompassing economic, social, and political rights. In many ways, what we consider to be our rights involves little more than freedom from government intrusion into our lives or, in essence, being left alone by the government. This includes many of the rights outlined in the Bill of Rights, those first 10 amendments to the U.S. Constitution such as freedom of speech, freedom of religion, and the right to peaceably assemble. But for some Americans, the consequence of being left alone by the government has been continued inequality and not being granted the same rights as others. Historically, the people who have had the most rights in the United States were white men, and certainly freedom is a concept that attracts the most support from people who are satisfied with the current state of their rights and privileges. For individuals who have historically been excluded from those rights and privileges, such as women and African Americans, freedom is tantamount to continued discrimination. For these people, government intervention is often a necessity for them to realize the same rights that were held by white men.

Americans have applied this notion of rights to many areas of their lives, and the question of whether or not some desired benefit actually constitutes a right can result in both personal and political disagreements. For many, access to adequate health care is a right, while to others, it is a privilege to be earned. Similarly, some people believe that having access to a public school is a fulfillment of a right to an education, while others think that all schools have to be funded equally for that right to be protected. Some ask whether access to education is actually a right, in the same way that freedoms of religion or speech are rights. Despite the application of the word "rights" to many aspects of American life, the definition of what actually constitutes Americans' rights can be a source of disagreement within the country's political environment.

At the most fundamental level, however, most people are in agreement on what constitutes Americans' political rights. Political rights are those that constitute the foundation of American citizenship, providing access to the mechanisms of government. They include the right to vote, the right to serve on juries, and the right to run for political elective office. While political rights may be seen as very fundamental rights in a democracy, it is important to note that they were withheld from women for a great deal of the history of the United States. The acquisition of political rights for women has come from struggles on various political fronts, including amending the U.S. Constitution, changing both federal and state laws, and taking cases through the federal court system.

The rationale for restricting the political rights of women is similar to the explanations given for the restriction of other rights. In short, the belief that men were more naturally suited for some activities than women was the basis for most of the discrimination faced by women. Specific to their lack of access to political rights, discrimination against women was justified by the beliefs that women were irrational, that women's natures were not suited for exercising political rights, that married women should not act in ways that were contrary to their husbands' wishes, and that the traditional domestic sphere of women did not prepare women adequately for taking on political roles. The disadvantages inherent in not having access to political rights was noted as early as 1776, when Abigail Adams wrote to her husband, future president of the United States John Adams, to "remember the ladies and be more generous and favorable to them than your ancestors."

The first concerted effort to address women's political rights occurred in 1848, when women's rights advocates Lucretia Mott and Elizabeth Cady Stanton organized a women's rights convention in Seneca Falls, New York. At the convention the Declaration of Sentiments and Resolutions, outlining the many ways that women's rights were being violated, was drafted and approved. The arguments that attendees made for women's rights could be considered ahead of their time; they argued that the differences between men and women, which were used as a justification for discrimination, were constructed by society and were not, as many people believe, ordained by God. As such, attendees argued that the rationale for discriminatory treatment of women was baseless and was used only to prevent women from exercising their due rights as American citizens. A similar argument emerged again in the 1970s' women's movement, but in the middle of the 19th century this was a radical idea.

In the years following the American Civil War, these women's rights advocates identified a potential avenue for gaining the right to vote. As the country considered the political rights of former slaves after the war, women hoped that they would be included in any decisions made that would enfranchise former slaves and define their rights. Once the Civil War had ended, Congress proposed three amendments to the Constitution, often referred to as the Reconstruction Amendments. The Thirteenth Amendment, ratified in 1865, freed the slaves and prohibited further slavery in the United States. The Fourteenth Amendment, ratified in 1868, defined citizenship and addressed the states' responsibilities in protecting the rights of citizens. A related discussion at this time involved the voting rights of former slaves. Women's rights advocates believed that this was an opportune time for women to gain their voting rights. In an 1867 meeting of the American Equal Rights Association, various speakers compared women's political situation to that of former slaves and argued that any rationale for giving black men the right to vote could just as accurately be made for women. However, when the issue of voting rights was finally addressed by the Fifteenth Amendment in 1870, women were omitted. The amendment prohibits the consideration of race, color, or previous condition of servitude in granting voting rights but does not mention sex. As abolitionist Frederick Douglass said, this was the "Negro's hour," and women would have to wait until a later time to achieve this fundamental right of citizenship.

This was a blow to the women's suffrage movement, and it wasn't until the second decade of the 20th century that the issue of women's voting rights rose again to the national agenda. Women's rights advocates had remained active during the 50 years following the Fifteenth Amendment's ratification; a women's suffrage amendment was actually introduced to Congress in 1878, a mere 8 years after black men received the constitutional right to vote. But it wasn't until 1917 that newly elected female member of Congress Jeanette Rankin pressed for Congress to study the issue of women's voting rights, arguing for the necessity of federal action to secure women's rights across the country. Congress formally proposed the Nineteenth Amendment in 1919 to secure voting rights for women, with the states ratifying the amendment a year later in 1920.

Voting is considered the cornerstone of political rights in a democracy, but there are other rights of citizenship that women have historically been denied. Once the Fourteenth Amendment was ratified, women's rights activists attempted to use the Equal Protection Clause as a vehicle for securing greater rights for women, from voting rights to protections from workplace discrimination. Well into the 20th century, the U.S. Supreme Court had ruled in numerous opinions that the Fourteenth Amendment's Equal Protection Clause did not extend to differential treatment of men and women, given that the amendment was clearly passed to protect the rights of former slaves. To address the exclusion of women from constitutionally protected political rights, women's rights advocate Alice Paul drafted the Equal Rights Amendment (ERA) to the U.S. Constitution in 1923. This amendment was introduced in every session of Congress until it succeeded in being formally proposed by Congress in 1972. While Alice Paul remained an active participant in the women's rights movement until her death in 1977, by the time the Congress gave serious consideration to the ERA in 1970, the torch had been passed to younger women leaders, such as Gloria Steinem, who testified to the Senate Judiciary Committee about the need to pass the ERA. Although Congress had passed the amendment in 1972, it never received enough support by the states to be ratified and added to the U.S. Constitution.

Although often portrayed as a burden rather than a right or responsibility of citizenship, jury duty was another political right that women had to fight to obtain. The Sixth Amendment to the Constitution requires that all criminal trials be decided by an "impartial jury." However, until 1975, many states systematically excluded women from jury duty, resulting in all-male juries. There were several concerns expressed about women jurors, ranging from women being too emotional and unable to handle the graphic nature of some cases to a woman's inability to serve on a jury and still perform her domestic responsibilities. However, advocates for women's rights argued that a jury cannot be impartial if it consists of only male jurors and does not represent a cross-section of the population. Interestingly, the case in which the Supreme Court ultimately decided that the exclusion of female jurors was unconstitutional was brought not by a woman defendant but by a man. In *Taylor v. Louisiana* (1975), a male defendant's legal counsel argued that men as well as women were discriminated against if the jury consisted of people from only one sex.

In many ways, the last aspect of political rights attained by women—running for and serving in elective office—was addressed when women received the right to vote. Prior to the Nineteenth Amendment, several states had already given women the right to vote, opening the door to women running for political office. In fact, the first woman to be elected to Congress, Jeannette Rankin, was elected in Montana in 1917 even before the Nineteenth Amendment's ratification. But just because women can run for office doesn't mean they will run for office or that they will be elected when they do run. Women face numerous hurdles to being elected. First and foremost is that women are less likely to run for office than are men. Either women don't ever consider it or if they do consider it they do not feel encouraged to take the steps to declare their candidacy. Women cannot get elected to office if there are no women on the ballot. Another hurdle, possibly related to the first, is that Americans' conception of leadership tends to correspond with traits that are associated with masculinity: rationality, assertiveness, risk taking, independence, and competitiveness. When women exhibit these traits, they are not often perceived favorably. Yet if women display more traditionally feminine traits, they are not perceived as strong leaders.

Similar barriers exist for women who hope to be appointed to political office. However, while the number of men in political office still greatly outnumbers women, the United States has witnessed several changes. At the federal level, the president is able to fill open seats in the executive and judicial branches, and many of these nominees must receive Senate confirmation. While presidents have nominated women for various executive branch positions, the number of women appointees has been few, and they have often been appointed to positions that are consistent with traits associated with femininity. For instance, the two most common cabinet-level offices filled by women include secretary of labor and secretary of health and human services. This has changed since the presidency of Bill Clinton, when he nominated the first women to serve in the positions of attorney general and secretary of state. In the federal judiciary women were slow to be appointed, and it wasn't until Ronald Reagan appointed Sandra Day O'Connor to the Supreme Court in 1981 that a woman served on the high court. O'Connor was the sole woman on the court for 12 years until President Clinton nominated Ruth Bader Ginsburg. President Barack Obama has nominated two women: Sonia Sotomayer and Elena Kagan.

Also in the 1980s, Geraldine Ferraro was nominated by Democratic presidential candidate Walter Mondale to serve as his running mate in the 1984 presidential election. Although the Mondale-Ferraro ticket was unsuccessful in its bid for the presidency, Ferraro's successful navigation of the political arena was an inspiration to other women who were considering a run for elective office. After her death in 2011, several female members of Congress spoke about the positive effect that Ferraro's career had on their decisions to run for office and serve in Congress.

Early Activists Issue a Call for Women's Rights

Seneca Falls Convention "Declaration of Sentiments and Resolutions"

July 19–20, 1848

In 1832 the New England Anti-Slavery Society was established, and unlike many abolitionist organizations, founder William Lloyd Garrison encouraged the full participation of women in the movement. Among the female members of the Anti-Slavery Society was Lucretia Mott and Elizabeth Cady Stanton. In 1840, Mott and Stanton both traveled to attend the World Anti-Slavery Convention in London with their husbands and had the opportunity to meet and talk when they were both denied admission to the conference for being women. Angered at the situation, they became friends, discussing their views on abolition and women's rights and subsequently working together on these issues. By 1848, they had organized the first convention to promote women's rights at Seneca Falls, New York. Two hundred people participated in the convention, at which Stanton drafted the Declaration of Sentiments and Resolutions, modeled on the Declaration of Independence. This reliance on the wording of the Declaration of Independence was intentional, drawing attention to the fact that the American revolutionaries' demands for freedom had clearly not applied to women. In short, the Declaration of Sentiments and Resolutions was designed to illustrate the hypocrisy of limiting women's rights in a country founded on individual freedoms.

Mott and Stanton drew attention to several practices that they thought were particularly oppressive to women. First, women were denied the right to vote, thus putting them in the same position of the revolutionaries who had protested taxation without representation against Great Britain. Second, women essentially lost their legal identity once they married, a practice known as feme covert, including rights to the property they brought into the marriage, the right to testify in court, and access to their children in the case of a divorce. Third, society has been structured by men to benefit men, in terms of access to jobs, wages, education, and roles within the church. Stanton and Mott believed that these were fundamental rights that were not dependent on a person's sex but were instead rights that women should expect by being human. In a few cases, there does seem to be an element of elitism in the list of grievances. For instance, Stanton implied that women should have more rights than native and foreigners, whom she defines as "ignorant and degraded."

When, in the course of human events, it becomes necessary for one portion of the family of man to assume among the people of the earth a position different from that which they have hitherto occupied, but one to which the laws of nature and of nature's God entitle them, a decent respect to the opinions of mankind requires that they should declare the causes that impel them to such a course.

We hold these truths to be self-evident: that all men and women are created equal; that they are endowed by their Creator with certain inalienable rights, that among these are life, liberty, and the pursuit of happiness; that to secure these rights governments are instituted, deriving their just powers from the consent of the governed. Whenever any form of government becomes destructive of these ends, it is the right of those who suffer from it to refuse allegiance to it, and to insist upon the institution of a new government, laying its foundation on such principles, and organizing its powers in such form as to them shall seem most likely to effect their safety and happiness. Prudence, indeed, will dictate that governments long established should not be changed for light and transient causes; and accordingly, all experience hath shown that mankind are more disposed to suffer, while evils are sufferable, than to right themselves by abolishing the forms to which they were accustomed. But when a long train of abuses and usurpations, pursuing invariably the same object evinces a design to reduce them under absolute despotism, it is their duty to throw off such government, and to provide new guards for their future security. Such has been the patient sufferance of the women under this government, and such is now the necessity which constrains them to demand the equal station to which they are entitled.

The history of mankind is a history of repeated injuries and usurpations on the part of man toward woman, having in direct object the establishment of an absolute tyranny over her. To prove this, let facts be submitted to a candid world.

He has never permitted her to exercise her inalienable right to the elective franchise.

He has compelled her to submit to laws, in the formation of which she had no voice.

He has withheld from her rights which are given to the most ignorant and degraded men—both natives and foreigners.

Having deprived her of this first right of a citizen, the elective franchise, thereby leaving her without representation in the halls of legislation, he has oppressed her on all sides.

He has made her, if married, in the eye of the law, civilly dead.

He has taken from her all right in property, even to the wages she earns.

He has made her, morally, an irresponsible being, as she can commit many crimes with impunity, provided they be done in the presence of her husband. In the covenant of marriage, she is compelled to promise obedience to her husband, he becoming, to all intents and purposes, her master—the law giving him power to deprive her of her liberty, and to administer chastisement.

He has so framed the laws of divorce, as to what shall be the proper causes of divorce; in case of separation, to whom the guardianship of the children shall be given; as to be wholly regardless of the happiness of women—the law, in all cases, going upon a false supposition of the supremacy of man, and giving all power into his hands.

After depriving her of all rights as a married woman, if single and the owner of property, he has taxed her to support a government which recognizes her only when her property can be made profitable to it.

He has monopolized nearly all the profitable employments, and from those she is permitted to follow, she receives but a scanty remuneration.

He closes against her all the avenues to wealth and distinction, which he considers most honorable to himself. As a teacher of theology, medicine, or law, she is not known.

He has denied her the facilities for obtaining a thorough education—all colleges being closed against her.

He allows her in Church, as well as State, but a subordinate position, claiming Apostolic authority for her exclusion from the ministry, and, with some exceptions, from any public participation in the affairs of the Church.

He has created a false public sentiment, by giving to the world a different code of morals for men and women, by which moral delinquencies which exclude women from society, are not only tolerated but deemed of little account in man.

"He has monopolized nearly all the profitable employments, and from those she is permitted to follow, she receives but a scanty remuneration. He closes against her all the avenues to wealth and distinction, which he considers most honorable to himself."

He has usurped the prerogative of Jehovah himself, claiming it as his right to assign for her a sphere of action, when that belongs to her conscience and to her God.

He has endeavored, in every way that he could, to destroy her confidence in her own powers, to lessen her self-respect, and to make her willing to lead a dependent and abject life.

Now, in view of this entire disfranchisement of one-half the people of this country, their social and religious degradation, in view of the unjust laws above mentioned, and because women do feel themselves aggrieved, oppressed, and fraudulently deprived of their most sacred rights, we insist that they have immediate admission to all the rights and privileges which belong to them as citizens of the United States.

These expectations of what the future would hold for women seeking the vote were astonishingly accurate. While efforts toward women's suffrage were witnessed after the Civil War, particularly with the passage of the Fifteenth Amendment, these efforts intensified by the late 1800s and early 1900s. Advocates for women's voting rights were met with opposition, ridicule, and open hostility. In addition to the more mainstream methods of political persuasion, such as petitions and media stories, some women's rights advocates engaged more drastic measures, such as hunger strikes and civil disobedience. The harsh treatment of these women is at least partially credited with changes in the public's perceptions of women's voting rights.

In entering upon the great work before us, we anticipate no small amount of misconception, misrepresentation, and ridicule; but we shall use every instrumentality within our power to effect our object. We shall employ agents, circulate tracts, petition the state and national legislatures, and endeavor to enlist the pulpit and the press in our behalf.

We hope this Convention will be followed by a series of Conventions, embracing every part of the country.

Firmly relying upon the final triumph of the Right and the True, we do this day affix our signatures to this declaration.

Source: Elizabeth Cady Stanton, *A History of Woman Suffrage,* Vol. 1 (Rochester, NY: Fowler and Wells, 1889), 70–71. Available at http://www.fordham.edu/halsall/mod/senecafalls.asp.

Women's Rights Leaders Champion Universal Voting Rights

Proceedings of the First Anniversary of the American Equal Rights Association

May 9–10, 1867

Address of Elizabeth Cady Stanton

> To discuss the question of suffrage for women and negroes, as women and negroes, and not as citizens of a republic, implies that there are some reasons for demanding this right for these classes that do not apply to "white males."

The obstinate persistence with which fallacious and absurd objections are pressed against their enfranchisement—as if they were anomalous beings, outside all human laws and necessities—is most humiliating and insulting to every black man and woman who has one particle of healthy, high-toned self-respect. There are no special claims to propose for women and negroes, no new arguments to make in their behalf. The same already made to extend suffrage to all the white men in this country, the same John Bright makes for the working men of England, the same made for the enfranchisement of 22,000,000 Russian serfs, are all we have to make for black men and women. As the greater includes the less, an argument for universal suffrage covers the whole question, the rights of all citizens. In thus relaying the foundations of government, we settle all these side issues of race, color and sex, end all class legislation, and remove forever the fruitful cause of all the jealousies, dissensions and revolution of the past. This is the platform of the American Equal Rights Association. "We are masters of the situation." Here black men and women are buried in the citizen. As in the war, freedom was the key-note of victory, so now is universal suffrage the key-note of reconstruction.

"Negro suffrage" may answer as a party cry for an effete political organization through another Presidential campaign; but the people of this country have a broader work on hand to-day than to save the Republican party, or, with some abolitionists, to settle the rights of races. The battles of the ages have been fought for races, classes, parties, over and over again, and force always carried the day, and will until we settle the higher, the holier question of individual rights. This is our American idea, and on a wise settlement of this question rests the problem whether our nation shall live or perish. . . .

In 1865 the Thirteenth Amendment to the Constitution was ratified, abolishing slavery in the United States. The amendment stopped short, however, of expressly giving American citizenship to former slaves. This didn't occur until the Fourteenth Amendment was ratified in 1868, a year after Elizabeth Cady Stanton appealed for voting rights in this speech at the Church of the Puritans in 1967. Stanton felt strongly that by defining women and black men as citizens of the United States, the Fourteenth Amendment was sufficient to provide these groups with the right to vote. As she had articulated 19 years earlier at the Seneca Falls Convention, she believed that suffrage was not a right to be bestowed by those who already had it but instead was a right of all citizens, independent of their race, color, or sex. The Fourteenth Amendment was not interpreted this way, however, and the Fifteenth Amendment to the Constitution was ratified in 1870, granting black men the right to vote.

In the enfranchisement of woman, in lifting her up into this broader sphere, we see for her new honor and dignity, more liberal, exalted and enlightened views of life, its objects, ends and aims, and an entire revolution in the new world of interest and action where she is soon to play her part. And in saying this, I do not claim that woman is better than man, but that the sexes have a civilizing power on each other. . . .

When woman understands the momentous interests that depend on the ballot, she will make it her first duty to educate every American boy and girl into the idea that to vote is the most sacred act of citizenship—a religious duty not to be discharged thoughtlessly, selfishly or corruptly; but conscientiously, remembering that, in a republican government, to every citizen is entrusted the interests of the nation. . . .

To many minds, this claim for the ballot suggests nothing more than a rough polling-booth where coarse, drunken men, elbowing each other, wade knee-deep in mud to drop a little piece of paper two inches long into a box—simply this and nothing more. . . .

Stanton's strategy here is to use the traditional roles of mother and wife as a rationale for why women needed the right to vote. It was also widely believed at the time that women were the more moral sex, and given their role as the primary caregiver for children, Stanton raised this idea to underscore the importance of women voting. She argued that if women could vote, they could better educate their children on the importance of voting and furthermore could balance the votes of men who have the right to vote but engage in immoral behavior and vote without thought. This is in rather stark contrast to the arguments she made in the Declaration of Sentiments and Resolutions, in which she downplayed the differences between men and women. This may illustrate a shift in Stanton's political strategy in an effort to more easily change public opinion to support women's suffrage.

Behold, with the coming of woman into this higher sphere of influence, the dawn of the new day, when politics, so called, are to be lifted into the world of morals and religion; when the polling-booth shall be a beautiful temple, surrounded by fountains and flowers and triumphal arches, through which young men and maidens shall go up in joyful procession to ballot for justice and freedom; and when our elections shall be like the holy feasts of the Jews at Jerusalem.

Through the trials of this second revolution shall not our nation rise up, with new virtue and strength, to fulfill her mission in leading all the peoples of the earth to the only solid foundation of government, "equal rights to all?" What an inheritance is ours! What boundless resources for wealth, happiness and development! With every variety of climate and production, with our mighty lakes and rivers majestic forests and inexhaustible mines, nothing can check our future prosperity but a lack of virtue in the people. . . .

While man talks of "equal, impartial, manhood suffrage," we give the certain sound, "universal suffrage." While he talks of the rights of races, we exalt the higher, the holier idea proclaimed by the Fathers, and now twice baptized in blood, "individual rights." To woman it is given to save the Republic. . . .

Resolved, That as republican institutions are based on individual rights, and not on the rights of races or sexes, the first question for the American people to settle in the reconstruction of the government, is the RIGHTS OF INDIVIDUALS.

Resolved, That the present claim for "manhood suffrage," masked with the words "equal," "impartial," "universal," is a cruel abandonment of the slave women of the South, a fraud on the tax-paying women of the North, and an insult to the civilization of the nineteenth century.

Resolved, That the proposal to reconstruct our government on the basis of manhood suffrage, which emanated from the Republican party and has received the recent sanction of the American Anti-Slavery Society, is but a continuation of the old system of class and caste legislation, always cruel and proscriptive in itself, and ending in all ages in national degradation and revolution.

I am glad to see that men are getting their rights, but I want women to get theirs, and while the water is stirring I will step into the pool. Now that there is a great stir about colored mens getting their rights is the time for women to step in and have theirs. I am sometimes told that 'Women ain't fit to vote. Why don't you know that a woman have Seven devils in her; and do you suppose a woman is fit to rule the nation?' Seven devils ain't no account: a man had a legion in him. [Great laughter] . . . [A]nd man is so self-ish that he has got women's rights and his own too and yet he won't give women their rights. He keeps them all to himself. . . .

Address by Sojourner Truth

I feel that if I have to answer for the deeds done in my body just as much as a man, I have a right to have just as much as a man.

> **There is a great stir about colored men getting their rights, but not a word about the colored women; and if colored men get their rights, and colored women not theirs, the colored men will be masters over the women, and it will be just as bad as it was before.**

"I am glad to see that men are getting their rights, but I want women to get theirs, and while the water is stirring I will step into the pool. Now that there is a great stir about colored mens getting their rights is the time for women to step in and have theirs."

Sojourner Truth was a former slave who became a leading proponent of abolition and women's rights. She was one of the first black women to successfully take a white man to court, in her case for selling her son illegally after slavery was abolished in New York state. Truth is best known for her 1951 speech "Ain't I a Woman," in which she powerfully, and for her time radically, questioned the inconsistent standards of femininity to which white women and black women were held. In 1964 she was invited to the White House by President Abraham Lincoln, and at the time of this speech she was helping draw large crowds to abolitionist rallies.

So I am for keeping the thing going while things are stirring; because if we wait till it is still, it will take a great deal to get it going again.

Sources: Address by Elizabeth Cady Stanton: Proceedings of the first anniversary of the American equal rights association held at the Church of the Puritans, New York, May 9 and 10, 1867. Phonographic report by H. M. Parkhurst (New York: R. J. Johnston, printer, 1867), 8–17. Available at http://memory.loc.gov/ammem/naw/nawshome.html.

Address by Sojourner Truth: Elizabeth Cady Stanton, Susan B. Anthony, and Matilda Joslyn Gage, *History of Woman Suffrage,* Vol. 2 (New York: Fowler and Wells, 1882), 193, 222.

A Congresswoman Expresses Support for a Federal Suffrage Amendment

Statement of Representative Jeannette Rankin

May 19, 1917

Statement of Miss Jeannette Rankin, a Representative in Congress from the State of Montana

Mr. Chairman and members of the committee, it has been too long assumed that woman suffrage can be gained State by State. We are now convinced that all of the women of the United States can not be enfranchised until a Federal suffrage amendment has been adopted.

We have one State, the State of New Mexico, whose constitution can not be amended for 25 years from the time the constitution was adopted. I think that will be in 20 years from now. . . . I think it is considered practically impossible to amend the constitution of New Mexico.

The constitutions in some of the States may be amended by a constitutional convention. There are 11 States which do not provide for a constitutional convention. In other States, the State of New Hampshire, for instance, the constitution can be amended only by a constitutional convention, which can be called only once in seven years. In four States the number of constitutional amendments that can be submitted to the voters at any one time is restricted. In Illinois it is restricted to one, in Kentucky to one, and in Arkansas to three. At one time the Legislature of Arkansas adopted a resolution for a woman suffrage amendment, but other amendments came up, and it was decided to vote on three which did not include the woman-suffrage amendment. Thus, even after the suffrage bill passed the legislature, it was defeated before it came before the voters. Thirteen States require that the amendment go through two successive legislatures before it can be submitted to the voters. A number of legislatures require a minimum vote, some two-thirds, some merely a majority, some three-fourths, and some three-fifths. Alabama require a three-fifths vote, and the legislature meets only once in four years. Mississippi and South Carolina require the approval of the legislature before and after the measure has been approved by the voters. On the referendum 11 States require a majority of all

Jeannette Rankin was the first woman elected to Congress, elected to the House of Representatives in 1916 two years after Montana gave women the right to vote. Born in 1880, she had an unusual life for a woman of this era. She graduated from the University of Montana with a degree in biology, although she later attended school to study social work. By 1910 she was active in the women's suffrage movement, working with the National American Women's Suffrage Association in New York before returning to Montana to pursue women's suffrage in her home state. After Montana granted women the right to vote in 1914, she ran for the House of Representatives and won the seat. She served one term before beginning work in the international peace movement and for the American Civil Liberties Union. In 1940 she was reelected to the House, serving one term from 1941 until 1943. Rankin was an outspoken suffragist and used her position in Congress to call for a constitutional amendment giving women the right to vote.

the votes cast at the election. In the past this has been a considerable obstacle, but the suffrage issue has become so popular in recent years that in California it carried by a majority of all the votes cast at the election, although such a majority was not required.

Unless specified by the U.S. Constitution, voting rights are determined by individual states, and in 1917 only 11 states had granted women full voting rights. Rankin's concern was that women would never fully have the right to vote if that right was dependent on the states. Instead, she argued that an amendment to the Constitution was a more efficient and effective route to women's suffrage. Additionally, it was clear to Rankin and other suffragists that women's suffrage would fall to men to decide, since they held all but one seat in Congress and were the only people who could vote in all but a handful of states. As Rankin makes clear in her statement, the tide was starting to turn toward women's suffrage by 1917. While certainly the decades-long efforts of suffragists contributed to this changing perception, there is some evidence that women's rights advocates were using voters' fears of the increasing immigrant population to advocate for greater women's participation in the political process.

When woman suffrage was not such a popular question it was hard to get the voters to vote on it; but now in most of the States we find that the men vote more readily on the question of woman suffrage than they do on the candidates.

In Indiana one decision of the court has been found which has made it necessary to get a majority of all those who are eligible to vote, which is manifestly impossible. In one State, the law requires that such an amendment shall be submitted but once in 10 years. In Michigan an amendment was submitted in 1913, and it will be 1923 before the question can be even considered. Other States fix the period of time which must elapse between an unfavorable vote and a reconsideration of an amendment by the people. In Pennsylvania and New Jersey it is five years, in Tennessee six years, and so on. These long periods of time militate largely against the effectiveness of a suffrage campaign. . . . These are just a few of the obstacles that exist in some of the States. It seems to me that these questions should be carefully considered by a woman suffrage committee before it is decided whether woman suffrage should be granted by Federal amendment or by the several States. I thank you.

Source: "Creating a Committee on Woman Suffrage in the House of Representatives," Hearing before the Committee on Rules, HR, 65th Congress, 1st Session, on H. Res. 12, May 19, 1917, 5–6.

Gloria Steinem Speaks Out for an Equal Rights Amendment

Hearings before a Senate Subcommittee on Constitutional Amendments

May 6, 1970

Statement of Gloria Steinem, Writer and Critic

I am here in support of the equal rights amendment. . . . Some protective legislation is gradually proving to be unenforceable or contrary to Title VII. It gives poor women jobs but serves to keep them poor. Restrictions on working hours, for instance, may keep women in the assembly line from becoming foremen.

No one is trying to say that there is no difference between men and women, only as I will discuss more in my statement that the differences between, the differences within the groups, male and female, are much, much greater than the differences between the two groups. Therefore, requirements can only be sensibly suited to the requirements of the job itself.

During the 12 years of working for a living, I have experienced much of the legal and social discrimination reserved for women in this country. I have been refused service in public restaurants, ordered out of public gathering places, and turned away from apartment rentals; all for the clearly-stated, sole reason that I am a woman. And all without the legal remedies available to blacks and other minorities. I have been excluded from professional groups, writing assignments on so-called "unfeminine" subjects such as politics, full participation in the Democratic Party, jury duty, and even from such small male privileges as discounts on airline fares. Most important to me, I have been denied a society in which women are encouraged, or even allowed to think of themselves as first-class citizens and responsible human beings.

However, after 2 years of researching the status of American women, I have discovered that in reality, I am very, very lucky. Most women, both wage-earners and housewives, routinely suffer more humiliation and injustice than I do.

As a freelance writer, I don't work in the male-dominated hierarchy of an office. (Women, like blacks and other visibly-different minorities, do better in individual professions such as the arts, sports, or domestic work; anything in which they don't have authority over white males.) I am not one of the

Gloria Steinem is a prominent women's rights activist who became an outspoken advocate for women's rights during the 1960s and 1970s. She helped create both *New York* and *Ms.* magazines, writing columns on political and feminist topics for both publications, including subjects that were considered taboo at the time, such as domestic violence and abortion. She was a particularly vocal advocate of the Equal Rights Amendment (ERA) and used her celebrity as a journalist to draw attention to the need for a constitutional protection against sex discrimination. In her testimony to Congress in support of the ERA, she articulates that it is a person's abilities that should determine suitability for a job and pay for doing that job, not a person's sex. She uses her own experiences in the male-dominated field of journalism to contrast the legal protections against discrimination that were based on race to those that were in place for women. At the time Steinem testified, the Fourteenth Amendment's Equal Protection Clause had not been interpreted to apply to issues of sex discrimination. Thus, besides the right to vote, there was nothing in the U.S. Constitution that guaranteed equal rights to women. Even now, the Fourteenth Amendment has not been applied to issues of sex discrimination as fully as it has been to other forms of discrimination, such as discrimination based on race.

millions of women who must support a family. Therefore, I haven't had to go on welfare because there are no day-care centers for my children while I work, and I haven't had to submit to the humiliating welfare inquiries about my private and sexual life, inquiries from which men are exempt. I haven't had to brave the sex bias of labor unions and employers, only to see my family subsist on a median salary 40 percent less than the male median salary.

I hope this committee will hear the personal, daily injustices suffered by many women—professionals and day laborers, women housebound by welfare as well as by suburbia. We have all been silent for too long. But we won't be silent anymore.

The truth is that all our problems stem from the same sex based myths. We may appear before you as white radicals or the middle-aged middleclass or black soul sisters, but we are all sisters in fighting against these outdated myths. Like racial myths, they have been reflected in our laws. Let me list a few.

That [women] are biologically inferior to men. In fact, an equally good case can be made for the reverse. Women live longer than men, even when the men are not subject to business pressures. Women survived Nazi concentration camps better, keep cooler heads in emergencies currently studied by disaster-researchers, are protected against heart attacks by their female sex hormones, and are so much more durable at every stage of life that nature must conceive 20 to 50 percent more males in order to keep some balance going.

Man's hunting activities are forever being pointed to as tribal proof of superiority. But while he was hunting, women built houses, tilled the fields, developed animal husbandry, and perfected language. . . .

However, I don't want to prove the superiority of one sex to another. That would only be repeating a male mistake. English scientists once definitively proved, after all, that the English were descended from the angels, while the Irish were descended from the apes; it was the rationale for England's domination of Ireland for more than a century. The point is that science is used to support current myth and economics almost as much as the church was.

The ERA was proposed by Congress only two years after Steinem testified, but it was ultimately ratified by only 35 of the 38 states needed to add it to the U.S. Constitution. The argument made by Steinem and other supporters of the ERA—that there were fewer differences between men and women than there were among individuals of the same sex—may have contributed in part to the ERA's failure to be ratified. Steinem's view countered many peoples' beliefs that men and women are inherently different and naturally play differing roles, both in the workplace and in the family. In fact, some of the most ardent opponents of the amendment were women, who argued that the ERA would eliminate many of the legal workplace protections that women had gained in the early 1900s and that it would diminish traditional women's roles. Although advocates of the ERA are still active in U.S. politics, the momentum for the amendment died after it failed to be ratified, and there have been no viable proposals to revive it in Congress.

What we do know is that the difference between two races or two sexes is much smaller than the differences to be found within each group. Therefore, in spite of the slide show on female inferiorities that I understand was shown to you yesterday, the law makes much more sense when it treats individuals, not groups bundled together by some condition of birth.

A word should be said about Dr. Freud, the great 19th century perpetuator of female inferiority. Many of the differences he assumed to be biological, and therefore changeless, have turned out to be societal, and have already changed. Penis envy, for instance, is clinically disappearing. Just as black people envied white skins, 19th century women envied penises. A second-class group envies whatever it is that makes the first-class groups first class.

Another myth, that women are already treated equally in this society. I am sure there has been ample testimony to prove that equal pay for equal work, equal chance for advancement, and equal training or encouragement is obscenely scarce in every field, even those—like food and fashion industries—that are supposedly "feminine." . . .

Women suffer from this second class treatment from the moment they are born. They are expected to be, rather than achieve, to function biologically rather than learn. A brother, whatever his intellect, is more likely to get the family's encouragement and education money, while girls are often pressured to conceal ambition and intelligence. . . .

I interviewed a New York public school teacher who told me about a black teenager's desire to be a doctor. With all the barriers in mind, she suggested kindly that he be a veterinarian instead.

The same day, a high school teacher mentioned a girl who wanted to be a doctor. The teacher said, "How about a nurse?"

Teachers, parents, and the Supreme Court may exude a protective, well-meaning rationale, but limiting the individual's ambition is doing no one a favor. Certainly not this country; it needs all the talent it can get. . . .

Similarly, it shouldn't deceive male observers into thinking that this is somehow a joke. We are 51 percent of the population; we are essentially united on these issues across boundaries of class or race or age; and we may well end by changing this society more than the civil rights movement. . . .

Finally, I would like to say one thing about this time in which I am testifying.

I had deep misgivings about discussing this topic when National Guardsmen are occupying our campuses, the country is being turned against itself in a terrible polarization, and America is enlarging an already inhuman and unjustifiable war. But it seems to me that much of the trouble in this country has to do with the "masculine mystique"; with the myth that masculinity somehow depends on the subjugation of other people. It is a bipartisan problem; both our past and current Presidents seem to be victims of this myth, and to behave accordingly.

"Women suffer from this second class treatment from the moment they are born. They are expected to be, rather than achieve, to function biologically rather than learn."

Although Steinem discusses issues that would .... never have been addressed in 1848, it is important to note the commonalities in the arguments she made as compared to those made by Elizabeth Cady Stanton in the Declaration of Sentiments and Resolutions. Steinem focuses on the barriers that have been set up for women due not to their inherent inferiority but instead to society's imposition of roles for women that keep them inferior to men. She also specifically notes the myth that women are more moral than men. While this claim may seem on the surface to be a compliment to women, historically it has been used to prevent women from engaging in jobs or activities that have been dominated by men.

Women are not more moral than men. We are only uncorrupted by power. But we do not want to imitate men, to join this country as it is, and I think our very participation will change it. Perhaps women elected leaders—and there will be many more of them—will not be so likely to dominate black people or yellow people or men; anybody who looks different from us.

Source: "The Equal Rights Amendment," Hearings before the Subcommittee on Constitutional Amendments of the Committee on the Judiciary, United States Senate, 91st Congress, 2nd Session, on S.J. Res. 61, May 5, 6, and 7, 1970, 331–334.

The U.S. Supreme Court Ends Gender-Based Exemptions for Jury Duty

Supreme Court Ruling in *Taylor v. Louisiana*

1975

When this case was tried, [Article] VII, [Section] 41 of the Louisiana Constitution, and Art. 402 of the Louisiana Code of Criminal Procedure provided that a woman should not be selected for jury service unless she had previously filed a written declaration of her desire to be subject to jury service. The constitutionality of these provisions is the issue in this case. . . .

The Sixth Amendment to the U.S. Constitution reads, in part, that "In all criminal prosecutions, the accused shall enjoy the right to a speedy and public trial, by an impartial jury of the State and district wherein the crime shall have been committed." What constitutes an "impartial jury," however, requires some interpretation, and until *Taylor v. Louisiana,* states were given considerable discretion in determining whether women had to be included in the venire, or jury pool, for a trial. For instance, in 1961 the Supreme Court had ruled in *Hoyt v. Florida* that a Florida law requiring women to register for jury service in order to be included in a jury pool, while men were automatically registered, was consistent with the Constitution. In 1975 the Supreme Court revisited the underlying question: whether or not the systematic exclusion of women from a jury pool violated the Sixth Amendment's mandate of an impartial jury, as applied to the states by the Fourteenth Amendment.

Appellant, Billy J. Taylor, was indicted by the grand jury of St. Tammany Parish, in the Twenty-second Judicial District of Louisiana, for aggravated kidnapping. On April 12, 1972, appellant moved the trial court to quash the petit jury venire drawn for the special criminal term beginning with his trial the following day. Appellant alleged that women were systematically excluded from the venire and that he would therefore be deprived of what he claimed to be his federal constitutional right to "a fair trial by jury of a representative segment of the community." . . .

Appellant's motion to quash the venire was denied that same day. After being tried, convicted, and sentenced to death, appellant sought review in the Supreme Court of Louisiana, where he renewed his claim that the petit jury venire should have been quashed. The Supreme Court of Louisiana, recognizing that this claim drew into question the constitutionality of the provisions of the Louisiana Constitution and Code of Criminal Procedure dealing with the service of women on juries, squarely held, one justice dissenting, that these provisions were valid and not unconstitutional under federal law. . . .

Appellant appealed from that decision to this Court. We noted probable jurisdiction . . . to consider whether the Louisiana jury selection system deprived appellant of his Sixth and Fourteenth Amendment right to an impartial jury trial. We hold that it did, and that these Amendments were violated in this case. . . . In consequence, appellant's conviction must be reversed.

The Louisiana jury selection system does not disqualify women from jury service, but, in operation, its conceded systematic impact is that only a very few women, grossly disproportionate to the number of eligible women in the community, are called for jury service. In this case, no women were on the venire from which the petit jury was drawn. The issue we have, therefore, is whether a jury selection system which operates to exclude from jury service an identifiable class of citizens constituting 53% of eligible jurors in the community comports with the Sixth and Fourteenth Amendments.

The State first insists that Taylor, a male, has no standing to object to the exclusion of women from his jury. But Taylor's claim is that he was constitutionally entitled to a jury drawn from a venire constituting a fair cross-section of the community, and that the jury that tried him was not such a jury by reason of the exclusion of women. Taylor was not a member of the excluded class, but there is no rule that claims such as Taylor presents may be made only by those defendants who are members of the group excluded from jury service. In *Peters v. Kiff* . . . (1972), the defendant, a white man, challenged his conviction on the ground that Negroes had been systematically excluded from jury service. Six Members of the Court agreed that petitioner was entitled to present the issue, and concluded that he had been deprived of his federal rights. Taylor, in the case before us, was similarly entitled to tender and have adjudicated the claim that the exclusion of women from jury service deprived him of the kind of fact finder to which he was constitutionally entitled.

We accept the fair cross-section requirement as fundamental to the jury trial guaranteed by the Sixth Amendment, and are convinced that the requirement has solid foundation. The purpose of a jury is to guard against the exercise of arbitrary power—to make available the common sense judgment of the community as a hedge against the overzealous or mistaken prosecutor and in preference to the professional, or perhaps overconditioned or biased response of a judge. . . . This prophylactic vehicle is not provided if the jury pool is made up of only special segments of the populace or if large, distinctive groups are excluded from the pool. Community participation in the administration of the criminal law, moreover, is not only consistent with our democratic heritage, but is also critical to public confidence in the fairness of the criminal justice system. Restricting jury service to only special groups or excluding identifiable segments playing major roles in the community cannot be squared with the constitutional concept of jury trial. . . .

We are also persuaded that the fair cross-section requirement is violated by the systematic exclusion of women, who,

> *". . . the fair cross-section requirement is violated by the systematic exclusion of women, who, in the judicial district involved here, amounted to 53% of the citizens eligible for jury service."*

in the judicial district involved here, amounted to 53% of the citizens eligible for jury service. This conclusion necessarily entails the judgment that women are sufficiently numerous and distinct from men, and that, if they are systematically eliminated from jury panels, the Sixth Amendment's fair cross-section requirement cannot be satisfied. . . .

There remains the argument that women as a class serve a distinctive role in society and that jury service would so substantially interfere with that function that the State has ample justification for excluding women from service unless they volunteer, even though the result is that almost all jurors are men. . . .

The States are free to grant exemptions from jury service to individuals in case of special hardship or incapacity and to those engaged in particular occupations the uninterrupted performance of which is critical to the community's welfare. . . . It would not appear that such exemptions would pose substantial threats that the remaining pool of jurors would not be representative of the community. A system excluding all women, however, is a wholly different matter.

It is untenable to suggest these days that it would be a special hardship for each and every woman to perform jury service or that society cannot spare *any* women from their present duties. This may be the case with many, and it may be burdensome to sort out those who should be exempted from those who should serve. But that task is performed in the case of men, and the administrative convenience in dealing with women as a class is insufficient justification for diluting the quality of community judgment represented by the jury in criminal trials.

Although this judgment may appear a foregone conclusion from the pattern of some of the Court's cases over the past 30 years, as well as from legislative developments at both federal and state levels, it is nevertheless true that, until today, no case had squarely held that the exclusion of women from jury venires deprives a criminal defendant of his Sixth Amendment right to trial by an impartial jury drawn from a fair cross-section of the community. . . .

Accepting as we do, however, the view that the Sixth Amendment affords the defendant in a criminal trial the opportunity to have the jury drawn from venires representative of the community, we think it is no longer tenable to

Although it can vary by locality, potential jurors are generally selected from among people who have driver's licenses and are registered to vote. If someone called for jury duty can adequately demonstrate to the court that jury duty will present a hardship, for instance because of extensive driving distance to the courthouse or because of old age or health conditions, she or he can be excused from service. Until *Taylor v. Louisiana,* it was commonly argued that women, as a group, needed an exemption from jury duty because of their family and household responsibilities. More specifically, the belief was that women and their husbands and families would be so burdened by jury duty that women should only be called to serve if they had specifically requested their names be included among potential jurors. This often resulted in few if any women serving on juries. The Supreme Court ruled that offering women a blanket exemption from jury duty solely because they were women resulted in juries that were not representative of the population as a whole and was thus a violation of the Sixth Amendment.

hold that women as a class may be excluded or given automatic exemptions based solely on sex if the consequence is that criminal jury venires are almost totally male. To this extent we cannot follow the contrary implications of the prior cases, including *Hoyt v. Florida.* If it was ever the case that women were unqualified to sit on juries or were so situated that none of them should be required to perform jury service, that time has long since passed. If at one time it could be held that Sixth Amendment juries must be drawn from a fair cross-section of the community but that this requirement permitted the almost total exclusion of women, this is not the case today. Communities differ at different times and places. What is a fair cross-section at one time or place is not necessarily a fair cross-section at another time or a different place. Nothing persuasive has been presented to us in this case suggesting that all-male venires in the parishes involved here are fairly representative of the local population otherwise eligible for jury service.

Source: *Taylor v. Louisiana,* 419 U.S. 522 (1975). Available at http://supreme .justia.com/cases/federal/us/419/522/case.html.

Nomination of Sandra Day O'Connor to the U.S. Supreme Court

Testimony at Confirmation Hearing before the U.S. Senate's Committee on the Judiciary

September 9–11, 1981

Opening Statement of Chairman Strom Thurmond

The Judiciary Committee will come to order.

It is a privilege to welcome each of you to the opening session of the Committee on the Judiciary to consider the nomination of Judge Sandra Day O'Connor of Arizona to serve as an Associate Justice of the Supreme Court of the United States. This is truly a historic occasion, as it is the first time in the history of our Nation that a President has nominated a woman to serve on this august body. Today we begin the consideration of this nomination.

Opening Statement of Senator Edward M. Kennedy

I, too, want to welcome the nominee to this committee, and say to Judge O'Conner that since the time that you received the President's endorsement, I think that you have seen both the worst of this city and the best of it—the worst in being the target of some of the single-issue constituencies who are going to urge your defeat, and the best in the fact that you have had the strong and unyielding support of a President of the United States, and strong bipartisan support from Members of the U.S. Senate who have been unflinching in support of your candidacy. . . .

As has been pointed out, for many years there have been women with the highest qualifications for the Nation's highest Court. Every American can take pride in President Reagan's commitment to select such a woman for this critical office but the broad support for Judge O'Connor in this hearing must not become a pretext to ignore the need for greater representation of women, not only on the Supreme Court but at every other level of the Federal judiciary and Federal Government.

Women hold less than 7 percent of all the Federal judgeships. In two centuries of Federal judicial history, only 50 women have been appointed to the lower Federal courts, and 44 of them are still serving there today. In fact, 33 of

When the Ninety-Seventh Congress began in January 1981, women held only 23 seats in the House of Representatives and the Senate. Despite this relatively small number, it represented an increase in the number of women serving in Congress from the previous term, when only 17 women had held seats in Congress. This increase by 6 women came exclusively from the Republican Party, the same year that Ronald Reagan, also a Republican, was elected to the presidency. Despite this increase in the number of women in Congress from his own party, President Reagan did not win among women voters in 1980, a fact that did not go unnoticed by the media. Perhaps due in part to this confluence of events regarding women and politics, Reagan chose to appoint the first woman to the Supreme Court, Sandra Day O'Connor, when Associate Justice Potter Stewart retired from the Court. The Senate Judiciary Committee held confirmation hearings in September 1981, where the historic nature of O'Connor's nomination was a key topic of discussion, with both Democrats and Republicans in the committee expressing their support for her.

them were approved by this committee during the past Congress. All of us who care about this issue look forward to the day when appointments to the Federal bench and to the other high public offices will not stand out as an historic event simply because the appointees are women.

By some, Judge O'Connor has been termed a judicial conservative. However, simplistic labels are inadequate to define a complex concept like judicial philosophy, let alone predict a vote in a future case. What we seek in the Federal courts are judges who will display legal excellence and personal integrity and sensitivity to individual rights.

It is offensive to suggest that a potential Justice of the Supreme Court must pass some presumed test of judicial philosophy. It is even more offensive to suggest that a potential Justice must pass the litmus test of any single-issue interest group. The disturbing tactics of division and distortion and discrimination practiced by the extremists of the "New Right" have no place in these hearings and no place in our Nation's democracy.

I look forward to Judge O'Connor's testimony and her response to the questions. Based on what I know today, I intend to support her nomination. I take pride in the opportunity to participate in these historic hearings.

Opening Statement of Senator Alan K. Simpson

"Historic" is overused here this morning but very appropriate. I have a special feeling about the situation since I happen to represent the State of high altitude and low multitude, where we had the first woman justice of the peace, we had the first woman Governor, and we also were the first State in the Union to give women the right to vote, an interesting thing at that time of our rather robust history.

Therefore, it is a historic occasion, the confirmation of a Supreme Court Justice. I think it achieves our very fullest and most solemn task in the constitutional advise and consent function of the Senate. . . .

[I]t is an extraordinary position, life tenure. The purpose of it, of course, was to allow the judiciary to operate freely without political tampering that so weighted down previous judicial systems. The judiciary then was to transcend the politics so properly part and parcel of the other two branches. . . .

Just a final personal note, Mr. Chairman. I am very impressed by this lady. I greatly enjoyed my first visit with

As a Republican, President Reagan would have appointed a nominee with a more conservative ideology, and O'Connor was considered a moderate conservative. The appointment of a conservative woman provided an interesting dynamic in the hearings, affecting senators and witnesses at the hearing in interesting yet subtle ways. First, because women voters tend to favor candidates from the Democratic Party, Democratic senators were inclined to support her nomination. In fact, it would have been difficult for Democrats to oppose the first women appointed to the Supreme Court regardless of her ideology because of the support they receive from women voters. Likewise, the feminist National Organization for Women also supported O'Connor, despite disagreeing with some of her earlier decisions as a judge. Second, any attack on the first woman nominee by a committee consisting entirely of men would have appeared unchivalrous. For instance, although Senator Kennedy insisted that a rigorous review of O'Connor's judicial philosophy would be inappropriate, this was a relatively common practice, and by the time Reagan appointed Robert Bork to the Supreme Court in 1988, Senator Kennedy took a lead role in rejecting Bork's nomination because of his conservative judicial philosophy. A witness from the antiabortion National Right to Life explained his concerns with O'Connor's moderate views on abortion rights but softened his stance by claiming that she was a "likeable" person.

her. She is an observant, bright, lucid, articulate, thoughtful, sharp, curious person. She has a nice touch of wit and a warm sense of humor which one sorely needs when the brittle, cold winds of ridicule and harsh judgment whistle around this place, I can tell you, and the place east of us across the pasture there. . . .

I do feel an extra special form of kinship with Judge O'Connor. My path that led me here is very similar to the one that she took, both serving as attorneys and assistant attorney general, and in the general practice of law and civic work, and legislators in the State legislature where you never become known as a statesman. You are just the guy or the gal that voted against the "red fox bill," and I know how tough that gets. The judge was also majority floor leader, and that is something I enjoyed so much, much better than being minority floor leader.

Therefore, you have a diverse and lively background and you are an involved and committed woman in both your public and your personal life. I commend you, who have served as attorney and judge and legislator, involved citizen, wife, mother. . . .

Enough: My time runs. However, I do feel that here is a person who brings a real touch of class to this office, this Government, this city, and this place. I think that we will all perceive that at the conclusion of the hearings. I shall be listening with great interest, and I welcome you, Judge. . . .

Testimony of Honorable Sandra Day O'Connor

Thank you, Mr. Chairman. . . .

Mr. Chairman and members of the Senate Judiciary Committee, I would like to begin my brief opening remarks by expressing my gratitude to the President for nominating me to be an Associate Justice of the U.S. Supreme Court, and my appreciation and thanks to you and to all the members of this committee for your courtesy and for the privilege of meeting with you.

As the first woman to be nominated as a Supreme Court Justice, I am particularly honored, and I happily share the honor with millions of American women of yesterday and of today whose abilities and whose conduct have given me this opportunity for service. As a citizen and as a lawyer and as a judge, I have from afar always regarded the Court with the reverence and with the respect to which it is so clearly

One of the perennial concerns by women who achieve a high level within their profession is that they are still evaluated in part by traits that are unrelated to their abilities to do a job. For instance, women who achieve high office may be considered more acceptable if they have also played traditional female roles and fit the norms of femininity. The assumption is that a woman in power isn't so outside the norm if she fits the feminine norm in other areas of her life. This can be seen in Senator Simpson's compliments to O'Connor's ability to balance her roles as wife and mother with her other responsibilities, his reference to her charm, and her ability to soften the typical harsh environment of Washington, D.C. This tendency to draw attention to typical feminine traits for high-positioned women certainly didn't end with Justice O'Connor's confirmation hearing. As first lady, Hillary Clinton dealt with similar issues when she was counseled by political advisers to wear pastel colors when she was with husband President Bill Clinton. As recently as April 2013, President Barack Obama was criticized for referring to California attorney general Kamala Harris as "by far, the best-looking attorney general" at a fund-raising event. Women's organizations criticized the president for continuing to employ a double standard in how a woman's success is ultimately measured.

entitled because of the function it serves. It is the institution which is charged with the final responsibility of insuring that basic constitutional doctrines will always be honored and enforced. It is the body to which all Americans look for the ultimate protection of their rights. It is to the U.S. Supreme Court that we all turn when we seek that which we want most from our Government: equal justice under the law.

If confirmed by the Senate, I will apply all my abilities to insure that our Government is preserved; that justice under our Constitution and the laws of this land will always be the foundation of that Government. . . .

O'Connor's nomination to the U.S. Supreme Court was unanimously confirmed by the Senate, and she was sworn in as an associate justice on September 21, 1981. For the next 25 years O'Connor occupied a moderate conservative position on the Court, although she also displayed a strong independent streak. She also became known as a key swing vote on many cases before the Supreme Court, including cases that upheld the legality of *Roe v. Wade* and *Bush v. Gore* (2000), which delivered the disputed 2000 presidential election to Republican nominee George W. Bush. O'Connor retired from the Court on January 31, 2006.

If confirmed, I face an awesome responsibility ahead. So, too, does this committee face a heavy responsibility with respect to my nomination. I hope to be as helpful to you as possible in responding to your questions on my background and my beliefs and my views. There is, however, a limitation on my responses which I am compelled to recognize. I do not believe that as a nominee I can tell you how I might vote on a particular issue which may come before the Court, or endorse or criticize specific Supreme Court decisions presenting issues which may well come before the Court again. To do so would mean that I have prejudged the matter or have orally committed myself to a certain position. Such a statement by me as to how I might resolve a particular issue or what I might do in a future Court action might make it necessary for me to disqualify myself on the matter. This would result in my inability to do my sworn duty; namely, to decide cases that come before the Court.

Finally, neither you nor I know today the precise way in which any issue will present itself in the future, or what the facts or arguments may be at that time, or how the statute being interpreted may read. Until those crucial factors become known, I suggest that none of us really know how we would resolve any particular issue. At the very least, we would reserve judgment at that time.

Source: *Nomination of Sandra Day O'Connor of Arizona to Serve as an Associate Justice of the Supreme Court of the United States.* Hearing before the Committee on the Judiciary, United States Senate, 97th Congress, 1st Session, September 9, 10, and 11, 1981, Serial No. J–97–51 (Washington, DC: U.S. Government Printing Office, 1982). Available at http://www.loc.gov/law/find/nominations/oconnor/hearing.pdf.

"Honoring Geraldine Ferraro"

Statements of Representatives
Carolyn Maloney and Carolyn McCarthy

April 5, 2011

Statement by Carolyn Maloney

Mr. Speaker, I rise with the New York delegation to honor the memory and many contributions of one of our favorite daughters, Geraldine Ferraro.

Last Thursday, New Yorkers poured out in great numbers to honor her at her funeral. Her three children—Donna, Laura, and John, Jr.—spoke eloquently and movingly in support and love of their late mother. And at the funeral and speaking in a eulogy beautifully for her, Vice President Mondale, Secretary of State Madeleine Albright, Secretary of State Hillary Rodham Clinton, Congresswoman Jane Harman, Senator Mikulski, and former President Clinton.

It would have thrilled her to see four women precede a President in eulogizing and speaking about her, two of whom were Secretaries of State, because it was her life that helped inspire and move women forward in our national life, not only in politics but in every area—business, finance. All areas of American life, Geraldine Ferraro inspired with her life and her historic run for Vice President of the United States.

With her passing, America lost a leader who was as wise as she was warm; a trailblazer who broke down barriers for women. For women everywhere, not just in the United States but across the world, Geraldine Ferraro was a champion and a heroine. For me, personally, she was a dear, dear friend and a mentor.

What seemed to non-Yorkers as a feisty and fast-talking woman seemed to us as just another mom from Queens. She inspired us with her personal story.

The daughter of Italian immigrants, raised by her seamstress mother after her father died at 8, she became a public school teacher, a lawyer—one of just two women in her law class—and a Member and leader of Congress, elected in 1978. She also, after her historic run, became a commentator on television, a delegate to the United Nations. She headed the World Conference in Beijing in 1995, and I was proud to be part of her delegation at the World Conference on Women.

Last August, on her 75th birthday, we renamed the Post Office in Long Island City in her honor. It used to be in her district; it is now in mine. And I was honored to be able to

Geraldine Ferraro was the first woman to run on a major party ticket as the vice presidential nominee, selected by Democratic presidential candidate Walter Mondale in 1984. Her choice by Mondale was strategic, reflecting a major shift that was taking place in the American electorate. Specifically, the presidential election of 1980 was the first time that the number of women voting in the presidential election outnumbered the number of men voting, and Mondale hoped to capitalize on this increased number of women voters by nominating a woman as his vice presidential candidate. Although the Mondale-Ferraro ticket lost to incumbent president Ronald Reagan, Ferraro represented an important first in American politics. Upon her death in 2011, Representatives Carolyn Maloney and Carolyn McCarthy honored her memory in the House of Representatives and articulated the pride and excitement that many women had felt upon Ferraro's nomination for vice president.

author the legislation and work with my New York colleagues and others to pass it. And she was so thrilled at that naming to see so many of her friends, not only from New York and her district but across the country, come in one place to honor her.

Later that day, which happened to also be Women's Equality Day, she rang the bell at the New York Stock Exchange in honor of the progress for women.

I know that a post office is only the start of the memorials to this wonderful, charming, talented trailblazer who continued blazing trails her entire life. I met with her shortly before she died, and she had a list of constituents she wanted helped and causes she wanted completed.

We do stand on her shoulders and women like her who came before us.

I will never forget, as an eager, young delegate to the 1984 Democratic National Convention, and I can tell you firsthand that Geraldine Ferraro thrilled us when she took the stage as the first woman ever nominated by a major political party to be its candidate for Vice President of the United States.

It was absolutely electrifying. She changed my life, and she changed the lives of women everywhere. She changed the aspirations of women and how they view themselves.

I will never forget being on the floor. Many of the men gave their delegate card to the women delegates who were part-time delegates. So the floor was filled with women. People were handing out cigars saying, "It's a woman." And when she went to the floor, there was literally applause for over 10 minutes.

I shall miss her dearly and shall honor her passing by redoubling my efforts to complete her unfinished work to pass the ERA. It is time to enshrine in our Constitution the high principle of gender equality that Geraldine Ferraro so courageously stood for in her life.

Geraldine, we will miss you, we honor you, and we thank you for your many, many contributions to American life.

Statement of Carolyn McCarthy

Mr. Speaker, I also am part of the New York delegation, and I want to talk about Geraldine Ferraro. My good colleague, Carolyn Maloney, basically laid out her life and all the good things that she did. I guess I want to talk about what she meant to so many of us that weren't even in politics back then.

I think the first time that I ever saw Geraldine or heard of Geraldine was when she was announcing that she was going to be running for Vice President. . . .

". . . Geraldine Ferraro thrilled us when she took the stage as the first woman ever nominated by a major political party to be its candidate for Vice President of the United States. It was absolutely electrifying. She changed my life, and she changed the lives of women everywhere. She changed the aspirations of women and how they view themselves."

She struck me as a unique figure on TV, a woman in a male-dominated profession. She had a smile. She had confidence. When she got onto that stage, you just knew this radiance that came out of her. For myself, I was not in politics, didn't follow politics too well, but she certainly gave a strong impression to me.

Her message was also full of hope. I happen to believe that, especially when we say to people, "If we can do this, we can do anything." I am one of those people that believe that. I am here in Congress. Everybody said I couldn't do that. Somehow I got here. Somehow I have stayed here. Somehow I keep fighting for my constituents back at home.

She inspired women to get involved. She inspired them to get involved in politics, whether at the staff level or as a candidate. And while I understood the importance of the event, I had no idea that I would be standing here praising this woman that I first saw on TV. As I said, I had no political ambitions. I was a nurse, just several miles away from the city where Geraldine was. Like most Americans, I did vote and I followed the news, but I never thought I would get involved in politics. . . .

Well, here I am in Congress, and I am proud to be following in the footsteps of Geraldine Ferraro. I wouldn't use the words, the kind words that people use for her on myself like "pioneer" or "trailblazer." I actually followed Geraldine and her advice to come to Washington and try to make a difference.

Like so many women in New York politics today, Geraldine helped me as I went through from private citizen to candidate to public official. She opened so many doors for me, introducing me to people that I needed to meet.

She was well known for this, for spending as much energy helping lift up others and having another woman follow. . . .

With only 17 percent of members of Congress being women, we still have a long way to go when it comes to equality in representation.

But certainly we couldn't be where we are today if it weren't for Geraldine.

Source: "Honoring Geraldine Ferraro," *Congressional Record,* Vol. 157, Number 48 (April 5, 2011). Available online at http://www.gpo.gov/fdsys/pkg/CREC-2011-04-05/html/CREC-2011-04-05-pt1-PgH2298-2.htm.

In 1941 the number of women in Congress reached double digits for the first time, with a total of 10 women serving in the House and Senate. In the four decades following that milestone, the number of women elected to Congress varied widely from election to election, increasing some years and decreasing in others. After 1980, an upward trend in the number of women elected seemed to be evident, and by 1984, the year Walter Mondale nominated Geraldine Ferraro, a total of 24 women served in Congress, 2 in the Senate and 22 in the House of Representatives, including Ferraro. Since 1984, the number of women serving in Congress has only increased or stayed the same from election to election. As stated by both Representatives Mahoney and McCarthy, there were women who were inspired to run for office after the visibility of Ferraro's candidacy, and historically we see that when more women run for office, the more likely they are to be elected.

Despite the inroads that women have made in being elected to Congress, it took 24 years for another woman to be nominated for the vice presidency. In 2008, Republican presidential candidate John McCain selected Alaska governor Sarah Palin to be his running mate for the presidency. Hillary Clinton, a U.S. senator from New York at the time, was a serious contender for the Democratic nomination for president in 2008, but she lost the nomination to Barack Obama, who was later elected to the presidency. Currently, no woman has been nominated by one of the two major parties to run for the presidency, and Ferraro and Palin are the only two women who have ever been on a presidential ticket of either the Republican Party or the Democratic Party.

Chapter 4

Women's Health and Reproduction

Introduction

In her 1920 book *Woman and the New Race,* reproductive rights activist Margaret Sanger stated that "Woman must have her freedom—the fundamental freedom of choosing whether or not she shall be a mother and how many children she will have. . . . No woman can call herself free who does not own and control her body. No woman can call herself free until she can choose consciously whether she will or will not be a mother." Sanger was a pioneer in women's reproductive rights during the early 20th century, focusing primarily on women's access to contraception and reproductive health care. While Sanger was at times a controversial figure, being arrested several times and working with organizations that promoted eugenics, she was clearly one of the most influential advocates for women's reproductive rights and health care. Although she thought it was important to empower women in a very practical way, namely to help them control the number of children they had, she also helped define the issue of reproduction more broadly as an issue of women's rights and, more specifically, as an issue of individual freedom.

Although the concept of individual freedom is closely associated with democratic governance, it has always been understood in the American political culture that personal freedom only extends so far, that our freedoms may be limited under certain conditions. The popular notion is that one's rights end where another's rights begin; in essence, a person's freedom to do what she or he wants to do does not extend past the point at which it infringes on someone else's rights. But this explanation of limits on individual freedom is incomplete. Individual freedoms may also be restricted if it is perceived to be in the best interest of society as a whole, or for the public good, to do so. This can be seen on issues as simple as state governments setting speed limits on roadways or the federal government regulating pollution levels to keep the public safe.

Conflict can arise, however, when there is disagreement over whether some issue is a personal decision, governed by individual liberty, or whether the issue is legitimately in the public sphere, decided by the government in the public's interest. This dichotomy between personal freedom and the public interest can be seen most dramatically in issues related to women's reproductive rights and health concerns. On numerous occasions, state governments and the federal government have had to address to what extent decisions about reproduction—whether, when, and how to have a child—are personal decisions and to what extent the public, via government action, has a legitimate interest in these decisions. The answer to this question often comes down to a person's views on some very complex issues, such as when life actually begins, when the unborn gain rights of citizenship, whether women have rights to bodily autonomy in matters of reproduction, and whether women can be fully equal to men when their experiences, especially in matters of reproduction, differ so widely.

This chapter considers nine issues that relate to women's reproductive rights and women's health. For the issues related to reproductive rights, including women's access to contraception and abortion, the core question for each is consistently the appropriate role for government in restricting the personal reproductive decisions of women. For the issues related to women's health, such as funding for maternal health programs and breast cancer research, a similar but less controversial question is raised regarding the appropriate role of the federal government to pay for health care programs.

The first issue considered originates in 1873, when Congress passed an antiobscenity law known as the Comstock Act. The law was named for its author Anthony Comstock, a U.S. postal inspector and ardent opponent of pornography and other "obscene, lewd, or lascivious" materials. One of the items specifically prohibited by the law was contraception, specifically devices that were designed to prevent or end pregnancy as well as the dissemination of information concerning how a person could control reproduction. Comstock used his position as a postal inspector to intercept material being sent through the mail that was considered illegal under the law. After passage of the Comstock Act, several states followed suit, passing their own versions, sometimes more restrictive, of antiobscenity laws. Although the law wasn't widely supported, it wasn't until after Sanger's arrest in 1916 for opening a birth control clinic that the federal courts began to interpret the law more loosely and allow access to contraception. In 1932 Sanger testified before a Senate committee on the need to overturn the Comstock Act, especially in regard to contraception. She described the need for contraception as both a health issue for women and an economic need for families. While the government's response wasn't immediate, the Comstock Act was eventually weakened to allow information about contraception to be mailed across state lines. The act's eventual demise did not, however, eliminate states' efforts to control access to contraception.

Sanger's focus on women's health was not without precedent. Eleven years prior to her testimony supporting repeal of the Comstock Act, Congress had passed the Sheppard-Towner Act, a law allowing the federal government to help states fund programs that were designed to improve maternal and infant health. In 1921 when the law was passed, childbirth was the second most common cause of death for women, and a third of all children died before their fifth birthday. Many states were attempting to improve these statistics by giving rural women in particular greater access to health care, but the programs were expensive, and many states' programs were underfunded and ineffective. Representative Horace Mann Towner and Senator Morris Sheppard authored a bill to assist state efforts by providing funding from the federal government. Although the bill ultimately passed, it was a tough sell, not because members of Congress were not concerned with women's and children's health but because of ideological disagreements over the appropriate role of the federal government in such programs. Representative Towner's testimony to the House Committee on Interstate and Foreign Commerce illustrates this particular concern by focusing on whether the federal government would be overstepping its bounds with such a law. While he prevails with the passage of the Sheppard-Towner Act, the law was repealed a mere eight years later, largely due to continued concerns about the legitimate role of the federal government.

Although the Comstock Act has never been completely repealed, in 1936 the Second Circuit Court of Appeals decided in *United States v. One Package* that the federal government could not intercept and confiscate packages that originated with a physician. This decision dealt a major blow to the federal government's ability to implement the Comstock Act, and it largely fell out of use. However, the court decision did not affect the various state antiobscenity laws around the country. Connecticut, in particular, was considered to have one of the most restrictive laws in place in regard to contraception use and dissemination. Passed in 1879, the law's constitutionality had been challenged several times, but it wasn't until the Supreme Court heard the case *Griswold v. Connecticut* in 1965 that state laws prohibiting contraception were struck down as a violation of the Fourteenth Amendment's Due Process Clause. The excerpt from the majority opinion in the case included in this chapter outlines the Court's decision that the Bill of Rights implicitly protects an individual's right to privacy and that the use of contraception, especially for married couples, is an act that falls in a zone of privacy. The Court broadened its decision to all persons in 1972 in *Eisenstadt v. Baird.*

More controversial than the issue of contraception is the issue of abortion, although the two issues are related. First, the vast majority of abortions occur due to an unplanned and unwanted pregnancy. Although some women may have an abortion to protect their health or life, this is rather rare; most women give quality-of-life and economic explanations for their decision to have an abortion. Contraception helps women prevent unwanted, unplanned pregnancies, and the more access women have to contraception, the fewer abortions take place. The second relationship between the two issues is the concept of a constitutional right to privacy. When the Supreme Court used this rationale for overturning Connecticut's contraception laws, it opened the door for other reproductive rights issues to be governed by an individual's right to privacy. In 1973 the Supreme Court used this rationale in its majority decision for the case *Roe v. Wade.* Although the Court's conclusions were not as definitive as those provided in *Griswold v. Connecticut,* the case did prohibit states from prohibiting abortions, at least in the early stages of pregnancy, because a woman's privacy rights included the right to end a pregnancy. For most people, however, the prevention of pregnancy is less controversial than the choice to end a pregnancy. Thus, the excerpt from the majority opinion in *Roe v. Wade* illustrates the difficulties inherent in deciding a case on abortion. These complexities opened the door for later cases involving abortion rights.

Roe v. Wade provided a catalyst for opponents of abortion to organize politically and influence policy decisions related to abortion. While there were localized anti-abortion groups prior to *Roe,* they weren't particularly organized on a national scale. *Roe v. Wade* changed that. The largest antiabortion organization, National Right to Life, was organized a mere four months after the Court opinion was released in January 1973. Often, having an issue to fight against provides more incentive to organize than does at an attempt to maintain the status quo. Consequently, within a year of the group's founding, the first March for Life rally was held in Washington, D.C., with thousands of participants. This antiabortion sentiment was echoed by some members of Congress, and in 1976 Representative Henry Hyde of Illinois introduced an amendment to an appropriations bill in the House of Representatives that would prohibit federal funds from being used for abortions. Hyde made an impassioned speech to his colleagues in support of his amendment, and the measure was ultimately passed. His statement is included in this chapter.

If one were to look only at the actions of the federal government in the decade following the Hyde Amendment, it would appear that the issue of abortion had largely dropped off the national agenda. For the most part, the only laws that Congress passed on abortion were updated versions of the Hyde Amendment or other prohibitions on the use of federal funds for abortions. Most of the political action taking place during the late 1970s and into the mid-1980s, however, was taking place at the state level. National Right to Life and other antiabortion groups employed a strategy to have laws passed at the state level to limit women's access to abortion. The constitutionality of several of these state laws was challenged before the Supreme Court.

Webster v. Reproductive Health in 1989 and *Planned Parenthood of Southeastern Pennsylvania v. Casey* in 1992 were two of the most influential post-*Roe* cases dealing with abortion. Excerpts from each of the majority opinions are included in this chapter. In *Webster,* a Missouri law prohibited state funds from being used for abortion purposes, including public funds for medical facilities, staffing, and counseling, unless a woman's life was endangered. Advocates for reproductive rights believed that Missouri's law contradicted provisions of *Roe v. Wade,* but the Supreme Court disagreed, stating that the law did not lessen a woman's right to have an abortion. This case heartened abortion opponents that the Court would eventually permit other state-imposed obstacles to abortions. In 1992 the Supreme Court in *Planned Parenthood v. Casey* confirmed opponents' hopes that states would be allowed to pass laws further limiting women's access to abortion. Pennsylvania established numerous requirements for women seeking an abortion, such as parental consent for minors, a husband's consent for married women, and a waiting period between consulting a physician and having the abortion. With the exception of the husband's consent, the Court ruled that such obstacles to an abortion were not a violation of a woman's constitutional rights.

Although *Roe* was not overturned in either of these cases and it was still considered unconstitutional for states to outright prohibit abortion in the early part of a pregnancy, almost all states had established various legal obstacles for women who wanted an abortion. By 2003, after years of only passing legislation that dealt with federal funds for abortions, Congress stepped up its own involvement by passing a law prohibiting certain late-term abortions. The type of abortion a woman can have is largely dependent on how long she has been pregnant. Abortions are much simpler earlier in the pregnancy, but as the pregnancy progresses, abortions become more complicated and controversial, especially as the fetus moves toward viability. For women in the second half of their pregnancy, one procedure available is medically referred to as intact dilation and extraction. Opponents of the procedure, however, refer to the procedure as a "partial birth abortion." Although this procedure accounts for only 0.17 percent of all abortions performed, it garnered a great deal of opposition even among people who were generally in favor of abortion rights. In 2003 Congress passed the Partial Birth Abortion Ban, prohibiting this particular abortion procedure. Statements from both a supporter and an opponent of this legislation are provided in this chapter, outlining the general arguments made in a congressional hearing before the Subcommittee on the Constitution in the House Committee on the Judiciary.

When possible, members of Congress would generally prefer to deal with issues that are less controversial than abortion, which may help explain why so few laws have been passed at the national level on that topic. More popular are issues on which everyone can agree. This was the case in 1991 when Congress considered the federal funding of research on breast cancer and supporting methods of early detection such as mammograms and other breast health services. While members of Congress must ultimately agree on how much to appropriate for even popular programs, the general opinion toward finding a cure for breast cancer was overwhelmingly positive. Part of the positive response for this aspect of women's health was due to the efforts of the Susan G. Komen Foundation to define breast cancer as a national problem that affects everyone. Pink ribbons have become almost synonymous with breast cancer support. At a 1991 Senate hearing before the Subcommittee on Aging of the Committee on Labor and Human Resources, television actress and breast cancer survivor Jill Eikenberry shared her experiences with breast cancer and encouraged members of Congress to support women's health by providing greater access to methods of early detection. An excerpt of her statement is provided.

Margaret Sanger Testifies on Birth Control

Statement from U.S. Senate Subcommittee Hearings on Birth Control Legislation

May 1932

Statement of Mrs. Margaret Sanger

Mr. Chairman, and gentlemen of the committee, the essential object of the committee on Federal legislation for birth control in supporting this bill, Senate 4582, is to amend the existing Federal laws which prevent the dissemination through the mails of information relating to the subject of contraception.

We want to make it possible for motherhood to be conscious and controlled. We want to make it possible for mothers to have safe, scientific information to prevent conception so that they may regulate the size of their family in consideration of the mother's health, of the father's earning capacity, and of the welfare of each child. . . .

We not only want motherhood to be a conscious and controlled function but we want parenthood to be something other than the consequences of a reckless, careless shiftlessness. We want parenthood to be regarded as a fine commission, a noble trust, a splendid assignment, and it can be so considered only when it becomes a conscious responsibility.

In the laws, which this bill, Senate 4582, will amend, contraceptive information has been classed with obscenity, pornography, and abortion. Information concerning contraception does not belong there. . . .

The need for better information, for more scientific data on this important subject has been recognized. And there has gradually arisen in this country a movement in favor of birth control.

We find to-day that parents consider birth control information not only a health measure, not alone an economic expedient, but a principle of social welfare by which the future advancement of the individual and the country itself is safeguarded. . . .

These federal laws interfere with the proper dissemination of information to prevent conception in 47 States of this Union although there are already laws in those States

Margaret Sanger was one of the earliest and most outspoken advocates of birth control rights in the early decades of the 20th century. Her actions were prompted by the federal Comstock Act (1873), which made it illegal to distribute information or devices through the U.S. Postal Service that were considered obscene or immoral, including information and devices related to birth control and abortion. Many states followed the federal government's lead by passing even more restrictive laws on the use and dissemination of birth control. Sanger tried on several occasions to get Congress to repeal the Comstock Act but was unsuccessful in her efforts. Ultimately she was able to accomplish more through the federal courts, which used a relatively loose interpretation of the law allowing physicians to distribute birth control to their patients.

Sanger employed an interesting strategy to bolster support for birth control in the United States. In addition to focusing on the advantages of birth control for families' economic needs and women's health concerns, she focused on birth control's contribution to the national interest. It is on this point that Sanger has been the subject of some criticism in that she lauded birth control's ability to protect American society from people considered less desirable, going so far as to align herself with proponents of the eugenics movement. Eugenics is a method of encouraging some groups of people to have children while discouraging or actually preventing others from procreating. In American history, African Americans, immigrants, incarcerated people, and those suffering from mental illness were the targets of eugenicists. Whether Sanger actually agreed with the eugenics movement or was simply using it to build support for birth control is still debated.

enabling physicians to give advice to patients in their regular practice, and there are in this country to-day over 50 legally operating birth-control clinics distributed over 12 states. These birth-control clinics are medically established and medically directed, and have been organized solely for the purpose of giving contractive information by the medical profession. . . .

Under the laws now, especially section 211 of the Criminal Code, it is a crime for me or for anyone to send to a mother, a sister, or relative situated in any of these States the address of any clinic lawfully operating in that State, even though such an individual may be poverty stricken or diseased, even though she may have a right under that State law to have this information for her health and for her family happiness. The Federal law makes it a crime for anyone to send through the United States mail the address of a physician or a clinic where such information may be obtained. This bill asks that there be an exception in these cases. . . .

Most of us believe that the original object of these laws was to prevent the dissemination of pornographic literature through the United States mails and to restrict its entrance into this country. We fully concur in the prevention of the distribution of pornographic or obscene literature. We believe, however, that it is unfair to classify medical and scientific information or literature in this class and to do so places a great hardship upon the general practice of the medical profession and upon our welfare agencies. The effect . . . is to increase the surreptitious circulation of unscientific or harmful information which tends to increase crime and to multiply abortions.

Sanger was speaking from personal experience. As a young nurse, she was approached by numerous young wives and mothers, asking how to control the size of their families. These women were often from poor families who could not afford to continue increasing the size of their families. Due to the Comstock Act and similar state laws, Sanger was unable to legally provide information that would help these families plan and space the number of children they would have. When one of her patients died of an attempted abortion after she had expressed to Sanger the desire to prevent another pregnancy, Sanger was moved to action to give women and families access to birth control.

The laws, in effect, have already been responsible for a great deal of harm, and I think if we could measure the injury that has been done to women, and were aware of their damaged conditions, physiologically and mentally, the harm far outweighs the good that these laws have accomplished.

We, Mr. Chairman, believe that the effect of keeping these laws on the statute book is to keep alive hypocrisy, evasion, and a general increasing disregard for laws. We believe that there is nothing to be gained by keeping such laws on the statute books when they are known to be inimical to the personal health of mothers, to the family happiness, and to the general welfare and progress of the Nation.

Source: Excerpt from "Birth Control," Hearings before a Subcommittee of the Committee on the Judiciary, U.S. Senate, Seventy-second Congress, 1st Session, on S. 4436, May 12–20, 1932, 2–5.

A Congressman Urges Action to Protect the Health of Women and Children

Statement of Horace M. Towner at "Public Protection of Maternity and Infancy" Hearings

December 1920

Statement of Hon. Horace M. Towner, a Representative in Congress from the State of Iowa

Mr. Chairman and gentlemen of the committee, this bill, as I presume you all know, is a bill for the protection of maternity and infancy. It is built upon the general plan of aid from the National Government to the States for the purpose of stimulating the States to greater activity in these regards and for the purpose as well of aiding them by contributions from the General Government. . . .

The first section of the bill provides that the amounts to be provided in the bill to be paid from the General Treasury shall be paid to the several States for the purpose of cooperating with the States in promoting the care of maternity and infancy in the several States. That is a general statement of the purposes of the bill.

I should call the attention of the committee to the fact that there are not appropriations provided in the bill; they are merely authorizations. It is hardly necessary for me to tell the members of the committee that an authorization does not necessarily impose any obligation on the General Government; an authorization usually is followed by an appropriation, but not by any means is that always the case.

Conditions exist under which it will be practically impossible that all of the authorizations provided shall be followed by appropriations. For instance, only those States that take advantage of the law will have the benefit of the law; it is not probable that all of the States—immediately, at least—will take advantage of the law. . . .

The provision in section 2 is that there shall be granted absolute amount, without condition, to each of the States, of

Horace Mann Towner was a Republican member of the House of Representatives from Iowa, elected in 1910 and serving until 1923. He, along with Texas Senator Morris Sheppard, authored the Maternity and Infancy Act of 1921, commonly known as the Sheppard-Towner Act. The act was a response to information and statistics emerging from the Children's Bureau, a federal agency established in 1912 to investigate and report on the welfare of children in the country. Julia Lathrop, the first director of the Children's Bureau, was the first woman appointed to head an agency in the U.S. government, and her 1912 appointment predated women's right to vote by eight years. By the time of her appointment, Lathrop already had a distinguished history of advocacy for women's and children's health issues. As the director of the Children's Bureau, she played an important supporting role in the passage of the Sheppard-Towner Act.

In an interesting political move, Representative Towner reminds members of Congress that passage of this bill would not bind the hands of the federal government financially. While this bill would authorize funds for state child welfare programs, an authorization merely provides legal permission for funds to be spent. An authorization provides no funding. To fund programs, the federal government must pass an appropriations bill, which specifically designates how much will be spent on a program. This process would have been well known to other members of Congress. One possible explanation for Townsend's testimony is that he was aware that the bill put some members of Congress in a political bind. The bill would have been popular with constituents but would also result in the federal government moving into a policy area historically controlled by the states, something that many members of Congress opposed for ideological reasons.

If the order of Representative Townsend's comments provides a clue to the obstacles he saw facing this bill, the expansion of the federal government into state governments' business was possibly the biggest barrier to its passage. He focuses on these concerns first, explaining why this did not pose a problem to American federalism. Only after these comments does he turn to the more emotional arguments regarding the protection of mothers' and children's health. For most supporters of the bill this was of course the primary goal, the goal that was overtly included in its title. Legislation, however, can be nuanced, and while this bill was specifically intended to protect women's and children's health, it also would have an effect on relations between the national and state levels of government. Townsend was strategic in his presentation of this bill's merits, supplementing his appeal to protect maternal and infant health with an appeal to patriotism, arguing that the United States should not be lagging behind other countries in the protection of mothers and children.

$10,000, if they accede to the general condition imposed that they shall organize a department or bureau or commission, or whatever it may be, that shall use it for the particular purposes specified. It does not require, so far as this authorization is concerned, that the States shall meet this expenditure with equal amounts. . . .

But I will say to the committee that, after all, the expenditure of this money from the General Government can not under any circumstances meet the requirement of certain of the States. In some of the States they will not only meet the amount which is given by the General Government but may multiply it five times or even ten times, in order to meet particular and peculiar conditions. The States are not alike; the conditions are not alike. The necessity for this legislation is not so great in some of them as it is in others. The States will, after all, have to be the determining factors as to how much money shall be expended with regard for the desired purpose. . . .

The only purpose of the bill is to simply provide, if we possibly can, that the amount expended by the General Government shall be used for the purposes for which it is intended; and the purpose is to help in the administration of the law and the expenditure of the amount just as far as it is possible to help the State. . . .

We want the States, as far as possible, to take this work in their hands. We want to aid them, because in some of the States they need aid. We want to stimulate them, because in some of the States they need stimulation. In one State already they have appropriated $3,800 for two years, or $1,900 a year, and they found, in trying to administer the law, that they could not get anybody at all to take charge of this work in their State who would be qualified for a less salary than $1,800, so that $1,800 out of the $1,900 was to be used for paying one person for superintending the work. Of course the amount was grossly inadequate and insufficient. They need aid there perhaps; they need stimulation certainly.

So all along the line that is the object and purpose of the bill. It is not to control it; the Government does not want to control it. Why should they?

The purpose is to reach the poor individuals who are suffering and who need this aid. The purpose is to save the lives of the 250,000 people who die every year because of need of aid.

If it was proposed here in Congress to save the lives of 250,000 from some impending calamity out in California, or in Alaska, or anywhere, there would be no hesitancy on the part of the Government in doing it. But because these mothers and these babies are dying right along from day to day and from year to year, and it does not occur all at once, for that reason we are not shocked. . . .

We know that the loss in the United States is shamefully large. We know that we are way down among the list of nations of the world in regard to this. In the year 1914, 14 of the different Governments of the world made a much better showing than this country did with regard to the proportion of these lives that were saved, and in 1918, 23,000 mothers died from these particular causes. We have made great advancement in reducing the mortality in the United States from diphtheria—I believe about 75 per cent—and in cases of typhoid fever we have reduced the mortality by about 50 per cent. . . .

With regard to many and, indeed, to most diseases we have had a reduction in almost all without aid from the General Government or the stimulation of the General Government to activity. And the result, of course, has been to reduce, as the years have gone by, very strongly and splendidly the mortality in those cases.

But unfortunately, in this class of cases, involving the mothers and children, the mortality has not been reduced. Unfortunately, owing to the want of stimulation or from some cause in the United States, we are perhaps the most backward among the civilized nations in that regard. We should meet these conditions, because, after all, it is an emergency case. These people who favor this legislation on the part of the General Government are not coming to you with regard to the cases in which progress is being made; but we are saying to you that the States have not met or can not meet these conditions. We are saying to you that England and other nations have met these conditions, because of the necessities which have arisen in those countries, and we are not doing it. We are in the condition in which it almost appears that, for want of activity and aid and encouragement and stimulation on the part of the National Government, we are allowing these thousands and tens of thousands of women and children to die that might be saved. . . .

I want to say this, gentlemen: I presume you gentlemen realize, as all of those who have had practical experience in public life do, the inertia that exists, expecially [sic] in the State legislature, with regard to this kind of legislation. And you gentlemen understand, I am quite sure, far

"With regard to many and, indeed, to most diseases we have had a reduction in almost all without aid from the General Government or the stimulation of the General Government to activity. . . . But unfortunately, in this class of cases, involving the mothers and children, the mortality has not been reduced. Unfortunately, owing to the want of stimulation or from some cause in the United States, we are perhaps the most backward among the civilized nations in that regard."

better than most men could understand, how it will stimulate them to activity, stimulate them to meet the demands of their real duty, if it can be said, when the proposition is presented to the legislature, "You will receive aid from the general Government in this matter." That has been the case in other instances where we have this kind of legislation, with this kind of a proposition of cooperative effort; and I am quite sure it will be made more promptly and more completely with regard to this legislation, if it shall pass, than it had ever been in the case of any other legislation. Because this more appeals to men, if they can really understand its appeal, than anything else I can imagine.

Source: Excerpt from "Public Protection of Maternity and Infancy," Hearings before the Committee on Interstate and Foreign Commerce of the House of Representatives, 66th Congress, 3rd Session, on H.R. 10925, December 20, 21, 22, 23, 28, 29, 1920, 5–12.

The U.S. Supreme Court Expands Contraceptive Rights on Privacy Grounds

Supreme Court Ruling in
Griswold v. Connecticut

1965

Appellant Griswold is Executive Director of the Planned Parenthood League of Connecticut. Appellant Buxton is a licensed physician and a professor at the Yale Medical School who served as Medical Director for the League at its Center in New Haven—a center open and operating from November 1 to November 10, 1961, when appellants were arrested.

They gave information, instruction, and medical advice to *married persons* as to the means of preventing conception. They examined the wife and prescribed the best contraceptive device or material for her use. Fees were usually charged, although some couples were serviced free.

The statutes whose constitutionality is involved in this appeal are [Sections] 53–32 and 54–196 of the General Statutes of Connecticut (1958 rev.). The former provides:

Any person who uses any drug, medicinal article or instrument for the purpose of preventing conception shall be fined not less than fifty dollars or imprisoned not less than sixty days nor more than one year or be both fined and imprisoned.

Section 54–196 provides:

Any person who assists, abets, counsels, causes, hires or commands another to commit any offense may be prosecuted and punished as if he were the principal offender.

The appellants were found guilty as accessories and fined $100 each, against the claim that the accessory statute, as so applied, violated the Fourteenth Amendment. . . .

[W]e are met with a wide range of questions that implicate the Due Process Clause of the Fourteenth Amendment. Overtones of some arguments suggest that *Lochner v. New York,* 198 U.S. 45, should be our guide. But we decline that invitation, as we did in *West Coast Hotel Co. v. Parrish,* 300 U.S. 379; *Olsen v. Nebraska,* 313 U.S. 236; *Lincoln Union v. Northwestern Co.,* 335 U.S. 525; *Williamson v. Lee Optical Co.,* 348 U.S. 483; *Giboney v. Empire Storage Co.,* 336 U.S.

Although the portion of the federal Comstock Act affecting contraception was overturned by the Supreme Court in *United States v. One Package of Japanese Pessaries* in 1936, the states still had discretion to pass laws regarding the use and distribution of contraception within their boundaries. Although most states had abandoned such laws by 1965, Connecticut maintained its prohibition on the use of contraception as well as the dissemination of devices or information. When the director and a physician employed by a Planned Parenthood clinic were arrested and fined for providing information and contraception to a married couple in their care, they appealed their conviction, arguing that Connecticut's law violated the Due Process Clause of the Fourteenth Amendment. Before the Court considered the actual merits of the case before them, it first outlined the precedent set by the Court for using the Fourteenth Amendment in similar legal questions.

490. We do not sit as a super-legislature to determine the wisdom, need, and propriety of laws that touch economic problems, business affairs, or social conditions. This law, however, operates directly on an intimate relation of husband and wife and their physician's role in one aspect of that relation.

The association of people is not mentioned in the Constitution nor in the Bill of Rights. The right to educate a child in a school of the parents' choice—whether public or private or parochial—is also not mentioned. Nor is the right to study any particular subject or any foreign language. Yet the First Amendment has been construed to include certain of those rights. . . .

In *NAACP v. Alabama* . . . we protected the "freedom to associate and privacy in one's associations," noting that freedom of association was a peripheral First Amendment right. Disclosure of membership lists of a constitutionally valid association, we held, was invalid "as entailing the likelihood of a substantial restraint upon the exercise by petitioner's members of their right to freedom of association."

In other words, the First Amendment has a penumbra where privacy is protected from governmental intrusion. In like context, we have protected forms of "association" that are not political in the customary sense, but pertain to the social, legal, and economic benefit of the members. *NAACP v. Button,* 371 U.S. 415, 430–431. In *Schware v. Board of Bar Examiners,* 353 U.S. 232, we held it not permissible to bar a lawyer from practice because he had once been a member of the Communist Party. The man's "association with that Party" was not shown to be "anything more than a political faith in a political party" . . ., and was not action of a kind proving bad moral character. . . .

Those cases involved more than the "right of assembly"—a right that extends to all, irrespective of their race or ideology. [*De Jonge v. Oregon,* 299 U.S. 353]. The right of "association," like the right of belief [*Board of Education v. Barnette,* 319 U.S. 624], is more than the right to attend a meeting; it includes the right to express one's attitudes or philosophies by membership in a group or by affiliation with it or by other lawful means. Association in that context is a form of expression of opinion, and, while it is not expressly included in the First Amendment, its existence is necessary in making the express guarantees fully meaningful.

The foregoing cases suggest that specific guarantees in the Bill of Rights have penumbras, formed by emanations from those guarantees that help give them life and substance. . . . Various guarantees create zones of privacy.

The Supreme Court recognizes that the language used in the U.S. Constitution and its amendments must often been interpreted to apply it to cases that come before the Court. For instance, there is no mention in the Constitution of whether states can make contraception illegal. As such, the Court has to illustrate that the Constitution is relevant to the case and that it provides some guidance on the question before the Court. For instance, in *Griswold v. Connecticut,* the Court argues that married couples have the right to privacy when deciding whether or not to use contraception, despite the fact that a right to privacy is never expressly mentioned in the Constitution. However, the Court argues that this right to privacy is in the "penumbra" of the Bill of Rights, meaning that privacy is consistent with the other rights articulated in the Constitution and thus can be used as a rationale for overturning Connecticut's law.

The right of association contained in the penumbra of the First Amendment is one, as we have seen. The Third Amendment, in its prohibition against the quartering of soldiers "in any house" in time of peace without the consent of the owner, is another facet of that privacy. The Fourth Amendment explicitly affirms the "right of the people to be secure in their persons, houses, papers, and effects, against unreasonable searches and seizures." The Fifth Amendment, in its Self-Incrimination Clause, enables the citizen to create a zone of privacy which government may not force him to surrender to his detriment. The Ninth Amendment provides: "The enumeration in the Constitution, of certain rights, shall not be construed to deny or disparage others retained by the people. . . ."

The present case, then, concerns a relationship lying within the zone of privacy created by several fundamental constitutional guarantees. And it concerns a law which, in forbidding the use of contraceptives, rather than regulating their manufacture or sale, seeks to achieve its goals by means having a maximum destructive impact upon that relationship. Such a law cannot stand in light of the familiar principle, so often applied by this Court, that a "governmental purpose to control or prevent activities constitutionally subject to state regulation may not be achieved by means which sweep unnecessarily broadly and thereby invade the area of protected freedoms." . . .

Would we allow the police to search the sacred precincts of marital bedrooms for telltale signs of the use of contraceptives? The very idea is repulsive to the notions of privacy surrounding the marriage relationship.

We deal with a right of privacy older than the Bill of Rights—older than our political parties, older than our school system. Marriage is a coming together for better or for worse, hopefully enduring, and intimate to the degree of being sacred. It is an association that promotes a way of life, not causes; a harmony in living, not political faiths; a bilateral loyalty, not commercial or social projects. Yet it is an association for as noble a purpose as any involved in our prior decisions.

Source: *Griswold v. Connecticut,* 381 U.S. 479 (1965). Available at http://caselaw.lp.findlaw.com/scripts/getcase.pl?court=US&vol=381&invol=479.

"Would we allow the police to search the sacred precincts of marital bedrooms for telltale signs of the use of contraceptives? The very idea is repulsive to the notions of privacy surrounding the marriage relationship."

The U.S. Supreme Court Legalizes Abortion

Supreme Court Ruling in *Roe v. Wade*

1973

In 1969, Texas resident Norma McCorvey became pregnant with her third child at the age of 21. McCorvey was a high school dropout at age 14 and was married at the age of 16. Her mother gained custody of McCorvey's first child, and McCorvey lost custody of her second child to the baby's father with whom she could have no contact. Upon becoming pregnant the third time, McCorvey was advised by her friends to get an abortion, despite being illegal in the state of Texas. Unable to obtain an abortion illegally, she consulted with lawyers who filed suit on her behalf, arguing that laws making abortion illegal were unconstitutional under the Constitution's protection of privacy. To protect McCorvey from the social stigma associated with abortion, she was known anonymously as "Jane Roe." In 1973 her case *Roe v. Wade*, with a similar case from Georgia, *Doe v. Bolton,* was heard by the U.S. Supreme Court. However, by the time the Supreme Court decided the case, McCorvey had given birth to her third child and placed it for adoption. She later became an ardent opponent of abortion.

This Texas federal appeal and its Georgia companion, *Doe v. Bolton* ... present constitutional challenges to state criminal abortion legislation. The Texas statutes under attack here are typical of those that have been in effect in many States for approximately a century.

The Georgia statutes, in contrast, have a modern cast, and are a legislative product that, to an extent at least, obviously reflects the influences of recent attitudinal change, of advancing medical knowledge and techniques, and of new thinking about an old issue.

We forthwith acknowledge our awareness of the sensitive and emotional nature of the abortion controversy, of the vigorous opposing views, even among physicians, and of the deep and seemingly absolute convictions that the subject inspires. One's philosophy, one's experiences, one's exposure to the raw edges of human existence, one's religious training, one's attitudes toward life and family and their values, and the moral standards one establishes and seeks to observe, are all likely to influence and to color one's thinking and conclusions about abortion.

In addition, population growth, pollution, poverty, and racial overtones tend to complicate and not to simplify the problem.

Our task, of course, is to resolve the issue by constitutional measurement, free of emotion and of predilection. We seek earnestly to do this, and, because we do, we have inquired into, and in this opinion place some emphasis upon, medical and medical-legal history and what that history reveals about man's attitudes toward the abortion procedure over the centuries. We bear in mind, too, Mr. Justice Holmes' admonition in his now-vindicated dissent in *Lochner v. New York,* 198 U.S. 45, 76 (1905):

[The Constitution] is made for people of fundamentally differing views, and the accident of our finding certain opinions natural and familiar or novel and even shocking ought not to conclude our judgment upon the question whether statutes embodying them conflict with the Constitution of the United States.

The Texas statutes that concern us here are [Articles] 1191–1194 and 1196 of the [Texas] State's Penal Code.

These make it a crime to "procure an abortion," as therein defined, or to attempt one, except with respect to "an abortion procured or attempted by medical advice for the purpose of saving the life of the mother." Similar statutes are in existence in a majority of the States. . . .

Jane Roe, a single woman who was residing in Dallas County, Texas, instituted this federal action in March 1970 against the District Attorney of the county. She sought a declaratory judgment that the Texas criminal abortion statutes were unconstitutional on their face, and an injunction restraining the defendant from enforcing the statutes.

Roe alleged that she was unmarried and pregnant; that she wished to terminate her pregnancy by an abortion "performed by a competent, licensed physician, under safe, clinical conditions"; that she was unable to get a "legal" abortion in Texas because her life did not appear to be threatened by the continuation of her pregnancy; and that she could not afford to travel to another jurisdiction in order to secure a legal abortion under safe conditions. She claimed that the Texas statutes were unconstitutionally vague and that they abridged her right of personal privacy, protected by the First, Fourth, Fifth, Ninth, and Fourteenth Amendments. By an amendment to her complaint, Roe purported to sue "on behalf of herself and all other women" similarly situated.

James Hubert Hallford, a licensed physician, sought and was granted leave to intervene in Roe's action. In his complaint, he alleged that he had been arrested previously for violations of the Texas abortion statutes, and that two such prosecutions were pending against him. He described conditions of patients who came to him seeking abortions, and he claimed that for many cases he, as a physician, was unable to determine whether they fell within or outside the exception recognized by Article 1196. He alleged that, as a consequence, the statutes were vague and uncertain, in violation of the Fourteenth Amendment, and that they violated his own and his patients' rights to privacy in the doctor-patient relationship and his own right to practice medicine, rights he claimed were guaranteed by the First, Fourth, Fifth, Ninth, and Fourteenth Amendments.

John and Mary Doe, a married couple, filed a companion complaint to that of Roe. They also named the District Attorney as defendant, claimed like constitutional deprivations, and sought declaratory and injunctive relief. The Does alleged that they were a childless couple; that Mrs. Doe was suffering from a "neural-chemical" disorder; that her physician had "advised her to avoid pregnancy until such time as her condition has materially improved" (although a

"Roe alleged that she was unmarried and pregnant; that she wished to terminate her pregnancy by an abortion . . ."

pregnancy at the present time would not present "a serious risk" to her life); that, pursuant to medical advice, she had discontinued use of birth control pills; and that, if she should become pregnant, she would want to terminate the pregnancy by an abortion performed by a competent, licensed physician under safe, clinical conditions. By an amendment to their complaint, the Does purported to sue "on behalf of themselves and all couples similarly situated." . . .

It is evident from the Court's inclusion of "privacy" and its discussion of the "penumbras" found in the Bill of Rights that the opinion in *Roe v. Wade* relied heavily on the precedent set by *Griswold v. Connecticut*. However, while the *Griswold* opinion was relatively brief, the Supreme Court wrote an expansive opinion for *Roe,* providing not only a history of abortion practices in the United States but also an extensive medical and legal analysis of abortion. The Court undoubtedly knew that its decision to overturn state prohibitions of abortion would be controversial, and the detailed opinion would at least provide the Court's rationale behind its decision.

The principal thrust of appellant's attack on the Texas statutes is that they improperly invade a right, said to be possessed by the pregnant woman, to choose to terminate her pregnancy. Appellant would discover this right in the concept of personal "liberty" embodied in the Fourteenth Amendment's Due Process Clause; or in personal, marital, familial, and sexual privacy said to be protected by the Bill of Rights or its penumbras . . . ; or among those rights reserved to the people by the Ninth Amendment. . . .

This right of privacy, whether it be founded in the Fourteenth Amendment's concept of personal liberty and restrictions upon state action, as we feel it is, or, as the District Court determined, in the Ninth Amendment's reservation of rights to the people, is broad enough to encompass a woman's decision whether or not to terminate her pregnancy. The detriment that the State would impose upon the pregnant woman by denying this choice altogether is apparent. Specific and direct harm medically diagnosable even in early pregnancy may be involved. Maternity, or additional offspring, may force upon the woman a distressful life and future. Psychological harm may be imminent. Mental and physical health may be taxed by child care. There is also the distress, for all concerned, associated with the unwanted child, and there is the problem of bringing a child into a family already unable, psychologically and otherwise, to care for it. In other cases, as in this one, the additional difficulties and continuing stigma of unwed motherhood may be involved. All these are factors the woman and her responsible physician necessarily will consider in consultation.

On the basis of elements such as these, appellant and some *amici* argue that the woman's right is absolute and that she is entitled to terminate her pregnancy at whatever time, in whatever way, and for whatever reason she alone chooses. With this we do not agree. Appellant's arguments that Texas either has no valid interest at all in regulating the abortion decision, or no interest strong enough to support any limitation upon the woman's sole determination, are unpersuasive. The Court's decisions recognizing a right of privacy also acknowledge that some state regulation in areas protected by that right is appropriate.

As noted above, a State may properly assert important interests in safeguarding health, in maintaining medical standards, and in protecting potential life. At some point in pregnancy, these respective interests become sufficiently compelling to sustain regulation of the factors that govern the abortion decision. The privacy right involved, therefore, cannot be said to be absolute.

A key aspect of the abortion controversy, both in 1973 and in contemporary times, is whether a fetus has rights and if so whether its rights supersede those of a woman to determine what she does with her own body. On one extreme is the thought that a woman's decision is absolute, that the state has no role to play in a woman's decision whether or not to have an abortion. At the other end of the spectrum is the idea that a human embryo, even as early as its conception, has the right to life and that this right takes precedence over the rights of the woman carrying that embryo. In between these two extremes are a wide range of views, including limits to abortion rights from people who tend to favor a woman's right to have an abortion as well as exceptions supported by other people who generally desire a prohibition on abortion. The Court deliberately fell somewhere in the middle of these extremes. Thus, while the Court said that states could not make abortion completely illegal, at least in the early stages of a pregnancy, it acknowledged that the state may have an increased interest in establishing the rights of a fetus the longer a pregnancy progresses.

In fact, it is not clear to us that the claim asserted by some *amici* that one has an unlimited right to do with one's body as one pleases bears a close relationship to the right of privacy previously articulated in the Court's decisions. . . .

We, therefore, conclude that the right of personal privacy includes the abortion decision, but that this right is not unqualified, and must be considered against important state interests in regulation. . . .

The pregnant woman cannot be isolated in her privacy. She carries an embryo and, later, a fetus, if one accepts the medical definitions of the developing young in the human uterus. . . . As we have intimated above, it is reasonable and appropriate for a State to decide that, at some point in time another interest, that of health of the mother or that of potential human life, becomes significantly involved. The woman's privacy is no longer sole and any right of privacy she possesses must be measured accordingly.

Source: *Roe v. Wade,* 410 U.S. 113 (1973). Available at http://caselaw .lp.findlaw.com/cgi-bin/getcase.pl?court=us&vol=410&invol=113.

Congressman Hyde Calls for an End to Federal Funding for Abortions

Statement of U.S. Representative Henry Hyde on the Hyde Amendment

June 24, 1976

On June 24, 1976, Representative Henry Hyde introduced an amendment to a spending bill that prohibited any federal funds from being used for abortion purposes. This amendment, referred to as the Hyde Amendment, has been added in various forms to federal appropriations bills every year since this initial amendment. Proposed three years after the *Roe v. Wade* Supreme Court decision, it was one of the first efforts by opponents of abortion to make the process of getting an abortion more difficult, since the Court had removed the option of making abortions completely illegal. Although the amendment simply prohibits government funds, such as those used toward health care for the poor, from being used to pay for abortions unless the woman was raped or her life is at risk, Representative Hyde's comments focus very heavily on his opposition to abortion, not simply on the government's funding of abortion.

The question of when life begins is a cornerstone of the abortion controversy, a fact acknowledged by the Supreme Court in *Roe v. Wade*. However, while the Supreme Court attempted to address this question in a dispassionate and objective fashion, Representative Hyde used much more emotional language regarding his thoughts on abortion and the beginning of human life. As an elected representative, Hyde has to be conscious not only of expressing his own views but also of representing the views of his constituents, who will ultimately decide whether or not he is reelected. While Hyde's rhetoric was clearly directed at voters who are opposed to abortion and believe that abortion is akin to murder, the amendment itself was a pretty safe political decision in that even people who favored the decision in *Roe v. Wade* were uncomfortable with the idea of abortions being paid for from taxpayer dollars, despite the fact that the government pays for other health care services for many people living in poverty.

Mr. Chairman, this amendment may stimulate a lot of debate—but it need not—because I believe most Members know how they will vote on this issue.

Nevertheless, there are those of us who believe it is to the everlasting shame of this country that in 1973 approximately 800,000 legal abortions were performed in this country—and so it is fair to assume that this year over a million human lives will be destroyed because they are inconvenient to someone.

The unborn child facing an abortion can best be classified as a member of the innocently inconvenient and since the pernicious doctrine that some lives are more important than others seems to be persuasive with the pro-abortion forces, we who seek to protect that most defenseless and innocent of human lives, the unborn—seek to inhibit the use of Federal funds to pay for and thus encourage abortion as an answer to the human and compelling problem on an unwanted child.

We are all exercised at the wanton killing of the porpoise, the baby seal. We urge big game hunters to save the tiger, but we somehow turn away at the specter of a million human beings being violently destroyed because this great society does not want them.

And make no mistake, an abortion is violent.

I think in the final analysis, you must determine whether or not the unborn person is human. If you think it is animal or vegetable then, of course, it is disposable like an empty beer can to be crushed and thrown out with the rest of the trash.

But medicine, biology, embryology, say that growing living organism is not animal or vegetable or mineral—but it is a human life.

And if you believe that human life is deserving of due process of law—or equal protection of the laws, then you cannot in logic and conscience help fund the execution of these innocent defenseless human lives.

101

If we are to order our lives by the precept of animal husbandry, then I guess abortion is an acceptable answer. If we human beings are not of a higher order than animals then let us save our pretentious aspirations for a better and more just world and recognize this is an anthill we inhabit and there are not such things as ideals or justice or morality.

Once conception has occurred a new and unique genetic package has been created, not a potential human being, but a human being with potential. For 9 months the mother provides nourishment and shelter, and birth is no substantial change, it is merely a change of address.

We are told that bringing an unwanted child into the world is an obscene act. Unwanted by whom? Is it too subtle a notion to understand it is more important to be a loving person than to be one who is loved? We need more people who are capable of projecting love.

We hear the claim that the poor are denied a right available to other women if we do not use tax money to fund abortions.

Well, make a list of all the things society denies poor women and let them make the choice of what we will give them.

Don't say "poor woman, go destroy your young, and we will pay for it."

An innocent, defenseless human life, in a caring and humane society deserves better than to be flushed down a toilet or burned in an incinerator.

The promise of America is that life is not just for the privileged, the planned, or the perfect.

Source: Statement by Representative Henry Hyde (R-IL), *Congressional Record,* June 24, 1976: 20410.

"We hear the claim that the poor are denied a right available to other women if we do not use tax money to fund abortions.
Well, make a list of all the things society denies poor women and let them make the choice of what we will give them."

The U.S. Supreme Court Upholds State Restrictions on Abortion Services

Supreme Court Ruling in *Webster v. Reproductive Health Services*

1989

Once the Supreme Court ruled in *Roe v. Wade* that a woman's access to abortion fell under the Constitution's rights to privacy, opponents of abortion began advocating for laws, both at the national and state levels, that would limit a woman's access to abortion without overtly making the procedure illegal. The Hyde Amendment was an early example of this strategy, making abortion less accessible, for example, to Medicaid recipients who relied on the government for health care costs. Several states began employing a similar strategy, prohibiting the use of state funds to be used for abortions by women on public assistance. Missouri took the prohibition further, preventing abortions and even abortion counseling from taking place in state-funded clinics and requiring all physicians to determine the fetus's viability, or likelihood of living, before performing an abortion. These provisions were founded on the notion, as articulated in the law's preamble, that human life begins at conception.

This appeal concerns the constitutionality of a Missouri statute regulating the performance of abortions.

The United States Court of Appeals for the Eighth Circuit struck down several provisions of the statute on the ground that they violated this Court's decision in *Roe v. Wade . . .* and cases following it. . . .

In June, 1986, the Governor of Missouri signed into law Missouri Senate Committee Substitute for House Bill No. 1596 (hereinafter Act or statute), which amended existing state law concerning unborn children and abortions. The Act consisted of 20 provisions, 5 of which are now before the Court. The first provision, or preamble, contains "findings" by the state legislature that "[t]he life of each human being begins at conception," and that "unborn children have protectable interests in life, health, and wellbeing." . . . The Act further requires that all Missouri laws be interpreted to provide unborn children with the same rights enjoyed by other persons, subject to the Federal Constitution and this Court's precedents. . . . Among its other provisions, the Act requires that, prior to performing an abortion on any woman whom a physician has reason to believe is 20 or more weeks pregnant, the physician ascertain whether the fetus is viable by performing such medical examinations and tests as are necessary to make a finding of the gestational age, weight, and lung maturity of the unborn child. . . .

The Act also prohibits the use of public employees and facilities to perform or assist abortions not necessary to save the mother's life, and it prohibits the use of public funds, employees, or facilities for the purpose of "encouraging or counseling" a woman to have an abortion not necessary to save her life. . . .

Decision of this case requires us to address four sections of the Missouri Act: (a) the preamble; (b) the prohibition on the use of public facilities or employees to perform abortions; (c) the prohibition on public funding of abortion counseling; and (d) the requirement that physicians conduct viability tests prior to performing abortions. . . .

The Act's preamble, as noted, sets forth "findings" by the Missouri legislature that "[t]he life of each human being begins at conception," and that "[u]nborn children have protectable interests in life, health, and wellbeing." . . . The Act then mandates that state laws be interpreted to provide unborn children with "all the rights, privileges, and immunities available to other persons, citizens, and residents of this state," subject to the Constitution and this Court's precedents. . . .

Certainly the preamble does not, by its terms, regulate abortion or any other aspect of appellees' medical practice. The Court has emphasized that *Roe v. Wade* "implies no limitation on the authority of a State to make a value judgment favoring childbirth over abortion." *Maher v. Roe,* 432 U.S. at 474. The preamble can be read simply to express that sort of value judgment.

We think the extent to which the preamble's language might be used to interpret other state statutes or regulations is something that only the courts of Missouri can definitively decide. . . .

Section 188.210 [of Missouri's law] provides that "[i]t shall be unlawful for any public employee within the scope of his employment to perform or assist an abortion, not necessary to save the life of the mother," while [Section] 188.215 makes it "unlawful for any public facility to be used for the purpose of performing or assisting an abortion not necessary to save the life of the mother."

The Court of Appeals held that these provisions contravened this Court's abortion decisions. . . . We take the contrary view.

[T]he State's decision here to use public facilities and staff to encourage childbirth over abortion "places no governmental obstacle in the path of a woman who chooses to terminate her pregnancy." . . . Just as Congress' refusal to fund abortions in *McRae* left "an indigent woman with at least the same range of choice in deciding whether to obtain a medically necessary abortion as she would have had if Congress had chosen to subsidize no health care costs at all," . . . Missouri's refusal to allow public employees to perform abortions in public hospitals leaves a pregnant woman with the same choices as if the State had chosen not to operate any public hospitals at all. The challenged provisions only restrict a woman's ability to obtain an abortion to the extent that she chooses to use a physician affiliated with a

Like most federal court cases, before *Webster v. Reproductive Health* came before the Supreme Court, it was first heard by a federal appeals court. In this case, the Eighth Circuit Court of Appeals had ruled that the Missouri statute barring public employees from performing abortions was unconstitutional, based on its reading of the opinion in *Roe v. Wade.* The Supreme Court disagreed with the appeals court's decision. Because the Supreme Court's membership changes over time, the decisions of the Court and its interpretation of laws and the Constitution may also vary. By 1989, the members of the Supreme Court were very different from the membership in 1973, and members were notably more conservative than the membership that had decided *Roe v. Wade.* Many opponents of abortion saw the changing ideological leanings of the Court as an opportunity to overturn, or at least weaken, the ruling in *Roe v. Wade.* In the case of *Webster v. Reproductive Health,* they were only partially successful in that the Court did not agree that the prohibition of abortion in public facilities was a constitutional violation of the right to privacy.

public hospital. This circumstance is more easily remedied, and thus considerably less burdensome, than indigency, which "may make it difficult—and in some cases, perhaps, impossible—for some women to have abortions" without public funding. . . . Having held that the State's refusal to fund abortions does not violate *Roe v. Wade,* it strains logic to reach a contrary result for the use of public facilities and employees. If the State may "make a value judgment favoring childbirth over abortion and . . . implement that judgment by the allocation of public funds," . . . surely it may do so through the allocation of other public resources, such as hospitals and medical staff.

The Court of Appeals sought to distinguish our cases on the additional ground that "[t]he evidence here showed that all of the public facility's costs in providing abortion services are recouped when the patient pays." . . . Absent any expenditure of public funds, the court thought that Missouri was "expressing" more than "its preference for childbirth over abortions," but rather was creating an "obstacle to exercise of the right to choose an abortion [that could not] stand absent a compelling state interest." We disagree. . . .

> *"Nothing in the Constitution requires States to enter or remain in the business of performing abortions. Nor, as appellees suggest, do private physicians and their patients have some kind of constitutional right of access to public facilities for the performance of abortions."*

Nothing in the Constitution requires States to enter or remain in the business of performing abortions. Nor, as appellees suggest, do private physicians and their patients have some kind of constitutional right of access to public facilities for the performance of abortions. . . .

The viability testing provision of the Missouri Act is concerned with promoting the State's interest in potential human life, rather than in maternal health. Section 188.029 creates what is essentially a presumption of viability at 20 weeks, which the physician must rebut with tests indicating that the fetus is not viable prior to performing an abortion. It also directs the physician's determination as to viability by specifying consideration, if feasible, of gestational age, fetal weight, and lung capacity. . . .

In *Roe v. Wade,* the Court recognized that the State has "important and legitimate" interests in protecting maternal health and in the potentiality of human life. . . . During the second trimester, the State "may, if it chooses, regulate the abortion procedure in ways that are reasonably related to maternal health." After viability, when the State's interest in potential human life was held to become compelling, the State may, if it chooses, regulate, and even proscribe, abortion except where it is necessary, in appropriate medical judgment, for the preservation of the life or health of the mother. . . .

In the first place, the rigid *Roe* framework is hardly consistent with the notion of a Constitution cast in general terms, as ours is, and usually speaking in general principles, as ours does.

The key elements of the *Roe* framework—trimesters and viability—are not found in the text of the Constitution, or in any place else one would expect to find a constitutional principle. Since the bounds of the inquiry are essentially indeterminate, the result has been a web of legal rules that have become increasingly intricate, resembling a code of regulations rather than a body of constitutional doctrine.

The Court, at this point in the opinion, calls into question the rigid trimester system in determining a state's interest in potential human life. Justice Blackmun argues that the trimester system has been given too much importance in deciding cases that followed *Roe v. Wade,* especially given the fact that there is nothing in the Constitution mandating a trimester determination of fetal viability. By overriding this key provision of *Roe v. Wade,* the Court's opinion opened the door to states setting limitations on when during a pregnancy abortions can take place.

[W]e do not see why the State's interest in protecting potential human life should come into existence only at the point of viability, and that there should therefore be a rigid line allowing state regulation after viability but prohibiting it before viability. . . .

Because none of the challenged provisions of the Missouri Act properly before us conflict with the Constitution, the judgment of the Court of Appeals is *Reversed.*

Source: *Webster v. Reproductive Health,* 492 U.S. 490 (1989). Available at http://www.law.cornell.edu/supct/html/historics/USSC_CR_0492_0490_ZO.html.

The U.S. Supreme Court Upholds Additional State-Level Abortion Restrictions

Supreme Court Ruling in *Planned Parenthood v. Casey*

1992

While the Supreme Court in *Webster v. Reproductive Health* had preserved the constitutionality of abortion under a right to privacy, it had clearly conveyed that states may enact laws making abortion a more difficult option in the interest of preserving unborn life. This decision gave opponents of abortion new hope that other types of obstacles could be placed before women seeking an abortion and that these obstacles would not be found unconstitutional. Three years after *Webster v. Reproductive Health,* the Supreme Court considered a Pennsylvania law that required various steps to be completed before an abortion could be performed. These included a counseling session 24 hours before an abortion procedure, parental consent for minors seeking an abortion, and a husband's consent if the woman seeking an abortion is married. Given the similar limitations on abortion being passed by other states at the time, the Court acknowledged in *Casey* that states needed better guidance on the legal limitations to abortion. In this case, the Court supported all of Pennsylvania's provisions with the exception of the need to acquire a husband's consent.

Liberty finds no refuge in a jurisprudence of doubt. Yet 19 years after our holding that the Constitution protects a woman's right to terminate her pregnancy in its early stages, *Roe v. Wade* . . . (1973), that definition of liberty is still questioned.

Joining the respondents as *amicus curiae,* the United States, as it has done in five other cases in the last decade, again asks us to overrule *Roe.* . . .

At issue in these cases are five provisions of the Pennsylvania Abortion Control Act of 1982 as amended in 1988 and 1989. . . . The Act requires that a woman seeking an abortion give her informed consent prior to the abortion procedure, and specifies that she be provided with certain information at least 24 hours before the abortion is performed. For a minor to obtain an abortion, the Act requires the informed consent of one of her parents, but provides for a judicial bypass option if the minor does not wish to or cannot obtain a parent's consent. Another provision of the Act requires that, unless certain exceptions apply, a married woman seeking an abortion must sign a statement indicating that she has notified her husband of her intended abortion. The Act exempts compliance with these three requirements in the event of a "medical emergency," which is defined in [Section] 3203 of the Act. . . . In addition to the above provisions regulating the performance of abortions, the Act imposes certain reporting requirements on facilities that provide abortion services. . . .

[A]t oral argument in this Court, the attorney for the parties challenging the statute took the position that none of the enactments can be upheld without overruling *Roe* v. *Wade.* . . . We disagree with that analysis; but we acknowledge that our decisions after *Roe* cast doubt upon the meaning and reach of its holding. Further, the Chief Justice admits that he would overrule the central holding of *Roe* and adopt the rational relationship test as the sole criterion of constitutionality. . . . State and federal courts as well as legislatures throughout the Union must have guidance as they seek to address this subject in conformance with the

Constitution. Given these premises, we find it imperative to review once more the principles that define the rights of the woman and the legitimate authority of the State respecting the termination of pregnancies by abortion procedures.

After considering the fundamental constitutional questions resolved by *Roe,* principles of institutional integrity, and the rule of *stare decisis,* we are led to conclude this: the essential holding of *Roe* v. *Wade* should be retained and once again reaffirmed.

It must be stated at the outset and with clarity that *Roe*'s essential holding, the holding we reaffirm, has three parts. First is a recognition of the right of the woman to choose to have an abortion before viability and to obtain it without undue interference from the State. Before viability, the State's interests are not strong enough to support a prohibition of abortion or the imposition of a substantial obstacle to the woman's effective right to elect the procedure. Second is a confirmation of the State's power to restrict abortions after fetal viability, if the law contains exceptions for pregnancies which endanger a woman's life or health. And third is the principle that the State has legitimate interests from the outset of the pregnancy in protecting the health of the woman and the life of the fetus that may become a child. These principles do not contradict one another; and we adhere to each. . . .

Men and women of good conscience can disagree, and we suppose some always shall disagree, about the profound moral and spiritual implications of terminating a pregnancy, even in its earliest stage. Some of us as individuals find abortion offensive to our most basic principles of morality, but that cannot control our decision. Our obligation is to define the liberty of all, not to mandate our own moral code. The underlying constitutional issue is whether the State can resolve these philosophic questions in such a definitive way that a woman lacks all choice in the matter, except perhaps in those rare circumstances in which the pregnancy is itself a danger to her own life or health, or is the result of rape or incest. . . .

From what we have said so far it follows that it is a constitutional liberty of the woman to have some freedom to terminate her pregnancy. We conclude that the basic decision in *Roe* was based on a constitutional analysis which we cannot now repudiate. The woman's liberty is not so unlimited, however, that from the outset the State cannot show its concern for the life of the unborn, and at a later point in fetal development the State's interest in life has sufficient force so that the right of the woman to terminate the pregnancy can be restricted. . . .

"The woman's liberty is not so unlimited, however, that from the outset the State cannot show its concern for the life of the unborn, and at a later point in fetal development the State's interest in life has sufficient force so that the right of the woman to terminate the pregnancy can be restricted."

Though the woman has a right to choose to terminate or continue her pregnancy before viability, it does not at all follow that the State is prohibited from taking steps to ensure that this choice is thoughtful and informed. Even in the earliest stages of pregnancy, the State may enact rules and regulations designed to encourage her to know that there are philosophic and social arguments of great weight that can be brought to bear in favor of continuing the pregnancy to full term and that there are procedures and institutions to allow adoption of unwanted children as well as a certain degree of state assistance if the mother chooses to raise the child herself. . . .

In *Casey,* the Court argues that the state's interest in preserving unborn life permits the state to require that certain actions take place prior to an abortion to help ensure that a woman's decision to have an abortion has been given appropriate consideration. Proponents of abortion rights have long criticized this argument as insulting to women in that it tacitly assumes that a woman who is considering an abortion would not have independently considered the ramifications of her decision unless the state had intervened. The Court, however, acknowledges that states may enact obstacles to obtaining an abortion as long as the burden is not "undue," or limiting a woman's access to the procedure simply for the sake of preventing the abortion entirely. Thus, because most of Pennsylvania's restrictions were purportedly made with the intent to better inform the woman's decision, they were not considered to be an unconstitutional violation of her rights to an abortion.

It follows that States are free to enact laws to provide a reasonable framework for a woman to make a decision that has such profound and lasting meaning. This, too, we find consistent with *Roe*'s central premises, and indeed the inevitable consequence of our holding that the State has an interest in protecting the life of the unborn. . . .

The fact that a law which serves a valid purpose, one not designed to strike at the right itself, has the incidental effect of making it more difficult or more expensive to procure an abortion cannot be enough to invalidate it. Only where state regulation imposes an undue burden on a woman's ability to make this decision does the power of the State reach into the heart of the liberty protected by the Due Process Clause.

The very notion that the State has a substantial interest in potential life leads to the conclusion that not all regulations must be deemed unwarranted. Not all burdens on the right to decide whether to terminate a pregnancy will be undue. In our view, the undue burden standard is the appropriate means of reconciling the State's interest with the woman's constitutionally protected liberty. . . .

A finding of an undue burden is a shorthand for the conclusion that a state regulation has the purpose or effect of placing a substantial obstacle in the path of a woman seeking an abortion of a nonviable fetus. A statute with this purpose is invalid because the means chosen by the State to further the interest in potential life must be calculated to inform the woman's free choice, not hinder it. And a statute which, while furthering the interest in potential life or some other valid state interest, has the effect of placing a substantial obstacle in the path of a woman's choice cannot be considered a permissible means of serving its legitimate ends. . . .

For the great many women who are victims of abuse inflicted by their husbands, or whose children are the victims of such abuse, a spousal notice requirement enables the husband to wield an effective veto over his wife's decision. Whether the prospect of notification itself deters such women from seeking abortions, or whether the husband, through physical force or psychological pressure or economic coercion, prevents his wife from obtaining an abortion until it is too late, the notice requirement will often be tantamount to the veto found unconstitutional in *Danforth*. The women most affected by this law—those who most reasonably fear the consequences of notifying their husbands that they are pregnant—are in the gravest danger.

The husband's interest in the life of the child his wife is carrying does not permit the State to empower him with this troubling degree of authority over his wife. . . .

Women do not lose their constitutionally protected liberty when they marry. The Constitution protects all individuals, male or female, married or unmarried, from the abuse of governmental power, even where that power is employed for the supposed benefit of a member of the individual's family. These considerations confirm our conclusion that [this provision of the law] is invalid.

Source: *Planned Parenthood of Southeastern Pennsylvania v. Casey,* 505 U.S. 833 (1992). Available at http://caselaw.lp.findlaw.com/scripts/getcase.pl?court= US&vol=505&invol=833.

The one provision of Pennsylvania's law that was overturned was the requirement that married women obtain the consent of their husbands before having an abortion. The Court's opinion on this issue was based on two factors. First, there are the practical concerns of a woman's well-being if she is in an abusive marriage and has to approach her husband for consent to an abortion. According to the Court, such a consent requirement might deter a woman entirely from having an abortion and, as such, is problematic under its earlier definition of "undue burden." Second, the Court claimed that giving a husband veto power over his wife's decision to have an abortion essentially gave the husband more power over his wife than the government itself was willing to exercise in regard to abortion rights.

Debating the Partial-Birth Abortion Ban Act of 2003

Statements of Representatives
Steve Chabot and Jerrold Nadler

March 25, 2003

The term "partial-birth abortion" is not a medical term; it is instead a political term used for a procedure medically referred to as "dilation and extraction" or D&X. The D&X procedure is a surgical abortion procedure that is generally performed after 20 weeks of pregnancy. While the reported number of D&X abortions is only approximate, most researchers agree that the number of D&X abortions is extremely small, less than 1 percent of all abortions. In fact, the vast majority of all abortions take place prior to the 12th week of pregnancy, and thus the Partial Birth Abortion Ban would have a very small effect on the number of abortions being performed. There was some strategic value to the law, however, for opponents of abortion. Because of the rather gruesome description of a D&X, the majority of Americans were opposed to the procedure, even Americans who considered themselves pro-choice on abortion rights. It was an antiabortion law that was relatively easy to pass in Congress and received support from both Democrats and Republicans.

Excerpt from Opening Statement by the Honorable Steve Chabot, Chair, Subcommittee on the Constitution

We have convened this afternoon to receive testimony on H.R. 760, the "Partial-Birth Abortion Ban Act of 2003."

On February 13th, on behalf of over 100 original cosponsors, I introduced H.R. 760, the "Partial-Birth Abortion Ban Act of 2003," which will ban the dangerous and inhumane procedure during which a physician delivers an unborn child's body until only the head remains inside the womb, punctures the back of the child's skull with a sharp instrument, and sucks the child's brain out before completing delivery of the now dead infant.

An abortionist who violates this ban would be subject to fines or a maximum of 2 years imprisonment or both. H.R. 760 also establishes a civil cause of action for damages against an abortionist who violates the ban, and includes an exception for those situations in which a partial birth abortion is necessary to save the life of the mother. On March 13, 2003 the Senate approved S.3, which is virtually identical to H.R. 760, by a 64 to 33 vote.

A moral, medical and ethical consensus exists that partial birth abortion is an inhumane procedure that is never medically necessary and should be prohibited. Contrary to the claims of those who proclaimed the medical necessity of this barbaric procedure, partial birth abortion is, in fact, a dangerous medical procedure. It can pose serious risks to the long-term health of women. As testimony received by the Subcommittee during the 107th Congress demonstrates, there is never any situation in which the procedure H.R. 760 would ban is medically necessary. In fact, 10 years after Dr. Martin Haskell presented this procedure to the mainstream abortion community, partial birth abortions have failed to become standard medical practice for any circumstance under which a woman might seek an abortion.

As a result, the United States Congress voted to ban partial birth abortions during the 104th, 105th and 106th Congresses, and at least 27 States enacted bans on the procedure. Unfortunately, the two Federal bans that reached President Clinton's desk were promptly vetoed.

To address the concerns raised by the majority opinion of the U.S. Supreme Court in *Stenberg* v. *Carhart,* H.R. 760 differs from these previous proposals in two areas.

First, the bill contains a new, more precise definition of the prohibited procedure to address the Court's concerns that Nebraska's definition of the prohibitive procedure might be interpreted to encompass a more commonly performed late second trimester abortion procedure. As previous testimony indicates, H.R. 760 clearly distinguishes the procedure it would ban from other abortion procedures.

The second difference addresses the majority's opinion that the Nebraska ban placed an "undue burden" on women seeking abortions, because it did not include an exception for partial birth abortions deemed necessary to preserve the "health" of the mother. The *Stenberg* court, based its conclusion on the trial courts factual findings regarding the relative health and safety benefits of the partial birth abortions—findings which were highly disputed. The Court was required to accept these findings because of the highly deferential, "clearly erroneous" standard that is applied to lower court factual findings. . . .

Despite overwhelming support from the public, past efforts to ban partial birth abortions were blocked by President Clinton. We now have a president who has promised to stand with Congress in its efforts to ban this barbaric and dangerous procedure. It is time for Congress to end the national tragedy of partial birth abortions and protect the lives of these helpless, defenseless little babies.

Excerpt from the Honorable Jerrold Nadler, Ranking Member, Subcommittee on the Constitution

Today we have a very bad combination: Members of Congress who want to play doctor, and Members of Congress who want to play Supreme Court. When you put the two together you have a prescription for some very bad medicine for women and for this country.

We have been through this debate often enough to know by now that you will not find the term partial birth abortion in any medical textbook. There are procedures that you will

"Despite overwhelming support from the public, past efforts to ban partial birth abortions were blocked by President Clinton. We now have a president who has promised to stand with Congress in its efforts to ban this barbaric and dangerous procedure."

find in medical textbooks, but apparently the authors of this legislation would prefer to use the language of propaganda rather than the language of science.

Prior to the 2003 Partial Birth Abortion Ban bill that ultimately was passed into law, Congress had passed two earlier versions in 1995 and 1997. Both of these bills were vetoed by President Clinton for not including provisions that allowed the procedure when done to protect the life and health of the woman. Further, in 2000 the Supreme Court heard a case involving a Nebraska law making it illegal for doctors to perform late-term abortions unless a woman's life was in danger. With a 5 to 4 decision, the Supreme Court ruled the law, as written, unconstitutional because it did not make an exception for a woman's health and was too broad in its application to various types of abortions. Justice O'Connor, the swing vote to overturn the Nebraska law, indicated, however, that had the law addressed these concerns, she would have upheld it. Supporters of the federal Partial Birth Abortion Ban of 2003 claimed that they had taken these issues into account, and as such the bill was constitutional. Opponents of the bill argued that if it was passed into law, it would be found to be unconstitutional. Ultimately the bill was passed and signed by President George W. Bush, and the Supreme Court did not rule it to be unconstitutional.

> **This bill, as written, fails every test the Supreme Court has laid down for what may or may not be a Constitutional regulation of abortion. It reads almost as if the authors went through the Supreme Court's recent decision in *Stenberg* v. *Carhart* and went out of their way to thumb their noses at the Supreme Court, and especially at Justice O'Connor, who is generally viewed as the swing vote on such matters, and who wrote a concurring opinion stating very specifically what exactly would be needed for her to uphold the statute.**

Unless the authors think that when the Court has made repeated and clear statements over the years of what the Constitution requires in this area, they are just pulling our collective legs, this bill has to be considered facially unconstitutional.

First and foremost, it does not include a health exception, which the Court has repeatedly said is necessary, even with respect to post viability abortions. The exception for a woman's life that is included in the bill is more narrowly drawn than is required by the Constitution, according to the Supreme Court, and will place doctors in the position of trying to guess just how grave a danger pregnancy is to a woman's life before they can be confident that protecting her will not result in jail time.

That is a test that doctors should not have to face. I know that some of my colleagues do not like the Constitutional rule that has been played down by the Supreme Court for 30 years, but that is the law of the land, and the supreme law of the land, and no amount of rhetoric, even if written into a piece of legislation, will change that. Even the Ashcroft Justice Department, in its brief in defending an Ohio statute now before the Court, has acknowledged that a health exception is required by law, which is not in this bill, of course. . . .

While I realize that many of the proponents of this bill view all abortion as tantamount to infanticide, that is not a mainstream view. This bill attempts to foist a marginal view on the general public by characterizing this bill as having to do only with abortions involving healthy, full-term fetuses.

If the proponents of this bill really want to deal with post-viability abortions in situations in which the woman's life and health are not in jeopardy, they should write a bill dealing with that issue. Although such a bill would be of marginal utility, since 41 States already ban post-viability abortions, except where the life or the health of the mother is in danger.

We now have a President who has expressed a willingness to sign this bill. He may get his chance. Unfortunately there are dire consequences for American women if this legislation passes. Perhaps here the role of Congress is to help the women take a back seat to the most extreme views of the anti-choice movement. Fortunately, those dire consequences will not be enforced long, because the Constitution still serves as a bulwark against such efforts.

But the majority is not interested, the majority in this Committee and this House is clearly not interested in a bill that could pass into law and actually be enforced as not contrary to the Constitution. What they want is an inflammatory piece of rhetoric, which even if passed, would be struck down by the Supreme Court. The real purpose of this bill that we are considering is not to save babies but elections.

To the dismay of pro-choice activists and reproductive rights supporters, the constitutionality of the Partial-Birth Abortion Ban Act of 2003 was upheld in 2007 in the U.S. Supreme Court by a vote of 5 to 4. The Court's ruling in the case of *Gonzales v. Carhart* reversed earlier courts of appeals decisions that had struck down the Partial-Birth Abortion Ban Act on constitutional grounds.

Source: "Partial Birth Abortion Ban Act of 2003," Hearing before the Subcommittee on the Constitution of the Committee on the Judiciary, House of Representatives, 108th Congress, 1st Session, on H.R. 760, March 25, 2003, 1–4.

A Breast Cancer Survivor Urges Increased Investment in Early Detection Programs

Actress Jill Eikenberry's Statement at "Why Are We Losing the War on Breast Cancer?" Senate Hearings

June 20, 1991

At the time of this hearing, Jill Eikenberry was a cast member on *L.A. Law,* a popular television series that ran from 1986 until 1994. She was diagnosed with cancer at the age of 44, just prior to the start of filming for the program, and became an ardent activist on issues related to breast cancer, such as research on treatments and early detection of the disease. Her testimony came a year after Congress had created the Breast and Cervical Cancer Mortality Prevention Act of 1990, instructing the Centers for Disease Control to create a program to fund early detection programs. As a celebrity, Eikenberry garnered a great deal of attention to the cause of breast cancer research and support, and in her testimony she encouraged Congress to adequately fund programs for early detection. She was willing to share her story in hopes that more women would take the steps necessary to protect their health and allow their physicians to discover cancer early, giving women the greatest chances of surviving the disease.

There are numerous treatments for breast cancer, including chemotherapy, radiation treatment, removal of the cancerous tissue, and removal of the entire breast, called a mastectomy. Feminists and observers of women's health care practices encourage women to play an active role in their own health care. There have been concerns that physicians may assert their expertise in ways that discourage women from questioning physicians' recommendations, even when the recommendations are alarming or invasive. Feminists have encouraged women to ask to whom is this recommendation most beneficial and to make sure that the answer is themselves. From a physician's standpoint, a mastectomy may be the safest route to remove cancer and requires the least precision in treatment, and certainly there are cases where a mastectomy is warranted. However, the recommendation to take off the breast may not be made with sensitivity to the great emphasis that American society places on women's breasts in terms of their desirability and femininity. Given this emphasis on women's bodies, removal of a breast may create significant emotional strain on a woman in addition to the physical stress on her body. Eikenberry ultimately plays a more active role in her own treatment options, seeks a second opinion, and makes an better-educated decision for the best approach to treat her cancer.

Statement of Jill Eikenberry

Thank you, Mr. Chairman and members of the committee. It is an honor to be asked to appear before you today and to sit at the table with my co-panelists . . . who have worked so hard in fighting breast cancer, Nancy Brinker and Zora Brown.

Five years ago, I was diagnosed with breast cancer. I was over 35, and had never had a screening mammogram. I had never practiced breast self-examination. I wasn't even regular about my pap smear. But on a routine visit to my gynecologist, she found something to concern her and scheduled a mammogram for me. . . .

I went to the mammography clinic with great trepidation. It was mobbed. I had an endless wait for the first initial test, and then because they needed more pictures, I had to wait longer.

The next step was a visit to the breast specialist, who looked at my x-rays and said I had cancer. And I will never forget that moment. My husband and I felt as if we were facing a firing squad.

The specialist said, "There are a few treatment options, but I would take the breast off. It is the procedure I do most often." And without hesitation, I said, "Take it off. I want to live." . . .

On the third day after my diagnosis, I got up and went to the screening of a movie that I had done months before. At the screening, I ran into a young actress with whom I had worked on the film. She took one look at me and said, "What happened?"

In spite of my plan to keep the whole thing under wraps, I told her the whole story in a burst of tears. She took me by the hand and led me to her mother, who after hearing my story dragged me to the ladies' room, hiked up her blouse, and said, look, this little scar on my breast is all that I have left to remind me of my breast cancer experience 11 years ago. And suddenly, there was a ray of hope in the tunnel, a ray of light. Maybe I wouldn't die.

The next day a friend called me and begged me to get a second opinion and do better research on my treatment options. My newfound hope gave me the energy to do that, and the next doctor said, no mastectomy is needed. You are a good candidate for a lumpectomy with radiation. I could save the breast.

Five years later, I am here before you cancer-free. I was one of the lucky ones. I am a survivor. The truth is that many of the women with breast cancer can be survivors.

Mr. Chairman, I was so happy to see that you and some of your colleagues have introduced a national Breast Cancer Challenge, a challenge to the [National Institutes of Health], medical researchers, and Congress. Needless to say, the research aspects of the Challenge are of the utmost importance. We must find a cure.

But one important thing we can do right now to reduce the mortality rate is to encourage women over 35 to get regular screening mammographies. As you stated, Mr. Chairman, medical experts have estimated that the breast cancer mortality rate could be reduced by 30 percent immediately if all women followed the guidelines for screening mammography, but currently only 17 percent of women follow those guidelines. And the question is, why?

I went public with my breast cancer 5 years ago when I produced an NBC documentary called "Destined to Live." We interviewed hundreds of breast cancer survivors and their families. We talked to some women, like my Aunt Treba, who has been cancer-free for 60 years—she is now 94—and some who had had surgery 2 weeks before. We talked about hope and we talked a lot about fear.

Because of going public with my breast cancer, I get three to four calls per week and hundreds of letters from women who are scared to death. Just the thought of cancer is terrifying. In fact, just going for a regular screening mammogram is daunting, because you are going to a special place to find out if you have cancer. No wonder so many women don't go.

We have to remove the onus of the test. It should be widely available in doctors' offices and clinics so that it becomes as routine and unfrightening as getting a pap smear. Now, I will grant you there are a lot of reasons that women don't get mammograms, but there are several things the Federal government can do to affect that behavior.

"Five years later, I am here before you cancer-free. I was one of the lucky ones. I am a survivor. The truth is that many of the women with breast cancer can be survivors."

Coverage of mammograms for breast cancer screening has become much more extensive since Eikenberry's appearance on Capitol Hill in 1991. The Affordable Care Act, also known as Obamacare, mandated mammogram coverage without copays or deductibles for most health insurance plans starting after August 1, 2012. Medicare now covers the full cost of annual mammogram procedures for all women enrollees age 40 and over. (Medicare eligibility extends to people with disabilities and end-stage renal disease as well as people who are age 65 and older.) In addition, all state Medicaid programs cover mammograms, and many states require private insurance companies to fully cover breast cancer screenings.

In addition to disparity in survival rates based on income levels, there are related disparities among women based on level of education and race. For instance, black women have consistently been more likely to die from breast cancer than white women, while Hispanic and Asian women had lower death rates than white women. Furthermore, the more education a woman has, the more likely she is to have a regular mammogram, leading to earlier detection and better survival rates. Eikenberry emphasized to the members of Congress that adequate funding was key to decreasing some of these disparities. In fiscal year 1991, Congress had appropriated $30 million to support states' efforts at early detection.

First, the Federal government should pay for adequate mammography coverage for all beneficiaries of Federal health programs. Last year, Congress provided Medicare coverage for screening mammography, but limited payments to $55 for all parts of the country, and limited the test to once every 2 years for women over 65.

I believe Congress should amend this law by paying for screening mammography through a fee schedule, and by paying for annual mammography for Medicare recipients over the age of 65. Certainly $55 is too low in many parts of California, where I live, where more than half of the facilities charge over $100.

As I said, I was one of the lucky ones. My husband and family were incredibly supportive. My surgery was relatively minimal, and my follow-up treatment, 6 weeks of radiation, was mild enough that I was able to go to the UCLA oncology lab every afternoon after filming *L.A. Law.* . . .

But what about all the women that don't have my resources? I think low-income women should have as much chance of surviving breast cancer as I did. Unfortunately, that is not the case.

The 5-year survival rate for women with breast cancer earning less than $15,000 per year is 64 percent. For women earning over $30,000 per year, the survival rate is much higher, 78 percent. . . .

Testimony in the House last year highlighted the sad fact that most low-income women who seek treatment for breast cancer are at the later stages of the disease, when survival rates are lower and treatment more difficult and more expensive. We must have access to screening for all low-income women. . . .

Many women that I have spoken to, and especially low-income and minority women, desperately need to know where they can go for information and support after they are diagnosed, and they need information on mammography, breast self-examination, and risk factors. This is another area where the government could do more toward meeting your challenge by reducing mortality.

Source: *Why Are We Losing the War on Breast Cancer? Hearing before the Subcommittee on Aging of the Committee on Labor and Human Resources,* U.S. Senate, 102nd Congress, 1st Session, on Examining Certain Issues Relating to the Study and Treatment of Breast Cancer, June 20, 1991, 8–11.

Chapter 5
Women and Violence

Introduction

In the United States, laws relating to violent crime generally fall under the jurisdiction of state governments, although the federal government has passed some legislation dealing with violent crime. A potential problem of having 50 separate criminal codes and multiple layers of law enforcement within each state is that crime often transcends those state boundaries or law enforcement jurisdictions. Unless the various agencies can communicate with each other, any trends in criminal behavior may go unnoticed, making law enforcement less effective. To better serve the communication needs of law enforcement, one of the roles played by the federal government is to collect crime statistics, allowing government officials and law enforcement professionals at all levels to see any trends that may extend beyond their boundaries. For instance, demographic information of both victims and perpetrators, such as their age, race, sex, socioeconomic status, and geographical region provide a snapshot of violent crime in the United States.

There is no single location in the federal government that collects all of this information. Instead, the collection of crime statistics is handled by various government offices, including the Federal Bureau of Investigation (FBI), the Department of Justice, and the Centers for Disease Control and Prevention (CDC), and each has its own method of collecting and reporting data. While this may not seem like the most efficient system, it is important to note that the creation of government agencies takes place over time as new needs are perceived and addressed by government. As a result of the piecemeal way of creating parts of the executive branch, one agency's responsibilities may overlap to some degree with the responsibilities of another agency.

Regardless of the source of data, one thing is clear: crime is gendered. Looking just at crime within the United States, statistics from all sources show that men are significantly more likely to be victims of violent crime than are women. For instance, when looking specifically at victims of murder, the FBI reports that more than three-quarters of murder victims in 2011 were male. Additionally, through the National Crime Victimization Survey, the Bureau of Justice Statistics in the

Department of Justice collects data on victims of rape or sexual assault, robbery, aggravated assault, and simple assault. Taking the combined statistics from these crimes, men are victims at a higher rate than women. In 2011, for every 1,000 men surveyed, 25.4 were the victims of nonfatal violent crimes. Women, on the other hand, were victims at a rate of 19.8 for every 1,000 women surveyed.

Yet despite being the victims of crime less frequently than men, women are much more likely to be the victim of particular types of crimes, including stalking, domestic violence, sexual violence, and crimes committed by an intimate partner. Statistics from the CDC clearly illustrate this trend. For example, while 18.3 percent of women in the United States have been raped at some point in their lives, the percent of men having been raped is 1.4 percent. Similarly, 16.2 percent of women have been stalked in their lifetime; for men, that statistic is 5.2 percent. One feature that distinguishes violence against women from crimes generally experienced by men is that women are more likely to be victims of a crime committed by an intimate partner. Among women, 35.6 percent report having experienced rape, stalking, or physical violence by an intimate partner, while the rate of men experiencing intimate partner violence is 28.5 percent. Women are also almost twice as likely than men to be murdered by an intimate partner.

The particular nature of crimes committed against women has prompted lawmakers to pass legislation specifically addressing female victims of crime, but this has been a relatively recent phenomenon. Until the 1970s, intimate partner violence, particularly when a man and woman were married, was often considered a private issue, and police officers were less likely to intervene if called to a residence because of a conflict. Even into the 1980s, most states defined rape in such a way that a husband could not legally rape his wife, even if the sex was forced. Although a state law might legally define rape as forced or nonconsensual sex, most states explicitly exempted a man having sex with his wife as falling under the definition of rape, regardless of the circumstances of that sex. It was thought that sex within marriage was an expectation and that a husband had the right to demand sex from his wife. It wasn't until the mid-1980s that this concept of marital sex was challenged in the courts. *People v. Liberta* (1984) was a landmark court case in the state of New York that challenged the notion that women lost their rights to bodily autonomy simply by being married. This case prompted many states to modify their laws on rape and sexual assault to legally permit the charge of rape within marriage. Clearly the boundaries between what was considered a private issue and what was considered a public issue changed with this court case.

Although Congress had passed some limited government programs to address domestic violence in the 1980s, it wasn't until the 1990s that the breadth of issues related to violence against women was placed on the national agenda. In 1990 Senator Joseph Biden of Delaware, chair of the Senate Committee on the Judiciary at the time, initiated a three-year study of the issues associated with violence against women. In the report published in 1993, Biden commented that through the process of investigation he had "become convinced that violence against women reflects as much a failure of our Nation's collective moral imagination as it does the failure of our Nation's laws and regulations. We are helpless to change the course of this violence unless, and until, we achieve a national consensus that deserves our profound public outrage" (U.S. Congress, Senate Committee on the Judiciary, 1993).

Although Biden had introduced an unsuccessful bill in 1991 to address these concerns, the committee's report, bolstered by substantial grassroots activism, prompted Congress to take up the issue again and pass comprehensive legislation. In 1994 the Violence Against Women Act (VAWA) was passed as part of the Violent Crime Control and Law Enforcement Act of 1994. The VAWA included several broad provisions, including many grants to help combat violence and provide services for victims and allowing crimes that were committed because of a person's sex to be tried in federal court as a civil rights violation. This last provision was not universally supported, and as early as 1992, Biden was countering opposition to the civil rights provision. Although that provision was kept in the bill that was ultimately passed in 1994, the U.S. Supreme Court ruled in 2000 that the provision was unconstitutional.

A study by the National Task Force to End Sexual and Domestic Violence Against Women indicated that the VAWA had a significant effect on combating violence and serving the needs of victims. However, as in other areas of the law, representatives often have to play catch-up as new trends develop. In the area of violence against women, the trend that was developing by the mid-1990s was the use of date rape drugs. A mere two years after the VAWA was passed, Congress was considering new legislation that criminalized the use of illegal drugs to commit sexual assault and imposed stiffer penalties for those who were convicted of the crime. Although the Drug-Induced Rape Prevention and Punishment Act of 1996 passed Congress with bipartisan support, it did not go as far as some members of Congress would have liked, stopping short of reclassifying the drug as a higher-risk illegal substance with the Drug Enforcement Agency (DEA). Statements by several members of the House of Representatives in support of the bill explained what this bill would and would not accomplish upon its passage.

Awareness of yet another aspect of violence against women had emerged by 2000: human trafficking. Trafficking of persons can take several forms, including forcing people into factory, domestic, and agricultural work as well as into prostitution. Despite the different manifestations of trafficking, at its base in any form is the commercial exploitation of forced human labor. According to the International Labor Organization as cited by a report from the U.S. Department of State, the number of people affected by trafficking in any form is estimated at 20.9 million; the number of people forced into sex work alone is 4.5 million. Out of the total number of trafficked persons, 55 percent are women, although the percentage increases to 98 percent when looking solely at victims of sex trafficking. In 2000, Congress considered the issue of trafficking and recognized that international victims of trafficking in the United States faced a unique barrier to freedom, which was a fear of deportation under the country's immigration laws. Congress passed the Trafficking Victims Protection Act in 2000, which considered the unique circumstances of immigrants exploited within the United States and offered some protections to victims against deportation. It was hoped that this would remove at least one barrier for victims to seek help.

Despite the bipartisan support for much antiviolence legislation, Congress has not passed all bills that have been introduced to address violence against women. Laws assisting law enforcement agencies in combating violence against women or providing funds for state and local support agencies have been generally well supported. However, when bills have taken steps to mandate private employers to provide certain economic protections to victims of domestic abuse, the traditional partisan divide between Republicans and Democrats seems to come into play. For instance, one means by which an abuser can maintain control over a partner is by making the victim economically dependent on the abuser. If a person is unable to support herself economically, she may remain with an abusive partner simply for the assurance that she has a source of food and shelter for herself and her children. Senator Patty Murray from Washington state attempted to address this reality of domestic violence by introducing legislation protecting the economic situation of victims of abuse. While the bill was introduced and referred to a Senate committee, the bill lacked support to have it brought to a vote. Despite the federal government's failure to protect the economic security of domestic abuse victims, several states have passed very similar laws that protect victims' ability to support themselves.

A New York Appeals Court Strikes Down a Marital Exemption for Rape

New York Court of Appeals Ruling in *People v. Liberta*

1984

At the time of this case, more than 40 states had some type of exemption to their rape or sexual assault laws in cases where the parties were married to one another. In essence, a man who forced a woman to engage in sexual behavior could be convicted of rape unless that woman was his wife. Forcible sex with one's wife was not legally considered rape, and in the case of the New York law, a wife was not even included in the legal definition of "a female" for purposes of defining rape. New York's law did recognize certain exceptions, however, and Mario Liberta was convicted of raping his wife, Denise, because the couple had been living apart due to a protective order against him. He appealed his conviction, arguing that the state's law on rape unconstitutionally violated both New York's and the U.S. Constitution's guarantee of equal protection under the law because the law applied differently to unmarried and married men as well as to men and women, since women couldn't be charged with rape. His hope was to have his conviction overturned by having the entire law found unconstitutional.

The defendant, while living apart from his wife pursuant to a Family Court order, forcibly raped and sodomized her in the presence of their 2 1/2 year old son.

Under the New York Penal Law a married man ordinarily cannot be prosecuted for raping or sodomizing his wife. The defendant, however, though married at the time of the incident, is treated as an unmarried man under the Penal Law because of the Family Court order. On this appeal, he contends that because of the exemption for married men, the statutes for rape in the first degree . . . and sodomy in the first degree . . . violate the *equal protection clause of the Federal Constitution*. . . .

The defendant also contends that the rape statute violates equal protection because only men, and not women, can be prosecuted under it. . . .

Defendant Mario Liberta and Denise Liberta were married in 1978. Shortly after the birth of their son, in October of that year, Mario began to beat Denise. In early 1980 Denise brought a proceeding in the Family Court in Erie County seeking protection from the defendant. On April 30, 1980 a temporary order of protection was issued to her by the Family Court. Under this order, the defendant was to move out and remain away from the family home, and stay away from Denise. The order provided that the defendant could visit with his son once each weekend.

On the weekend of March 21, 1981, Mario, who was then living in a motel, did not visit his son. On Tuesday, March 24, 1981 he called Denise to ask if he could visit his son on that day. Denise would not allow the defendant to come to her house, but she did agree to allow him to pick up their son and her and take them both back to his motel after being assured that a friend of his would be with them at all times. The defendant and his friend picked up Denise and their son and the four of them drove to the defendant's motel.

When they arrived at the motel the friend left. As soon as only Mario, Denise, and their son were alone in the motel room, Mario attacked Denise, threatened to kill her, and forced her to perform fellatio on him and to engage in sexual intercourse with him. The son was in the room during the entire episode, and the defendant forced Denise to tell their son to watch what the defendant was doing to her.

The defendant allowed Denise and their son to leave shortly after the incident. . . . Denise, after going to her parents' home, went to a hospital to be treated for scratches on her neck and bruises on her head and back, all inflicted by her husband. She also went to the police station, and on the next day she swore out a felony complaint against the defendant. On July 15, 1981 the defendant was indicted for rape in the first degree and sodomy in the first degree.

Section 130.35 of the Penal Law provides in relevant part that "A male is guilty of rape in the first degree when he engages in sexual intercourse with a female . . . by forcible compulsion." "Female," for purposes of the rape statute, is defined as "any female person who is not married to the actor." . . . *Section 130.50 of the Penal Law* provides in relevant part that "a person is guilty of sodomy in the first degree when he engages in deviate sexual intercourse with another person . . . by forcible compulsion." "Deviate sexual intercourse" is defined as "sexual conduct between persons not married to each other consisting of contact between the penis and the anus, the mouth and penis, or the mouth and the vulva." Thus, due to the "not married" language in the definitions of "female" and "deviate sexual intercourse," there is a "marital exemption" for both forcible rape and forcible sodomy. For purposes of the rape and sodomy statutes, a husband and wife are considered to be "not married" if at the time of the sexual assault they "are living apart . . . pursuant to a valid and effective: (i) order issued by a court of competent jurisdiction which by its terms or in its effect requires such living apart, or (ii) decree or judgment of separation, or (iii) written agreement of separation." . . .

As noted above, under the Penal Law a married man ordinarily cannot be convicted of forcibly raping or sodomizing his wife. This is the so-called marital exemption for rape. . . . The assumption, even before the marital exemption was codified, that a man could not be guilty of raping his wife, is traceable to a statement made by the 17th century English jurist Lord Hale, who wrote: "[The] husband cannot be guilty of a rape committed by himself upon his lawful wife, for by their mutual matrimonial consent and contract the wife hath given up herself in this kind unto her husband, which she cannot retract" (1 Hale, History of Pleas of the Crown, p 629). Although Hale cited no authority for his

"Denise, after going to her parents' home, went to a hospital to be treated for scratches on her neck and bruises on her head and back, all inflicted by her husband."

statement it was relied on by State Legislatures which enacted rape statutes with a marital exemption and by courts which established a common-law exemption for husbands. . . .

Presently, over 40 States still retain some form of marital exemption for rape. While the marital exemption is subject . . . to an equal protection challenge, because it classifies unmarried men differently than married men, the equal protection clause does not prohibit a State from making classifications, provided the statute does not arbitrarily burden a particular group of individuals. . . .

Early legal scholars such as William Blackstone in the late 1800s believed that marital relations fell within a realm of privacy that precluded government action. This assumption about the privacy of marriage applied both to a family's economic issues as well as to the sexual relations between a husband and wife. Thus, while rape was a legitimate concern for government action, sexual behavior within marriage fell outside the authority of government, regardless of the nature of those sexual relations. This was furthered by the societal view that a wife had no right to refuse her husband's demands for sex. One of the successes of the American women's rights movement was the reevaluation of what issues should remain private and what issues should be open to government action. The feminist view that women had rights to bodily autonomy went beyond the reproductive rights issues raised in the 1960s and 1970s and included the overturning of states' marital exemptions for rape. Although South Dakota removed the exemption in 1975, North Carolina didn't amend its laws to make rape within marriage a crime until 1993.

We find that there is no rational basis for distinguishing between marital rape and nonmarital rape. The various rationales which have been asserted in defense of the exemption are either based upon archaic notions about the consent and property rights incident to marriage or are simply unable to withstand even the slightest scrutiny.

We therefore declare the . . . marital exemption for rape in the New York statute to be unconstitutional.

Lord Hale's notion of an irrevocable implied consent by a married woman to sexual intercourse has been cited most frequently in support of the marital exemption. . . . Any argument based on a supposed consent, however, is untenable. Rape is not simply a sexual act to which one party does not consent. Rather, it is a degrading, violent act which violates the bodily integrity of the victim and frequently causes severe, long-lasting physical and psychic harm. . . . To ever imply consent to such an act is irrational and absurd. Other than in the context of rape statutes, marriage has never been viewed as giving a husband the right to coerced intercourse on demand. . . . Certainly, then, a marriage license should not be viewed as a license for a husband to forcibly rape his wife with impunity. A married woman has the same right to control her own body as does an unmarried woman. . . . If a husband feels "aggrieved" by his wife's refusal to engage in sexual intercourse, he should seek relief in the courts governing domestic relations, not in "violent or forceful self-help". . . .

The other traditional justifications for the marital exemption were the common-law doctrines that a woman was the property of her husband and that the legal existence of the woman was "incorporated and consolidated into that of the husband". . . . Both these doctrines, of course, have long been rejected in this State. Indeed, "[nowhere] in the common-law world—[or] in any modern society—is a woman regarded as chattel or demeaned by denial of a separate legal identity and the dignity associated with recognition as a whole human being". . . .

Rape statutes historically applied only to conduct by males against females, largely because the purpose behind the proscriptions was to protect the chastity of women and thus their property value to their fathers or husbands. . . . New York's rape statute has always protected only females, and has thus applied only to males. . . . Presently New York is one of only 10 jurisdictions that does not have a gender-neutral statute for forcible rape. . . .

The other portion of the law challenged by Mario Liberta was its application only to males. As the New York statute was written, a woman could not be prosecuted for raping a man. By 1984 most states had amended their laws to be gender neutral, applying to both sexes equally. New York, however, had not yet made this change to its law, and Mr. Liberta argued that its application only to men meant that the law was unconstitutional. In an interesting decision, the New York Court of Appeals ruled that only those provisions of the law providing for the unequal treatment of married and unmarried persons and men and women were unconstitutional but that the remainder of the law was constitutional. As such, while the court agreed with Mr. Liberta's argument, it did not overturn his conviction. The U.S. Second Circuit Court of Appeals later agreed with the New York appeals court decision when Mr. Liberta appealed in the federal court system.

The fact that the act of a female forcibly raping a male may be a difficult or rare occurrence does not mean that the gender exemption satisfies the constitutional test. A gender-neutral law would indisputably better serve, even if only marginally, the objective of deterring and punishing forcible sexual assaults. The only persons "benefitted" by the gender exemption are females who forcibly rape males. . . .

Accordingly, we find that *section 130.35 of the Penal Law* violates equal protection because it exempts females from criminal liability for forcible rape.

Source: *People v. Liberta,* No. 597, Court of Appeals of New York, 64 N.Y.2d 152, 474 N.E.2d 567, 485 N.Y.S.2d 207 (1984).

Senator Biden Urges Passage of the Violence Against Women Act

Senator Joseph Biden's Statement to the House Subcommittee on Crime and Criminal Justice

February 6, 1992

Statement of Hon. Joseph Biden, a Senator in Congress from the State of Delaware

As you know, Mr. Chairman—you and I have worked together on a lot of crime issues—I try not to beat around the bush. . . . Quite frankly, I would be dumbfounded if there were disagreement on 90 percent of the titles [in this bill]. But we should probably get right to the nub of the controversy.

Prior to becoming the vice president under President Barack Obama in 2009, Joseph Robinette "Joe" Biden was a U.S. senator from 1973 until 2009. In the Senate, Biden took the lead on several major crime bills and has claimed that the Violence Against Women Act of 1994 (VAWA) was one of his most significant accomplishments. In this particular hearing, Biden spoke to a committee in the House of Representatives to discuss the VAWA, which had already passed in the Senate. He specifically discusses one provision of the legislation in which female victims of crime could file a civil suit in federal court if the crime was committed because of their sex. While the bill was largely supported by both political parties, the civil rights provision had met with some opposition, most notably by conservative U.S. Supreme Court chief justice William Rehnquist. Rehnquist, appointed as an associate justice by President Richard Nixon in 1971 and as chief justice in 1986 by President Ronald Reagan, held very strong convictions about the appropriate constitutional division of power between the federal government and state governments. In the case of the civil rights provision of the VAWA, he believed that Congress had overstepped its constitutional boundaries into areas of the law best left to the state governments.

We have got a Chief Justice who, I respectfully suggest, does not know what he is talking about, when he criticizes this legislation. What he is referring to is the one section of the bill that refers to making violence against women a hate crime, providing a civil rights remedy; that is the most controversial section of the bill. . . .

I thought I understood this issue. I thought violent crime was an equal opportunity employer. I thought violent crime had been rising at an equal rate across the board whether you were rich or poor, black or white, male or female. But I was dumbfounded—in February 1990, when reading the statistics from the National Bureau of Justice Statistics—to learn that from 1974 to 1987, violent crimes against males in the age category of 20 to 24 dropped, if my memory serves me correctly . . . 12 percent—dropped—yet violent crime against women 20–24 went up over 50 percent during that same time period. Something was awry. Something is seriously wrong. I suspect many women as well as men in this body thought that the violence, the climate of violence in the American streets, made no distinction between women and men. In fact, it did.

[T]he bulk of our bill . . . deals with matters relating to Federal law enforcement—from providing dollars to achieve better lighting in areas of high intensity crime straight through to providing that a stay-away order issued in one State should be enforced in all States.

Now, the Chief Justice and others have suggested that the bill may burden the Federal courts unnecessarily. Let me tell you something.

We have, under title XVIII of the U.S. Code, provisions making it a Federal crime if you move across a State line with falsely made dentures—dentures. We cover a myriad, a host of crimes—for example, if you take a cow across State lines, if you rustle a cow, it is a Federal crime. And I hear the outrageous assertion from some on the bench that we should tolerate a system in which a State court in Pennsylvania tells a man who has battered, or is likely to batter his wife, "You must stay away," but when that woman crosses the State line into Delaware, that order has no effect whatsoever—is unenforceable. This notion that what is ordered in the State court in Pennsylvania should be enforceable in Delaware is, I don't think, any radical expansion.

While Senator Biden's comparison certainly had emotional appeal, there is a notable difference between the examples he provided of federal laws involving dentures and cows and the proposed civil rights legislation in the VAWA. Article 1, Section 8, of the U.S. Constitution includes the Interstate Commerce Clause, which allows Congress to regulate commerce across state lines. While dentures and cows clearly fall within the realm of commerce that may move from state to state, Congress has used the clause to expand its power into the area of civil rights legislation, such as the passage of the Civil Rights Act of 1964. For many conservatives, this expansion of the powers of the federal government has been a source of concern; critics of the VAWA questioned whether Congress could legitimately expand its powers further into issues that had generally fallen under the domain of the states. Later in his testimony Biden made more apt comparisons, comparing women to other groups of people protected by federal civil rights legislation, but to further strengthen his position, he emphasized the bill's overwhelming bipartisan support.

If we can take care of cows, maybe the vaulted chambers of the Supreme Court could understand it may make sense to worry about women—some of whom you are going to hear from today. . . .

As you know, Mr. Chairman, and many of you, I first introduced the Violence Against Women Act in the Senate in June 1990. . . . I might add a point on that study you mentioned, Mr. Chairman, from Rhode Island where it said one-quarter of all the young men in junior high school age believed that if a man spends $10 on a woman he is entitled to force sex on her. That is startling. What is even more startling is that one-fifth of the girls thought the same thing. Twenty percent of the girls—and I say "girls" advisedly—seventh grade, eight grade, and ninth grade—said that if a man spends $10, he has a right to force sex. We have a cultural problem in this country.

But I would respectfully suggest, no one State law—notwithstanding all of your and my adherence to the notion that the State should control law enforcement—is likely to change nationwide attitudes. So, Mr. Chairman, we had four hearings on my side of this Chamber . . . and we voted out this bill unanimously on two occasions. It is bipartisan, Mr. Sensenbrenner. Strom Thurmond and Joe Biden, the ultimate odd couple, both strongly support the legislation. Orrin Hatch and Ted Kennedy—I can go down the list; we have an unusually divided committee—unanimously voted this out.

"We talk about 'domestic' violence as if we are talking about 'domesticated' cats or 'domesticated' wild animals. 'Domestic' connotes somehow that this violence is gentle; 'domestic' connotes somehow that it is not horrible."

But clearly, as I said from the outset, the most controversial provision . . . is the civil rights provision. This provision gives a civil rights remedy for gender motivated crimes. It goes beyond sending the perpetrator of the violent act to jail, or whatever punishment under the Criminal Code is appropriate. . . .

The legislation has been supported by a broad cross section of interests—law enforcement groups like the National Association of Attorneys General; by victims groups, including hundreds of rape crisis centers and battered women's shelters across the Nation; and by many women advocates. . . . When we had before us the admitting physicians of two of the largest hospitals in America dealing with crisis problems and emergency wards, we learned that one of the top reasons why women come into an emergency ward off the top is because they have been beaten up. We talk about "domestic" violence as if we are talking about "domesticated" cats or "domesticated" wild animals. "Domestic" connotes somehow that this violence is gentle; "domestic" connotes somehow that it is not horrible. . . .

The reason we have to put in the bill the part that everyone, including the Chief Justice, is so fixated on—the civil rights provision—is that there have to be additional remedies for a woman. . . . It is not sufficient that a woman merely be able to have the satisfaction that her attacker is punished under the criminal justice system. She does not control that process—as the prosecutors on the bench can tell you—the prosecutor does. There has to be something to give the woman back the right of control, for her to say, "I have chosen to bring a civil action against this person." . . .

If you look at the section of the bill that deals with what satisfies the burden to carry the civil rights remedy, you will see that the crime has to be motivated by the fact that the person is a woman or by gender. A black man or woman who is indiscriminately beaten and/or the victim of violence, and/or the victim of rape, cannot under our present civil rights law say, "My civil rights were violated, because I'm black and someone who wasn't black did me harm." He or she must show that the reason they were picked as the victim is because they are black, and that that attacker does not like or attacks black people or has said that before he attacked. Remember the fellow up in Canada who said something like, "These women engineering students that I have killed, all women, are bad; they got into engineering school; I did not; I hate women." That would qualify as a hate crime against women. . . .

This country has a long tradition in which civil rights laws have been used to fight discriminatory violence beginning in 1871 with the first antilynching laws.

No one would say today that laws barring violent attacks motivated by race or ethnicity fall outside the Federal courts' jurisdiction. Then why are they saying that violent discrimination motivated by gender is not a traditional civil rights violation? This jurisdictional argument is just the latest in a series of strawmen raised to prevent the bill from moving forward. . . .

Every day we ignore the problem, thousands of women— literally thousands—are raped and battered in this country, and every day we fail to respond we help perpetuate the awful silence of thousands more survivors who never tell anyone of these crimes.

Source: *Violence against Women: Hearing before the Subcommittee on Crime and Criminal Justice of the Committee on the Judiciary,* House of Representatives, 102nd Congress, 2nd Session, February 6, 1992, Serial No. 42 (Washington, DC: U.S. Government Printing Office, 1992), 7–12. Available at http://niwaplibrary.wcl.american.edu/reference/additional-materials/ vawa-legislative-history/violence-against-women-act-hearings-and-reports/ vawa-related-hearings-1992/House%20Judiciary%20Hearing-%20 February%206-%201992.pdf.

Six years after passage of the VAWA, the U.S. Supreme Court, still headed by Chief Justice Rehnquist, ruled that the civil rights provision of the VAWA was unconstitutional and overturned that portion of the law. In *United States v. Morrison* (2000), Christy Brzonkala, a female student at Virginia Polytechnic Institute, claimed that two male students had raped her. At the university's student hearing, Antonio Morrison admitted to having nonconsensual sex with Brzonkala and was subsequently suspended from the university for two semesters. It was also reported that Morrison had bragged about drugging women and forcing them to have sex with him. When the university later reversed Morrison's punishment, Brozonkala filed a civil suit in a federal district court claiming that Morrison's sexual behavior had been motivated by a general animus toward women and was thus a civil rights violation. Morrison's counsel argued in federal district court that the civil rights portion of the VAWA was an unconstitutional expansion of federal powers. The district court agreed, ruling in favor of Morrison, and the decision was subsequently upheld by the U.S. Court of Appeals and the U.S. Supreme Court. The VAWA was reauthorized in 2000 and 2005, but in 2012 Congress allowed it to lapse due to disagreement over portions of the proposed reauthorization that extended the law's protections to gay and lesbian people, immigrants, and Native Indian women.

Bipartisan Support for the Drug-Induced Rape Prevention and Punishment Act

Statements of Representatives Bill McCollum, Charles Schumer, and Sheila Jackson Lee

September 25, 1996

Statement of Representative Ira William "Bill" McCollum (R-FL)

Although the act of giving drugs or alcohol to someone without that person's knowledge is not a new phenomenon, law enforcement professionals began seeing a new trend by the mid-1990s of women being drugged and sexually assaulted while incapacitated. Flunitrazepam, considered the first date rape drug, is a powerful sedative, and its effects are intensified when mixed with alcohol. Although flunitrazepam is legal in some countries, in the United States manufacturing and importing it into the country are illegal. The Drug-Induced Rape Prevention and Punishment Act of 1996 was introduced in April 1996. Representative Bill McCollum was a sponsor of the legislation, and like other bills related to violence against women, it had strong bipartisan support, as evidenced by the supporting statements from both Republican and Democratic representatives. The bill ultimately passed in both chambers and was signed into law on October 13, 1996.

Mr. Speaker, they call it "the forget pill" or "the date-rape drug." Technically known as flunitrazepam, better known by its trade name Rohypnol, this inexpensive drug is being used by sexual predators to incapacitate their victims before they are raped.

Rohypnol is colorless, odorless, tasteless and dissolves quickly and easily in alcohol. In fact, alcohol enhances the drug's intoxicating effects, and leaves the victim utterly helpless and vulnerable to rape.

Mr. Speaker, what makes the use of this drug even more vile and contemptible is that victims are likely to suffer amnesia. This makes it impossible for them to recount to law enforcement the circumstances surrounding the rape. These victims suffer the knowledge that they have been sexually assaulted—they just can't remember or explain how it happened.

The distribution and abuse of this drug is a particularly big problem in my home State of Florida. From 1990 to 1992, there were 14 State and local law enforcement cases involving flunitrazepam, and the drug was found almost exclusively in the Dade County area. By 1995, the number of cases had escalated to in excess of 480. Moreover, as law enforcement encounters indicate, the drug has now spread all over the State of Florida.

This drug has been frequently found at nightclubs and college parties. It is also horrifying to learn that distribution of this drug has been discovered at junior and senior high schools—in Florida, as well as in numerous other States. The drug has also been adopted by street gang members across the country. In Texas, street gangs have been known to administer Rohypnol to females in order to commit gang rape as part of the initiation into a gang.

131

Although it is approved in other countries for short-term treatment of anxiety and sleep disorders, this drug is not currently approved by the Food and Drug Administration for marketing in the United States.

According to the Drug Enforcement Administration [DEA], Rohypnol is being smuggled in from Mexico and other Latin American countries.

This drug is currently listed as a Schedule IV drug on the Controlled Substances Act. Schedule IV drugs are drugs with accepted medical uses and low potential for abuse. The DEA has suggested that the drug be moved to Schedule I—which are drugs with no currently accepted medical uses in the United States and which have a high potential for abuse. The difficulty in deciding whether to reschedule flunitrazepam is that the drug has some accepted medical uses—it is prescribed legally in 64 other countries. This bill will substantially increase the penalties for manufacturing or distributing flunitrazepam, to give law enforcement the muscle it needs to prosecute these cases. However, it also directs the Administrator of the DEA to conduct a thorough study on the appropriateness and desirability of rescheduling flunitrazepam to a Schedule I controlled substance. The Administrator is given 6 months to conduct this study, and I fully expect Congress to revisit this issue when that report is completed. As chairman of the Crime Subcommittee, I intend to hold a hearing on the DEA's report shortly after it's received.

It is entirely possible that other drugs may now exist, or may come along in the future, which have the same properties as Rohypnol. This legislation addresses those drugs, by making it illegal to possess a controlled substance with the intent to administer that substance to facilitate a crime of violence. If a victim is under the age of 14, the penalties are even higher. This bill ensures that whatever new "date-rape drug" may come along, the penalties are there for any sexual predator who may try and use it.

The bill also directs the Sentencing Commission to recommend additional penalties for the distribution of various quantities of flunitrazepam, and authorizes the Attorney General to create educational materials regarding the use of controlled substances in furtherance of rapes.

Mr. Speaker, we have a short time left in this Congress, and it would be a tragedy if we did not pass such a significant and important piece of legislation. This bill can help put a stop to the abhorrent practice of incapacitating women for the purpose of sexual assault. I commend the gentleman from New York [Mr. Solomon] for being the force responsible for

All substances developed for a medicinal purpose must be approved for use in the United States by the Food and Drug Administration (FDA). Pharmaceutical companies must research and test any new drug they develop and demonstrate that it is both effective and safe, and drugs must be approved by the FDA before they can be legally sold in the United States. Illegal drugs, on the other hand, come under the jurisdiction of the Drug Enforcement Administration (DEA), which enforces federal drug laws. The DEA classifies illegal drugs into schedules, or categories, based on criteria such as potential for abuse. In this case, members of the House of Representatives considered reclassifying flunitrazepam, allowing prosecutors to request stiffer penalties for people found using the drug. It was hoped that harsher sentencing would curb the use of these drugs in committing sexual assault.

getting this bill to the floor today. I strongly urge my colleagues to support this bill.

Statement of Representative Charles Ellis "Chuck" Schumer (D-NY)

Mr. Speaker, the bill before us is a watered down version of what the full Judiciary Committee approved just last week. At that time, the committee voted to raise the drug's classification from what is known as schedule four—with relatively weak penalties—to schedule one—with the toughest penalties applicable to any controlled substance.

Somehow, between then and today, the majority was persuaded to weaken this bill, and to take out the rescheduling provision.

There is no way to describe this but a cave in to the demands of the pharmaceutical industry.

I regret that the majority backed down in the face of heavy, behind-the-scenes lobbying and brought this weak measure to the floor.

Nevertheless, because it does substantially increase penalties for the use of controlled substances in crimes of violence, including rape, I will support the measure and urge my colleagues to vote for it.

However, I hope that the next Congress, perhaps with a change in leadership, will stand up to the special interests and get even tougher on this dangerous drug. Maybe we will even do it without a change in leadership because it is the right thing to do no matter who takes over.

Statement of Representative Sheila Jackson Lee (D-TX)

Mr. Speaker, I thank the gentleman from New York, Mr. Schumer. And might I say that there is much to say about this, but I will certainly contain my remarks.

This is a very serious matter that is made more serious by a recent incident in my community. I hope this brings home the importance of this legislation, albeit I am concerned with the mysterious way that it has changed from being a schedule 4 circumstance to a schedule 1. . . .

The FDA has begun the administrative process of moving this drug from schedule 4 to schedule 1, to put the drug in the same category that carries the same penalties as LSD and heroin. But, unfortunately, we found that even after this bill passed through the

---

Even for relatively noncontroversial bills, the legislative process can be long, and bills can undergo many changes. For instance, a Senate bill introduced by Senator Joe Biden in March 1996 specifically mandated that flunitrazepam be rescheduled by the DEA so that the drug would receive stronger controls. Representative Schumer relates in his statement to the House of Representatives that the Committee on the Judiciary had also decided to mandate a reclassification of the drug but that by the time the bill was being considered by the House, the language had been changed to simply require the DEA to study the need to reschedule flunitrazepam, a change the Schumer condemns as weakening the bill. His concerns may have been warranted, as the DEA ultimately recommended against rescheduling flunitrazepam to higher classification.

Committee on the Judiciary, it seems to have been reworded and reworked, and so this drug today remains a schedule 4 drug, not because anyone actually believes it is safe as the other schedule 4 drugs like Valium, but because a drug company has successfully lobbied, to the detriment of women and girls across the country.

I will simply say, Mr. Speaker, that I certainly have the confidence that we will go back and correct this. I certainly hope the life of this young, and vigorous young lady, does not go in vain. I also hope that we add to this effort certainly the importance of prevention and education, programs like the Safe and Drug-free Schools, DARE programs, explaining to our teenagers that the utilization of any drug is not the way to go, but recognizing that the date rape drug is usually dropped on an unsuspecting victim.

It is important that we focus on this drug, focus on this legislation, and in fact, maybe at another day, emphasize the level that it should be at, which should be schedule 4. . . .

Although the DEA ultimately opted against reclassifying flunitrazepam, the drug's manufacturers took voluntary steps to make its detection easier when it was added to a drink. By 1999, Congress had to revisit the issue of date rape drugs, as gamma hydroxybutyrate (GHB) and to a lesser extent ketamine were becoming more commonly used. Representative Jackson Lee was instrumental in having GHB classified as a Schedule I illegal drug, the highest classification. In the Hillory J. Farias and Samantha Reid Date-Rape Drug Prohibition Act of 2000, Congress did not leave the classification of GHB to the FDA or the DEA but instead mandated at what schedule it would be placed.

Mr. Speaker, I rise today in support of H.R. 4137. Unfortunately, violence against women is a major problem in our country today and one of its most devastating forms is that of date rape. While this is an issue that has plagued us for a long long time, it is the emergence of a drug called Rohypnol, which was the catalyst for this legislation. This legislation also applied to "GHB" another such drug that caused the recent tragic death of a teenager in Texas. . . .

While this drug represents a particular problem within a larger issue this bill is much broader since it criminalized the use of any controlled substance with the intent to commit sexual assault. This bill also sets stiff penalties for those who are convicted of such crimes and attempts to protect children by inflicting prison sentences of up to 20 years for those perpetrators whose victims are 14 years old or younger.

I applaud the efforts of Mr. Solomon to address this dire social issue at least partially, if not completely. For it cannot be refuted that while Rohypnol is used for the purposes of sexual assault, its use represents only a small fraction of sexual assaults.

Regardless, I support this bill and what it attempts to do. I stand with the other Members on both sides of the aisle, in the fight against violence against women, in whatever form it takes. This bill is only another battle in the long, arduous war that we are fighting and that we will one day win.

Source: "Drug-Induced Rape Prevention and Punishment Act of 1996," *Congressional Record,* Volume 142, Number 134, Wednesday, September 25, 1996, House of Representatives, H11122–H11126. Available online at http://www.gpo .gov/fdsys/pkg/CREC-1996-09-25/html/CREC-1996-09-25-pt1-PgH11122-2.htm.

Congress Passes the Trafficking Victims Protection Act

Excerpts from Conference Report
Testimony of Senators Sam Brownback
and Paul Wellstone

October 11, 2000

Testimony from Senators Sam Brownback and Paul Wellstone

Mr. BROWNBACK.

In 1865, the Thirteenth Amendment to the U.S. Constitution was ratified to outlaw slavery and involuntary servitude in the United States. For most people, slavery in the United States is a fact of history, an era of buying and selling human beings that ended more than a century ago. However, while the nature of human trafficking has changed in modern times, it undoubtedly still exists. While slavery of black people largely involved forced agricultural and household labor, the center of this modern manifestation of slavery is forced prostitution, although other sorts of labor also exist. Republican senator Sam Brownback and Democratic senator Paul Wellstone cosponsored the Trafficking Victims Protection Act of 2000. Because the House version of the bill differed from the bill passed in the Senate, the two chambers agreed to a compromise version of the bill, called a conference report. These two senators spoke on behalf of the conference report, which ultimately passed both chambers of Congress and was signed into law by President Bill Clinton.

Our Government estimates that between 600,000 and 2 million women are trafficked each year beyond international borders. They are trafficked for the purpose of sexual prostitution by organized crime units and groups that are aggressively out making money off the trafficking of human flesh. It is wrong. This bill seeks to deal with that wrong and that tragedy that has occurred and is occurring around the world today.

This is significant human rights legislation that this body is going to pass. I hope, predict, and pray that it will pass today. . . .

Our anti-trafficking bill is the first complete legislation to address the growing practice of international "trafficking" worldwide. This is one of the largest manifestations of modern-day slavery internationally. Notably, this legislation is the most significant human rights bill of the 106th Congress, if passed today, as hoped for. This is also the largest anti-slavery bill that the United States has adopted since 1865 and the demise of slavery at the end of the Civil War. Therefore, I greatly anticipate this vote today in the Senate on this legislation.

Senator Wellstone's and my trafficking bill, which passed in the Senate on July 27 of this year, was conferenced to reconcile the differences with the House bill, and the conference report was filed on October 5, Thursday, of last week.

In 1994, Congress passed the VAWA. Often when Congress passes legislation, the law will include an end date by which time Congress must revisit the legislation and reauthorize it or the law will expire. In 2000, Congress was in the process of reauthorizing the VAWA at the same time that the Trafficking Victims Protection Act was being considered. The conference committee that worked to reconcile House and Senate versions of the bill suggested pairing the bill on human trafficking with the VAWA. Although victims of human trafficking may be female or male, the vast majority of victims are women and girls. As such, packaging the trafficking law with reauthorization of the VAWA seemed like a good way to broadly address the issues of violence faced by women and girls in the United States.

The final conference package contains four additional pieces of legislation which are substantially appropriate to our bill. Most significant among those bill amendments is the Violence Against Women Act, known as VAWA, which provides relief and assistance to those who suffer domestic violence in America. . . .

135

Trafficking is the new slavery of the world. These victims are routinely forced against their will into the sex trade, transported across international borders, and left defenseless in a foreign country. This bill also addresses the insidious practice known as "debt bondage," wherein a person can be enslaved to the money lender for an entire lifetime because of a $50 debt taken by the family for an emergency. This is a common practice in countries throughout the South Asian region. . . .

This new phenomenon of sex trafficking is growing exponentially. Some report that it is, at least, $7 billion per year illicit trade, exceeded only by the international drug and arms trade. Its victims are enslaved into a devastating brutality against their will, with no hope for release or justice, while its perpetrators build criminal empires on this suffering with impunity. Our legislation will begin to challenge these injustices. . . .

Sex trafficking is among the most common forms of the new slavery and typically entails shorter periods of bondage, usually asking for 5 to 6 years, or whenever something like AIDS or tuberculosis is contracted, after which the victim is thrown out on the street, broken, without community or resources, left to die. I have met with people caught in that condition.

Women and children are routinely forced against their will. Sex traffickers favor girls aging in the range of 10 to 13.

I have a number of other things I could say, but my time is limited. I know a number of people want to speak on this bill. I ask to reserve the remainder of my time. I will turn the floor over to Senator Wellstone.

SENATOR WELLSTONE: I thank my colleague, Senator Brownback, for his very gracious remarks. It has been an honor to work with him on this legislation. I think a very strong friendship has come out of this effort. . . .

Our Government estimates that 2 million people are trafficked each year. Of those, 700,000 women and children, primarily young girls, are trafficked from poor countries to rich countries and sold into slavery, raped, locked up, physically and psychologically abused, with food and health care withheld. Of those, as many as 50,000 immigrants are brought into the United States each year, and they wind up trapped in brothels, sweatshops, and other types of forced labor, abused and too fearful to seek help.

Traffickers exploit the unequal status of women and girls, including harmful stereotypes of women as property and sexual objects to be bought and sold. Traffickers have also

"Our Government estimates that 2 million people are trafficked each year. Of those, 700,000 women and children, primarily young girls, are trafficked from poor countries to rich countries and sold into slavery, raped, locked up, physically and psychologically abused, with food and health care withheld."

taken advantage of the demand in our country and others for cheap, unprotected labor. For the traffickers, the sale of human beings is a highly profitable, low-risk enterprise as these women are viewed as expendable and reusable commodities. . . .

Trafficking has become a major source of new income for criminal rings. It is coldly observed that drugs are sold once while a woman or a child can be sold 10 or 20 times a day.

In the United States, Thai traffickers who incarcerated Thai women and men in sweatshops in El Monte, CA, are estimated to have made $8 million in 6 years. Further, Thai traffickers who enslaved Thai women in a New York brothel made about $1.5 million over 1 year and 3 months. . . .

All of these cases reflect a new condition: Women whose lives have been disrupted by civil wars or fundamental changes in political geography, such as the disintegration of the Soviet Union or the violence in the Balkans, have fallen prey to traffickers.

Seeking financial security, many innocent persons are lured by traffickers' false promises of a better life and lucrative jobs abroad. Seeking this better life, they are lured by local advertisements for good jobs in foreign countries at wages they could never imagine at home. However, when they arrive, these victims are often stripped of their passports, held against their will, some in slave-like conditions, in the year 2000.

Rape, intimidation, and violence are commonly employed by traffickers to control their victims and to prevent them from seeking help.

There are times when well-intentioned laws have unintended consequences. For instance, laws concerning illegal immigration, and the punishments for violating those laws, are often based on a premise that a person freely chooses to come to and remain in the United States illegally. As the immigration laws were structured at the time, many victims of human trafficking fit the description of illegal immigrants, since many victims are from other countries, lured to the United States with hopes of a better life, or are brought to the United States against their will. Once in the country, they are caught between a horrific experience of slavery and the fear that if they seek help, they will be arrested and face deportation. The Trafficking Victims Protection Act attempted to remedy this disincentive to seek help by including provisions that would allow victims to seek justice without fear of punishment by the government.

Through physical isolation and psychological trauma, traffickers and brothel owners imprison women in a world of economic and sexual exploitation that imposes a constant threat of arrest and deportation, as well as violent reprisals by the traffickers themselves to whom the women must pay off ever-growing debts. That is the way this works.

Many brothel owners actually prefer foreign women, women who are far from help and from home, who do not speak the language, precisely because of the ease of controlling them. Most of these women never imagined they would enter such a hellish world, having traveled abroad to find better jobs or to see the world. . . .

Trafficking abuses are occurring not just in far-off lands but here at home in America as well. The INS has discovered

250 brothels in 26 different cities which involve trafficking victims. This is from a CIA report. This is the whole problem of no punishment—being able to do this with virtual impunity. . . .

Teenage Mexican girls were held in slavery in Florida and the Carolinas, and they were forced to submit to prostitution.

Russian and Latvian women were forced to work in nightclubs in the Midwest. . . . This is in our country. The women were told that if they refused to work in sexually exploitive conditions, the Russian Mafia would kill their families. . . .

Trafficking in persons for labor is an enormous problem as well. The INS has also worked on cases involving South Asian children smuggled into the United States to work in slavery-like conditions. In one case, about 100 Indian children, some of them as young as 9 or 10, were brought into New York and shuffled around the country to work in construction and restaurants—ages 9 and 10, in the United States; today, in the United States—2000. . . .

The bitter irony is that quite often victims are punished more harshly than the traffickers because of their illegal immigration status, their serving as prostitutes, or their lack of documents, which the traffickers have confiscated in order to control the victims. . . .

The Victims of Violence and Trafficking Protection Act of 2000 establishes, for the first time, a bright line between the victim and the perpetrator. It punishes the perpetrator and provides a comprehensive approach to solving the root problems that create millions of trafficking victims each year.

This legislation aims to prevent trafficking in persons, provide protection and assistance to those who have been trafficked, and strengthen prosecution and punishment for those who are responsible for the trafficking. . . .

By way of conclusion, I say to my colleagues, starting with Senator Brownback, I believe with passage of this legislation—I believe it will pass today and the President will sign it—we are lighting a candle. We are lighting a candle for these women and girls and sometime men forced into forced labor.

Source: "Trafficking Victims Protection Act of 2000—Conference Report," *Congressional Record,* Volume 146, Number 126, Wednesday, October 11, 2000, Senate, S10164–S10188.

"The bitter irony is that quite often victims are punished more harshly than the traffickers because of their illegal immigration status, their serving as prostitutes, or their lack of documents, which the traffickers have confiscated in order to control the victims."

Proposed Legislation to Address the Economic Impact of Domestic Violence

Statements of Senators Patty Murray and Johnny Isakson at "Too Much Too Long?" Senate Hearings

April 17, 2007

Opening Statement of Senator Patty Murray

Two weeks ago, in my home State, a 26-year-old woman who worked at the University of Washington was killed at her workplace by an ex-boyfriend. She had filed a restraining order and warned her friends and co-workers to be on the lookout for him. The following day at the CNN Building in Atlanta, a hotel employee was killed by an ex-boyfriend. Many other cases of abuse, stalking, harassment and homicide don't make the nightly news but they do end lives, they hurt businesses and they alarm communities.

Patty Murray was elected to the Senate in 1992, the first woman to serve in the Senate from Washington state. Even among Democratic senators, she is considered very liberal and has promoted numerous issues related to women's rights during her career. In this particular case, Murray addressed the economic consequences of domestic violence, a consequence that receives considerably less attention than does the physical consequences of domestic violence. While certain aspects of domestic violence were included in the original VAWA and its subsequent reauthorizations, there was no protection against the loss of a job or loss of income due to domestic violence. Murray attempted to remedy this omission in the law by proposing the Survivors Empowerment and Economic Security Act; however, the bill was not ultimately passed in the Senate.

Each day, we get terrible reminders that domestic violence does not stay at home. It follows people into their workplace, posing safety, financial and legal problems for the victims, employers and other workers. If we ignore it, the horrible toll of domestic violence in the workplace will continue unchecked. But if we confront it, we can make progress.

My goal today is to gather the facts about the size and scope of the problem and to discuss solutions, including a bill that I am introducing today called the Survivors Empowerment and Economic Security Act, which I first introduced with my very good friend, the late Senator Paul Wellstone. . . .

Together, we crafted this bill with input from domestic violence survivors, advocates, workplace experts and our Senate colleagues and I want to thank all of our witnesses for coming today, for sharing their expertise and experiences with us. . . .

I've been working on domestic violence for a very long time and we have made progress. We've updated our Federal laws and invested in prevention, intervention and persecution. We've made domestic violence something that no one talked about to something that is everybody's business but I am frustrated that we have not made as much progress addressing the economic factors that allow abuse to continue.

As I discuss domestic violence today, I am referring to domestic violence, dating violence, sexual assaults and stalking. Its victims can be men or women.

When domestic violence follows victims into the workplace, it reveals a key connection between safety and economic independence. For many victims of domestic violence, a steady paycheck is the only thing that keeps them from relying on their abuser. We know, in fact, economic security and independence is the most accurate indicator of whether a victim will be able to stay away from an abuser.

For people who have not suffered from domestic violence or abuse, a common question posed is why a victim would stay with an abusive partner. Abusers often force victims into situations that create a measure of dependence on the very person who is doing the abuse. This can include distancing the victim emotionally and/or physically from friends and family, preventing transportation or communication by taking the victim's driver's license or cell phone, and creating economic dependence by taking the victim's debit or credit cards or preventing the victim from working. When the victim is employed, the abuser can create additional problems by negatively affecting the victim's job performance. It is this economic dependence that Senator Murray and the subcommittee were considering and hoping to address in this hearing.

But too often, victims are entirely dependent on their abuser for food and shelter for themselves and their families. And too often, abusers try to undermine a victim's ability to work, harass their victims in the workplace or worse. If we want to end domestic violence in the workplace or anywhere else, we need to address the economic barriers that trap victims in abusive relationships.

Let me share a few statistics that show the challenge that we face. Domestic violence impacts the productivity of employees and the success of businesses. Each year, domestic violence results in an estimated 8 million missed days of work nationwide and each year, domestic violence causes up to 50 percent of victims to lose their jobs, making them more dependent on their abuser. Many times employers just don't know how to handle a situation where an abuser is coming to the workplace or causing an employee to miss their work.

Unfortunately, more than 70 percent of U.S. workplaces have no formal program or policy that addresses workplace violence, let alone domestic violence. Only 4 percent of our employers provide training on domestic violence.

Some companies make the wrong choice and fire the worker. But making the employee go away does not make the problem go away. In fact, it can make it much harder for that person to get help if they do not have the financial security that a job provides. So we need to help our employers understand the right things to do.

If I look at these challenges, I see a series of locked doors. A victim wants to leave an abuser but she can't support herself so the economic door is locked. A survivor wants to go to court to get a protection order but she can't get time off work. Another door is locked. A survivor needs medical insurance or a job but she is discriminated against. More locked doors. My bill will unlock the doors that trap victims in abusive relationships and it will lift the economic barriers that allow abuse to continue.

Let me share four ways the Survivors Empowerment and Economic Security will help. First, it allows victims to take time off from work without penalty from their employers to appear in court, seek legal assistance and get help with safety planning. Second, it ensures that if a victim must leave a job because of abuse, that person is then eligible for unemployment compensation. Third, it prohibits employers or insurance providers from basing hiring or coverage decisions on a victim's history of abuse. Too many victims today cannot get a job or the insurance they need because insurance companies reject abuse victims. Finally, the bill addresses the punitive elements of the welfare system that penalize victims who are fleeing dangerous situations, also called the Family Violence Option. . . .

We owe it to the millions of victims of domestic violence, sexual violence and stalking to address this problem head on. People should not be forced to choose between financial security and physical security. Together we can help to stop this cycle of violence and the toll it takes on families, on communities and our society but we have to change the law and that's what I hope we can do together, starting with this hearing this morning.

Opening Statement of Senator Isakson

Domestic violence is illegal and it's wrong. There is also no doubt that domestic violence can and often does affect the workplace. As Chairman Murray just mentioned, in my hometown of Atlanta, Georgia, just earlier this month, Ms. Clara Riddles was fatally wounded while working at the Omni Hotel in the CNN Center. According to police, her former boyfriend entered the lobby, grabbed her by the hair and then shot her three times.

All of us seek to prevent it. Effective interventions require consistent and coordinated efforts by police and prosecutors, counselors and the courts.

Until 2012, the VAWA consistently enjoyed broad bipartisan support. Although legislation addressing violence against women has generally remained above the partisan fray, as is often said, the devil is in the details; while an issue may have widespread support in general, political differences may surface when the specific details of an issue are considered. When reading Senator Isakson's statement, one can see his concern with details of the legislation that probably led to the death of Senator Murray's bill. While Murray's bill would be designed to assist victims of domestic violence, a goal on which most could agree, the burden of compliance would fall on employers who employ victims of domestic violence. There are often concerns with any new legal and economic responsibilities put into the hands of employers, and this seems to contribute to Isakson's unease with the bill. Despite the fact that this bill died in the Senate, at least 15 states have passed similar legislation.

The Violence Against Women Act made great strides in this area, originally passed by the Congress in 1995 and reauthorized in 2005, the act authorizes the Department of Justice to coordinate with State governments as well as international governments on matters concerning violence against women.

In 2003, President Bush launched the Family Justice Center Initiative. The Initiative attempts to address the problem of victims having to seek help in an often fragmented system by providing comprehensive services for victims at one single location, including medical care, counseling, legal enforcement assistance, social services, employment assistance and housing assistance.

As an employer for 22 years of almost 1,000 women, 800 independent contractors and 200 employees, I am not unfamiliar with the effect that domestic violence can have on those individuals or the workplace. And I am happy to cooperate in encouraging exactly what Chairman Murray stated in her remarks and that is to help employers to do the right thing.

As an employer, I always tried to do the right thing and quite frankly, I find almost in all cases, employers always try to do the right thing because their assets are their employees.

I look forward to working with the Chairman on this legislation when it is introduced. I haven't had the chance to read it yet. My only cautions that I would raise is first of all, the caution with regard to any provisions on unlimited jury awards or creating an environment where the legal action against the companies takes place because of allegations. Second, I worry about the unintended consequences of people who have been abused not being employed because of the fear that because they were abused, they might be a problem in the workplace.

We don't want to pass a law that has the unintended consequence of causing that to happen by having employers judge people out of fear of either legal action of some consequence and therefore, they don't employ someone they might otherwise have employed.

I know many employers of all sizes and all sectors in the American economy. I do not know of one, however, who would be unsupportive or hostile to any employee who was suffering from domestic abuse.

I want to thank Chairman Murray for the introduction of this legislation and the calling of this hearing today and I look forward to working with her as the legislation develops.

". . . I worry about the unintended consequences of people who have been abused not being employed because of the fear that because they were abused, they might be a problem in the workplace."

Source: *Too Much, Too Long? Domestic Violence in the Workplace,* U.S. Senate, Subcommittee on Employment and Workplace Safety of the Committee on Health, Education, Labor, and Pensions, 110th Congress, 1st Session, April 17, 2007. Available at http://www.gpo.gov/fdsys/pkg/CHRG-110shrg34939/html/CHRG-110shrg34939.htm.

Chapter 6

Women's Rights
in the 21st Century

Introduction

When reading a historical account of women's rights, it is easy to see the issues as just that, history. Many women and girls live in a United States in which the rights of women seem like givens, the status quo. It is easy to ask whether we still need feminism when so much has already been accomplished.

With all that has already been accomplished for women's rights, one might ask whether there are still issues of women's rights that need to be addressed in the United States. Given some of the issues that have been raised in the political arena since 2011, the answer appears to be yes. In each of the areas discussed in earlier chapters, including women and work, education, politics, health and reproduction, and violence, government officials are still discussing issues that have implications for women. In this chapter some of these current issues are considered, placing them in the context of issues discussed in earlier chapters and reflecting on how the political dialogue and decision making on women's rights issues have changed.

Women and their expanding roles in the workplace occupied much of feminists' attention in the 20th century. Although societal norms had traditionally defined women by their family and domestic roles, their movement into the workforce has effectively changed the norm. The majority of women in the United States work outside the home, and the percentage of women who work is not much lower than the percentage of men who work. It is clear that women have made progress in working outside the home and in having their rights to work protected by law and judicial interpretation of the Fourteenth Amendment, but it is also clear that there is still work to be done. One factor in particular that illustrates this fact is the continuing wage gap between men and women. By 2013, women were making on average 77 cents for every dollar made by men.

In 2007 the Supreme Court ruled against Lilly Ledbetter, a woman who claimed that she had been discriminated against by her employer, Goodyear Tire and

Rubber. While it was evident that she had indeed been a victim of discrimination when pay raises had been granted, the Court claimed that Ledbetter had waited too long to file a complaint, based on the Court's narrow interpretation of Title VII of the Civil Rights Act of 1964. Within a year of the Court's ruling, Congress was considering an amendment to Title VII to more clearly articulate its intent that sex discrimination in pay decisions is illegal, effectively limiting the Court's ability to make similar decisions. Although Congress passed the Lilly Ledbetter Fair Pay Act in 2009, the issue of the wage gap was still being discussed as recently as 2013. President Barack Obama wants to see even greater protections for women against pay discrimination. While the Paycheck Fairness Act has been considered in both chambers of Congress, to date it has yet to be passed. Both of these proposals, the one that passed and the one that has not, are discussed in this chapter.

Women's and girls' education is still being discussed as well. Most little girls who started school after 1972 never experienced the types of limitations in their education that were experienced by their mothers and grandmothers. For the most part, girls in the United States today grow up believing that they can move into any field of study they want and that they can participate in the same school activities as boys. This is the result of Congress passing Title IX in 1972 prohibiting sex discrimination in educational opportunities. But simply prohibiting discrimination against female students does not mean that individual girls and women will be immune to gender norms and societal expectations for them. Thus, while women are not limited in what they can study and have clearly embraced the breadth of programs offered by schools and universities, it is also accurate to note that the majority of students in teacher education and nursing programs, that is, traditional female fields, are still women. Similarly, most computer science and engineering students are men. Although male and female students cannot be prohibited from studying in any discipline, they may simply self-select into disciplines that have traditionally been the domain of their particular gender.

This issue has been the topic of considerable discussion in recent years. In particular, the number of women in the disciplines of science, technology, engineering, and mathematics (STEM) has garnered much attention. Several factors speak to the gendered nature of these disciplines. First, the number of men studying and working in these fields is significantly higher than the number of women. While more women study these disciplines now than did prior to Title IX's passage, they are still in the minority. Second, looking just at the women who have been educated in these fields, these women are significantly more likely to drop out of these careers than are men. It is not that women cannot succeed in these positions but that the research expectations associated with these jobs often do not reflect the reality of women's lives or their personal goals to have a family. Rather than lose so many women in STEM careers, women who may find the next breakthrough technology or cure for a disease, President Obama's administration requested that the National Science Foundation modify its guidelines for research grants to better reflect a balance between work and personal life for grant recipients. The National Science Foundation is the country's largest provider of research grants in the STEM fields, and it is hoped that this effort will create an environment more hospitable to female researchers and encourage more girls and women to study these disciplines.

Similar to the areas of work and education, much has changed in the political world since women gained the right to vote in 1920. At least in national elections, women have had greater voter turnout than men since 1980, and the so-called gender gap in candidate preference has been instrumental in getting several candidates elected to office. Although it has been a slow process, more women are running for office now than they did in the 1980s and 1990s, and more are getting elected. By 2013, more women were serving in Congress than ever before. Similarly, women are being appointed to positions in the federal judiciary and the executive branch more than in the past, and they have been selected for powerful positions, such as secretary of state and the Speaker of the House of Representatives. Yet despite the clear gains in the number of women serving in public office, women are not close to reaching parity with men in terms of their numbers in government.

Perhaps as important as the numbers, however, is to ask whether the women in office are influencing public policy. On this question, the answer is clearly yes. Although she was not the first woman to serve in the position of secretary of state, Hillary Clinton exemplifies the inroads that women have made into government and politics. Before her appointment to the State Department in 2009, she played a more traditional role for women in politics, serving as the first lady of the state of Arkansas for 12 years and the first lady of the United States for 8 years when her husband Bill Clinton served as the governor of Arkansas and the president of the United States. Hillary Clinton, however, was not a traditional first lady. She was a lawyer with a prestigious law firm in Arkansas and played substantive policy roles in both of her first lady positions. In 2000 she was elected to the Senate by voters in New York and served on several powerful committees, such as the Committee on Armed Services and the Committee on the Budget. She ran for the Democratic nomination for president in 2008 but was defeated by Obama. When Obama was ultimately elected president, he asked Clinton to serve as his secretary of state, the third woman to hold the position. Although like most people in the position she faced some criticism during her term, the public has overwhelmingly had a positive impression of her and the job she did, and she was lauded in Congress when she ended her term.

While women's rights in the areas of work, education, and politics have had setbacks here and there, for the most part rights in these areas have expanded relatively consistently over time. However, for the last two policy areas—reproductive rights and violence against women—it is more difficult to make that same assertion. Laws and court cases can assert women's rights in the legal realm, but reproductive rights and violence are both very complex social issues that are hard to fully address through legislation. Women's reproductive rights, especially in regard to contraception and access to abortion services, are still in place, but they are also still active topics in the political arena, and the security of these rights is by no means stable. It is easy to argue that access to abortion is one of the most volatile political issues in the federal government and in state governments today. States have taken numerous steps to limit women's access to abortion, despite the fact that the right to have an abortion is still in place. These laws differ from state to state, but states may mandate that various actions take place before an abortion can take place, such as a waiting period, a counseling session, an offer to listen to the embryo's heartbeat, an ultrasound, and a transvaginal ultrasound. Not all of these actions are medically necessary, and they are clearly adopted to dissuade a woman from having an abortion.

However, since the Supreme Court has not taken steps to overturn the decision in *Roe v. Wade,* antiabortion groups are attempting to outlaw abortion by more indirect means. The most common tactic currently being pursued is to change state laws or constitutions to legally define a "person" to include all unborn humans, from the moment of their conception. The idea is that persons, as the term is defined by law, enjoy the protection of law. Thus, abortion would legally be murder, since it takes the life of a person. To date several states have placed the question on the ballot for a vote, but it has not passed in any state. The initiative proposed in the state of Mississippi is addressed in this chapter. For organizations such as Personhood USA, the 2011 Mississippi personhood initiative seemed like the proverbial ace in the hole. Mississippi is an extremely conservative state, and the state's one remaining abortion clinic is under constant threat of closure. It was widely expected that the ballot initiative would pass, yet even in Mississippi, the personhood initiative failed. Personhood Mississippi is planning to reword its proposed constitutional amendment and petition to have it placed on the 2014 ballot.

When the Violence Against Women Act (VAWA) was passed in 1994, it was praised by Republicans and Democrats alike. Twice it was reauthorized with overwhelming support from legislators of both parties. Yet when the law expired in 2011, it took Congress more than a year to pass legislation reauthorizing the law. For the last policy statement of this chapter, the sponsor of the legislation expresses his shock that a law that had done so much good for women had been allowed to expire. Clearly, something has changed in the political environment. One explanation is the increased politicization of gendered violence. In 2011 when a Toronto police officer suggested to a women's group that they could prevent rape by not dressing like "sluts," it prompted worldwide outrage at the tendency to blame victims for sexual crimes committed against them. As recently as March 2013, a CNN journalist was criticized for her sympathetic coverage of two Steubenville, Ohio, high school students who were convicted of raping a 16-year-old female classmate. No mention was made of the victim and the effect of the sexual assault on her; instead, the reporter lamented the effect that the conviction would have on the boys.

It would be too simple to say that the tendency toward victim blaming and so-called slut shaming caused the delay in reauthorizing the VAWA. But they both may reflect a change in the perceived worth of combating crimes against women, especially crimes of a sexual nature. If there are people who think that women are "asking for it" by dressing a certain way, drinking too much, or going to certain parties, it is not a stretch to think that policy makers may not perceive the sense of urgency to combat crime against women, especially women who do not conform to society's norms. Because the conflict over the VAWA's 2012 reauthorization was due to sections of the bill adding protections for immigrant women, Native American women, and the LGBT community, it at least appears that there were members of Congress who thought some women were more deserving of protections than others.

Critical Assessments of the Supreme Court's
Ledbetter v. Goodyear Decision

Statements of Representative George Miller and Lilly Ledbetter at "Justice Denied?" House Hearings

June 12, 2007

Title VII of the Civil Rights Act of 1964 states that "It shall be an unlawful employment practice for an employer . . . to discriminate against any individual with respect to his compensation, terms, conditions, or privileges of employment, because of such individual's race, color, religion, sex, or national origin." In 1998 when Lilly Ledbetter discovered that her employer, Goodyear, was paying her a fraction of the salary that men were paid in the same position, she sued for sex discrimination under Title VII. Although she initially won her suit in district court, in 2007 the Supreme Court overturned the decision and ruled in favor of Goodyear. The Court's opinion was based on a later section of the law, which states that an employee has 180 days from a discriminatory act to file a complaint with the Equal Employment Opportunity Commission (EEOC). The difficulty in this case was identifying that discriminatory act. Was it Goodyear's decision to give Ms. Ledbetter lower raises than men, which took place before the 180-day deadline, or did every paycheck from Goodyear constitute a violation of the law? The Court ruled that the decisions to give Ledbetter lower raises may have been discriminatory, but since they took place prior to the 180-day filing requirement, her current case was not viable.

Justice Samuel Alito wrote the Court opinion of which Representative Miller is so critical. An appointee of President George W. Bush, Alito in *Ledbetter v. Goodyear* wrote that "current effects alone cannot breathe life into prior, uncharged discrimination. . . . Ledbetter should have filed an EEOC charge within 180 days after each allegedly discriminatory pay decision was made and communicated to her. She did not do so, and the paychecks that were issued to her during the 180 days prior to the filing of her EEOC charge do not provide a basis for overcoming that prior failure." In essence, he says that the burden of proof to demonstrate sex discrimination falls on the employee. It was this narrow reading of Title VII's guidelines for filing a complaint that prompted Congress to amend the law. Since the Supreme Court made its decision based on a narrow reading of the law, Congress opted to change the wording of the law, preempting a similar decision being made by any future court.

Statement of Representative George Miller, Chair, House of Representatives Committee on Education and Labor

The Supreme Court's ruling in Ledbetter v. Goodyear is a painful step backward for civil rights in this country. It makes it more difficult for workers to stand up for their basic rights at work. This is unacceptable.

Title VII of the Civil Rights Act was intended to protect the civil rights of every American. When employers violate their employees' civil rights, the Civil Rights Act sought to ensure that those employers would be held accountable. . . .

Lilly Ledbetter worked at Goodyear over 19 years. While it appears that her salary at the start of her career was comparable to what her male colleagues were earning, her salary slipped over time. When she retired as a supervisor in 1998, her salary was 20 percent lower than that of the lowest-paid male supervisor. . . .

A jury found that Goodyear discriminated against Ms. Ledbetter. She was awarded $3.8 million in back pay and damages. This amount was reduced to $360,000, the Title VII damage cap.

Despite the fact that the jury found Goodyear guilty of discrimination, a sharply divided Supreme Court, in a 5–4 opinion, decided that, while Ms. Ledbetter had been discriminated against, her claim was made too late.

Title VII requires that employees file an Equal Employment Opportunity Commission charge within the 180 days of the unlawful employment practice. Ms. Ledbetter filed within 180 days of receiving the discriminatory pay from Goodyear, but a slim majority of the Supreme Court found that because Ms. Ledbetter did not file within 180 days of a discriminatory decision to write those discriminatory paychecks, her time had run out. She could not recover anything; Goodyear owed her nothing.

A slim majority of the Supreme Court shunned reason in order to satisfy its own narrow, ideological agenda. Reason and justice, however, demand a different result.

Discrimination does not just occur when the initial decision to discriminate is made. You may not know when the decision to discriminate against you is made. You may not recognize it when it was made.

Discrimination occurs both when the employer decides to discriminate and then when the employer actually discriminates by, for example, paying you less because you are a woman, an African-American, or older than other employees.

Ms. Ledbetter was discriminated against with nearly every paycheck she received.

The impact of the court's decision extends far beyond Ms. Ledbetter's case. It has far-reaching implications for an individual's right to receive equal pay for equal work.

Victims of pay discrimination often do not realize that they have been discriminated against for a long time. The reality of the workplace is that most workers don't know what their co-workers are making. Many employers, as Goodyear did, prohibit employees from discussing their pay with others. And social norms also keep employees from asking the question.

In addition, employers hold significant power over the employees. So even if an employee suspects discrimination, they will likely wait to sue until they know for sure.

With the Ledbetter decision, the court is telling employers that to escape responsibility, all they need do is keep the discrimination hidden and run out the clock.

Employers with a history of pay discrimination will be allowed to lawfully continue to discriminate against employees in protected categories, including sex, race, religion and national origin.

If the employee missed the deadline to sue when the employer made the decision, according to this Supreme Court the employee must live with the pay discrimination for the rest of her tenure with that employer.

This case is a clear indication that the court does not understand pay discrimination, nor does it reflect what the Congress intended when we passed the Civil Rights Act in 1964 or its amendments in 1991.

Women have made great strides in the workplace. They are leaders in business, government and academia. And for the first time in history, a woman is serving as the speaker of House of Representatives.

"With the Ledbetter decision, the court is telling employers that to escape responsibility, all they need do is keep the discrimination hidden and run out the clock."

Yet despite this progress that women have made, they continue to be held back by wage discrimination. We know that women are earning only 77 cents for every dollar earned by men. On average, women's wages constitute more than one-third of their family's income.

Women still have a steep hill to climb for pay parity. Thanks to this misguided Supreme Court decision, that hill just got a lot steeper. . . .

As Justice Ginsberg [*sic*] suggests, the ball has now fallen into Congress's court. And make no mistake: Congress intends to act to correct the Supreme Court's grievous insult to American workers.

Statement of Lilly Ledbetter, *Plaintiff in Ledbetter v. Goodyear* and Former Goodyear Employee

Good afternoon. Thank you, Mr. Chairman and Mr. Ranking Member, for inviting me. My name is Lilly Ledbetter. It is an honor to be here today to talk about my experience trying to enforce my right to equal pay for equal work.

I wish my story had a happy ending, but it doesn't. I hope that this committee can do whatever is necessary to make sure that in the future what happened to me does not happen to other people who suffer discrimination like I did. . . .

My story began in 1979, when Goodyear hired me to work as supervisor in the tire plant in Gadsden, Alabama.

Toward the end of my career, I got the feeling that maybe I wasn't getting paid as much as I should, or as much as the men. But there was no way to know for sure, because pay levels were kept strictly confidential.

I only started to get some hard evidence of discrimination when someone anonymously left a piece of paper in my mailbox at work showing what I got paid and what three other male managers were getting paid.

When I later complained to EEOC, just before I retired, I found out that while I was earning about $3,700 hundred per month, all the men were earning $4,300 to $5,200 per month. This happened because, time and again, I got smaller raises than the men. And over the years, those little differences added up and multiplied.

At the trial, the jury found that Goodyear had discriminated against me in violation of Title VII. The jury awarded me more than $3 million in back pay and punitive damages, but the law required the court to reduce my award to $360,000.

As evidenced by the date of this hearing, Congress considered amending Title VII of the Civil Rights Act of 1964 within months of the Supreme Court's ruling. In particular, an amendment would clarify that the 180-day clock to file a claim of discrimination would begin after any pay period that was affected by a discriminatory act. Thus, every new paycheck would be a new act of discrimination by the employer. At the time, President George W. Bush and his allies in Congress were opposed to any new legislation, fearing that an amendment to the law would fuel new discrimination lawsuits. This opposition was enough to forestall any effort in Congress to remedy the Court's reading of Title VII during Bush's administration. On January 8, 2009, Senator Barbara Milkulski introduced the Lilly Ledbetter Fair Pay Act to the Senate, less than two weeks before Barack Obama's presidential inauguration. Nine days after taking office, President Obama signed the bill into law. The Lilly Ledbetter Fair Pay Act of 2009 was the first law Obama signed after taking office.

The Supreme Court took it all away. They said I should have complained every time I got a smaller raise than the men, even if I didn't know what the men were getting paid and even if I had no way to prove the decision was discrimination.

They said that once 180 days passes after the pay decision is made, the worker is stuck with unequal pay for the rest of her career, and that there is nothing illegal about that under Title VII.

Justice Ginsberg [*sic*] hit the nail on the head when she said that the majority's rule just doesn't make sense in the real world. You can't expect people to go around asking their coworkers how much they are making.

Plus, even if you know some people are getting paid a little more than you, that is no reason to suspect discrimination right away. Especially when you work at a place like I did, where you are the only woman in a male-dominated factory, you don't want to make waves unnecessarily. You want to try to fit in and get along.

It was only after I got paid less than men again and again, without any good excuse, that I had a case that I could realistically bring to EEOC or to the court.

Every paycheck I received I got less than what I was entitled to under the law. The Supreme Court said that this didn't count as illegal discrimination, but it sure feels like discrimination when you are on the receiving end of the smaller paycheck and you are trying to support your family with less money than what the men are getting for doing the same job.

According to the Supreme Court, if you don't figure things out right away, the company can treat you like a second-class citizen for the rest of your career. And that is not right.

The truth is, Goodyear continues to treat me like a second-class worker to this day because my pension and my Social Security is based on the amount I earned while working there. Goodyear gets to keep my extra pension as a reward for breaking the law.

My case is over, and it is too bad that the Supreme Court decided the way that it did. I hope, though, that Congress won't let this happen to anyone else. I would feel that this long fight was worthwhile if at least at the end of it I knew that I played a part in getting the law fixed so that it can provide real protection to real people in the real world.

"Every paycheck I received I got less than what I was entitled to under the law. The Supreme Court said that this didn't count as illegal discrimination, but it sure feels like discrimination when you are on the receiving end of the smaller paycheck and you are trying to support your family with less money than what the men are getting for doing the same job."

Source: *Justice Denied? The Implications of the Supreme Court's Decision in Ledbetter v. Goodyear Employment Discrimination Decision,* U.S. House Committee on Education and Labor, June 12, 2007, 110th Congress, 1st Session (Washington, DC: U.S. Government Printing Office, 2007). Available at http://www.gpo.gov/fdsys/pkg/CHRG-110hhrg35806/pdf/CHRG-110hhrg35806.pdf.

Obama Endorses the Paycheck Fairness Act

President Barack Obama's Remarks on Wage Equality

June 4, 2012

The year after the Lilly Ledbetter Fair Pay Act of 2009 was passed, members of Congress attempted to close another legal loophole allowing men and women to be paid differently for the same work. In 1963 Congress passed the Equal Pay Act, which essentially said that men and women doing the same work must receive equal pay for that work. However, there were four exceptions written into the law. The first three exceptions are rather straightforward, stating that men and women can receive different pay when the difference is based on seniority, merit, or the quality or quantity of one's work. The last exception, however, is vague, stating that a difference in pay can exist if it is based on "any other factor other than sex." This language is broad enough that the courts have interpreted it broadly, dismissing cases of sex discrimination, for instance, because employers claimed that the necessities of the market require them to offer male employees higher pay to attract them to certain jobs. To prevent the courts from circumventing congressional intent for the Equal Pay Act, the Paycheck Fairness Act would require that any factors used to determine employee pay be directly related to the position.

A version of the Paycheck Fairness Act was introduced in the Senate by Hillary Clinton on January 8, 2009, the very day the Lilly Ledbetter Fair Pay Act was introduced. Although a similar bill passed in the House of Representatives in early 2009, it did not pass in the Senate, and by the end of the 111th Congress, the bill had died. President Obama indicated at the time that he would continue to encourage Congress to pass a bill that would help eliminate the wage gap between men and women, and several versions of the bill were introduced in 2011 and 2012. In these remarks, Obama specifically references S. 3220, a bill introduced by Senator Barbara Mikulski on May 22, 2012.

[T]omorrow Congress is going to have a chance to vote on the "Paycheck Fairness Act." I don't have to tell you how much this matters to families across the country. All of you are working day in, day out, to support the basic principle, equal pay for equal work.

And we've made progress. But we've got a lot more to do. Women still earn just 77 cents for every dollar a man earns. It's worse for African American women and Latinas. Over the course of her career, a woman with a college degree is going to earn hundreds of thousands of dollars less than a man who is doing the same work.

So at a time when we're in a make-or-break moment for the middle class, Congress has to step up and do its job. If Congress passes the "Paycheck Fairness Act," women are going to have access to more tools to claim equal pay for equal work. If they don't, if Congress doesn't act, then women are still going to have difficulty enforcing and pressing for this basic principle.

And we've got to understand, this is more than just about fairness. Women are the breadwinners for a lot of families, and if they're making less than men do for the same work, families are going to have to get by for less money for childcare and tuition and rent, small businesses have fewer customers. Everybody suffers.

So that's why we moved forward with the Lilly Ledbetter Fair Pay Act. That's why I established a National Equal Pay Task Force to help crack down on violations of equal pay laws. Earlier this year, the Department of Labor announced the winners of a national competition for equal pay apps that give women interactive tools and key information to help them determine if they're getting paid fairly.

So we're going to be releasing this afternoon a formal administration policy message supporting the "Paycheck Fairness Act," and we're going to call on Congress to do the right thing. But let's face it. Congress is not going to act because I said it's important; they're going to act because you guys are making your voices heard.

So Senators have to know you're holding them accountable. Everything that they're going to be hearing over the next 24 hours can make a difference in terms of how they vote.

We've got a long way to go, but we can make this happen, and together, we can keep moving forward. So let's make sure hard work pays off, responsibility is rewarded.

NOTE: The President spoke at 12:15 p.m. via conference call from the White House.

Source: President Obama's Remarks on Wage Equality, *Daily Composition of Presidential Documents,* June 4, 2012, DCPD No. 201200448. Available at http://www.gpo.gov/fdsys/pkg/DCPD-201200448/pdf/DCPD-201200448.pdf.

The White House Urges Passage of Equal Pay Legislation

White House Fact Sheet on the Paycheck Fairness Act

June 4, 2012

Today, the President continues to advocate for passage of the Paycheck Fairness Act, a comprehensive bill that strengthens the Equal Pay Act of 1963, which made it illegal for employers to pay unequal wages to men and women who perform substantially equal work. The Paycheck Fairness Act is commonsense legislation that, among other things, would achieve the following:

- Better align key Equal Pay Act defenses with those in Title VII.
- Bring remedies available under the Equal Pay Act into line with remedies available under other civil rights laws.
- Make the requirements for class action lawsuits under the Equal Pay Act match those of the Federal Rules of Civil Procedure.
- Protect employees who share their own salary information at work from retaliation by an employer.

President Obama's declaration of support for the Paycheck Fairness Act amounted to a last-ditch effort to generate public support for the bill. The White House hoped that by publicizing the vote—an important one to women's groups—Republicans could be convinced to forego a threatened filibuster of the legislation.

The existing legal tools available to remedy pay discrimination are not enough, so Congress needs to pass the Paycheck Fairness Act now.

Source: The White House, Office of the Press Secretary, "Fact Sheet: Fighting for Equal Pay and the Paycheck Fairness Act," June 4, 2012. Available at http://www.whitehouse.gov/the-press-office/2012/06/04/fact-sheet -fighting-equal-pay-and-paycheck-fairness-act.

Obama Criticizes Senate Republicans for Filibustering the Paycheck Fairness Act

President Barack Obama's Statement on Senate Action on Paycheck Fairness Legislation

June 5, 2012

This afternoon Senate Republicans refused to allow an up-or-down vote on the "Paycheck Fairness Act," a commonsense piece of legislation that would strengthen the Equal Pay Act and give women more tools to fight pay discrimination.

It is incredibly disappointing that in this make-or-break moment for the middle class, Senate Republicans put partisan politics ahead of American women and their families. Despite the progress that has been made over the years, women continue to earn substantially less than men for performing the same work. My administration will continue to fight for a woman's right for equal pay for equal work, as we rebuild our economy so that hard work pays off, responsibility is rewarded, and every American gets a fair shot to succeed.

Source: President Obama's Statement on Senate Action on Paycheck Fairness Legislation, *Daily Composition of Presidential Documents,* June 5, 2012, DCPD No. 201200452. Available at http://www.gpo.gov/fdsys/pkg/DCPD-201200452/pdf/DCPD-201200452.pdf.

Ultimately the Senate was unable to bring S. 3220 to a vote, and it died at the end of the 112th Congress, much like it had died in the 111th Congress. The legislation generated considerable opposition from Republicans in the Senate primarily due to a concern that tightening the Equal Pay Act's exclusions would open the door to litigation against employers, thus making it more expensive to run a business. It was feared that this added expense of running a business would increase unemployment and stifle the economy, making it more difficult for the country to rebound from the recession. Advocates for the Paycheck Fairness Act argue, however, that the legislation is necessary to protect women's rights to equal pay, especially as families have become more economically reliant on women working outside the home. As a show of continued support for the bill, Senator Mikulski reintroduced the bill on January 23, 2013.

The National Science Foundation Revises Its Workplace Flexibility Policies

White House Press Release

September 26, 2011

While women and girls often had to fight for equal educational opportunities in the United States, they have made significant gains in education since Title IX was passed in 1972. The statistics are impressive. Every year since 1981–1982, the number of bachelor's degrees earned by women outnumbered those earned by men, and by 2010 approximately 60 percent of all bachelor's degrees awarded in the United States were to women. The numbers are similar for master's and doctorate degrees. More women have earned master's degrees every year since 1985–1986, and since 2006–2007 more women have earned their doctorates. These gains in girls' and women's educations have even prompted some to ask whether there is a crisis in men's and boys' education. However, while women have been attaining higher education at a higher rate than men, they have not made the same sorts of gains in certain disciplines. The science, technology, engineering, and mathematics (STEM) disciplines are still the stronghold of men, and even as more women seek education in the STEM fields, the number of women moving into these careers has not grown similarly. The Obama administration took steps in 2011 to address this continuing disparity in men's and women's education and academic careers.

Today, White House Council on Women and Girls Executive Director Tina Tchen, White House Office of Science and Technology Policy Director John P. Holdren, and National Science Foundation (NSF) Director Subra Suresh announced the "NSF Career-Life Balance Initiative," a 10-year plan to provide greater work-related flexibility to women and men in research careers.

Among the best practices that NSF will expand Foundation-wide, are ones that will allow researchers to delay or suspend their grants for up to one year in order to care for a newborn or newly adopted child or fulfill other family obligations—maximizing current policy to facilitate scientists' reentry into their professions with minimal loss of momentum.

"Jump-starting girls' interest in science, technology, engineering and math—the so-called STEM subjects—and boosting the percentage of women employed in science and engineering is not just the right thing to do but is also the smart thing to do for America's future and the economy," said Tina Tchen.

"Too many young women scientists and engineers get sidetracked or drop their promising careers because they find it too difficult to balance the needs of those careers and the needs of their families," said Subra Suresh. "This new initiative aims to change that, so that the country can benefit from the full range and diversity of its talent." . . .

"If we're going to out-innovate and out-educate the rest of the world, we've got to open doors for everyone," said Mrs. Obama. "We need all hands on deck, and that means clearing hurdles for women and girls as they navigate careers in science, technology, engineering and math."

NSF—which is the leading source of Federal grants for many fields of basic research crucial to US technology development and job creation, including computer science, mathematics, and the social sciences—is also calling upon universities and research institutes to adopt similar policies for their employees and grantees.

Women today currently earn 41% of PhD's in STEM fields, but make up only 28% of tenure-track faculty in those fields. Reducing the dropout rate of women in STEM careers is especially important in the quest for gender equality because women in STEM jobs earn 33 percent more than those in non-STEM occupations and the wage gap between men and women in STEM jobs is smaller than in other fields.

TNSF has launched targeted workplace flexibility efforts in the past, but the new initiative is the first to be applied Foundation-wide to help postdoctoral fellows and early-career faculty members more easily care for dependents while continuing their careers.

The new initiative will offer a coherent and consistent set of family-friendly policies and practices to help eliminate some of the barriers to women's advancement and retention in STEM careers. It will:

- Allow postponement of grants for child birth/adoption—Grant recipients can defer their awards for up to one year to care for their newborn or newly adopted children.
- Allow grant suspension for parental leave—Grant recipients who wish to suspend their grants to take parental leave can extend those grants by a comparable duration at no cost.
- Provide supplements to cover research technicians—Principal investigators can apply for stipends to pay research technicians or equivalent staff to maintain labs while PIs are on family leave.
- Publicize the availability of family friendly opportunities—NSF will issue announcements and revise current program solicitations to expressly promote these opportunities to eligible awardees.
- Promote family friendliness for panel reviewers—STEM researchers who review the grant proposals of their peers will have greater opportunities to conduct virtual reviews rather than travel to a central location, increasing flexibility and reducing dependent-care needs.
- Support research and evaluation—NSF will continue to encourage the submission of proposals for research that would assess the effectiveness of policies aimed at keeping women in the STEM pipeline.
- Leverage and Expand Partnerships—NSF will leverage existing relationships with academic institutions to encourage the extension of the tenure clock and allow for dual hiring opportunities.

The Administration has been highly focused on the goal of increasing the participation of women and girls in STEM

While women have made gains in education and the workplace, it is interesting to note that the traditional concerns of family and motherhood continue to influence women's career paths and opportunities. There are different responses to women's concerns about balancing family and career. One approach would be that women have to make a choice: they cannot have demanding occupations such as those seen in STEM fields and still expect to have the time to devote to family life. However, opponents of this view state that if the expectations of academic institutions and the research traditions of STEM disciplines serve as barriers to women in ways that they do not for men, then these expectations and traditions should be changed. The thought is that women should not be disadvantaged by institutions when the institutions themselves can simply be changed to accommodate women's experiences. As the largest source of grants for STEM research, the NSF is in an ideal position to encourage systemic change for people working in these disciplines, and while the NSF Career-Life Balance Initiative is planned to encourage more women to stay in STEM careers, the policy changes apply to both men and women.

". . . the President's $4.35 billion Race to the Top competition, which rewards states that develop strategies to broaden the participation of women and girls and others underrepresented in science and engineering."

fields. The White House has encouraged and celebrated the participation of girls and women in STEM fields through initiatives like Educate to Innovate, which, among other goals, focuses on improving STEM education for underrepresented groups, including girls, and the President's $4.35 billion Race to the Top competition, which rewards states that develop strategies to broaden the participation of women and girls and others underrepresented in science and engineering. To achieve this, states applying for these funds receive competitive preference if they demonstrate efforts to address barriers to full participation of women and girls in these fields.

The President has appointed a strong team of women leaders to his Cabinet and White House staff, including several female scientists including EPA Administrator Lisa Jackson (an engineer), National Oceanic and Atmospheric Administration Administrator Jane Lubchenco (a marine scientist), US Geological Survey Director Marcia McNutt (a geophysicist), and Director of the Defense Department's Defense Advanced Research Projects Agency (DARPA) Regina Dugan (a mechanical engineer).

The White House has also been committed to making the government a model employer in the area of workplace flexibility. In March of 2010, The President's Council of Economic Advisors issued its first ever report on the economic benefits of workplace flexibility, concluding that it strengthens a company's bottom line while helping workers meet the needs of their families and stay in the workforce. The President hosted a White House Forum on Workplace Flexibility and the Department of Labor led subsequent efforts around the country to promote workplace flexibility and generate best practices in the private sector. To strengthen the government's position as a model employer in this area, the President signed the Telework Enhancement Act, which requires Federal agencies to take a number of significant steps to promote the use of telework, including appointing a senior telework managing officer in each Federal agency.

Several independent organizations and academic associations today announced initiatives in coordination with NSF and the White House, adding momentum to a nationwide shift that promises to strengthen the US economy and job security even as it strengthens families across the country. Among them:

• The White House Council on Women and Girls and Office of Science and Technology Policy are launching a "Women in STEM Speakers Bureau." Designed to spark the interest of girls in grades 6–12 through engagement with women-scientist role models at the top of their fields, the Speakers Bureau will deploy top Administration female STEM specialists to roundtables with students across the country.

- The National Alliance for Partnerships in Equity will announce an expansion of its signature initiative, the STEM Equity Pipeline, to provide professional development training for high-school and community college faculty and staff in STEM fields.

- The Association for Women in Science is launching a new initiative that brings together representatives from government, industry, and academia with the goal of improving STEM workplaces to promote gender equality and retention, re-entry, and re-training for women.

- The National Girls Collaborative Project will announce the FabFems Project to promote career development for young female STEM students through an online networking platform that will include female educators and professionals in STEM fields.

- The American Association of University Women will announce the expansion of successful regional programs aimed at engaging girls in STEM subjects to a national level.

- The Association of American Universities and the Association of Public Land-grant Universities will commit to looking for ways that the many institutions they represent can do more to develop, support, and promote more flexible work and learning environments for those in STEM and other disciplines.

"The Association for Women in Science is launching a new initiative that brings together representatives from government, industry, and academia with the goal of improving STEM workplaces to promote gender equality and retention, re-entry, and re-training for women."

Source: "The White House and National Science Foundation Announce New Workplace Flexibility Policies to Support America's Scientists and Their Families," The White House, Office of the Press Secretary, September 26, 2011. Available at http://www.whitehouse.gov/the-press-office/2011/09/26/white-house-and-national-science-foundation-announce-new-workplace-flexi.

Tributes to Secretary of State Hillary Clinton

Statements of Senators Tom Harkin
and Bill Nelson

January 29, 2013

Since women obtained the right to vote in
1920, the number of women serving in political office is still a small fraction of the total
positions in government. After the 2012
national election, the number of women serving in Congress did increase slightly: in the
House of Representatives, 77 women were
elected, up from 73 in the previous Congress; in the Senate, the number of women
increased from 17 to 20. Yet women still
comprise only 18 percent of the total seats
in Congress. However, elective office is only
one way to serve in government, and other
women have served in the federal government as presidential appointees in both the
executive and judicial branches of government. At the time of these comments, Hillary
Clinton was finishing her term as secretary
of state during President Obama's first term
of office. Prior to her appointment, she was
elected to the Senate from New York and had
held several unofficial posts as first lady when
her husband, Bill Clinton, was president. As
the third woman to serve as secretary of state,
Ms. Clinton's popularity may illustrate that
women are becoming more accepted in high-
level posts in the federal government.

Statement of Senator Tom Harkin

Madam President, on what is her final day as Secretary of State, I would like to express my admiration and gratitude to Hillary Rodham Clinton for the extraordinary job she has done over the last 4 years. I agree wholeheartedly with President Obama who said she has been one of the finest Secretaries of State in our Nation's history.

When she took on this responsibility in January 2009, Hillary Clinton was already one of the most celebrated and accomplished women in the world. Certainly her reputation and renown have been tremendous assets as she worked to restore America's standing in the world.

Over the last 4 years, Hillary Clinton has been the ultimate workhorse public servant as opposed to the showhorse. This comes as no surprise to me and other former colleagues in the Senate. We know she is a leader of extraordinary substance and a talent with an amazing work ethic.

Secretary of State Clinton has set records as the most traveled Secretary for time in office, visiting some 42 countries just in the last year alone. She will be remembered for her tireless efforts to promote the empowerment of women worldwide and for her many demonstrations that "smart power" and assertive diplomacy can be far more effective than so-called "hard power" and military interventions.

I am especially grateful to Secretary of State Clinton for insisting on robust assistance to Haiti in the wake of the devastating earthquake of 2010. In addition, following my visit to Vietnam in 2010, and just prior to her own visit, we talked and I had urged her to pledge America's commitment to helping Vietnam clean up the sites contaminated by Agent Orange. She agreed wholeheartedly, and this is one way she has been very successful in repairing the breach with our former adversary and doing what is right and just for the victims of Agent Orange in Vietnam.

I have many fond memories of Hillary Clinton's 8 years here in the Senate. During that entire tenure, we served together on the Committee on Health, Education, Labor, and Pensions. In that role, as in her previous role as First Lady, she was an outspoken advocate for health care reform, fighting tirelessly to secure quality affordable health care for all Americans. Although she was no longer in the Senate when the Affordable Care Act passed and was signed into law, she shares enormous credit for laying the groundwork of that historic achievement.

Hillary Clinton has been a wonderful friend to my wife Ruth and to me, and, of course, from her many campaigns in my State, she has so many friends all across the State of Iowa.

So she is retiring from the Department of State, but we all know that by no means is she a retiring person. There are many vivid chapters yet to be written in the story of Hillary Rodham Clinton.

I wish her a richly deserved rest and much success and happiness in the years ahead. . . .

Statement of Senator Bill Nelson

Madam President, I want to speak about the extraordinary public service that has been rendered by the Secretary of State and whose long record of public service I want to commend. I rise on behalf of my friend, our former colleague, our honorable Secretary of State, Hillary Clinton.

She has represented the United States. She is a world figure. She has represented America to the world, especially with her diligence, her grace, her hard work, and her incredible diplomatic skills. She has traveled to 112 countries. She has racked up 1 million miles, met with thousands of foreign dignitaries. She has reached nearly every corner of the globe and made history on the way.

In each assignment she has left an indelible mark empowering women, supporting sustainable development, supporting the establishment of civil societies, and promoting the tenets of democracy: one man, one vote; one woman, one vote; human rights; and the rule of law.

I might also note that she particularly has underscored the plight of women. Of course, we know we see societies that live almost in another time and age centuries before in the way they treat women. The Secretary of State has tried to help modernize those societies.

Madeleine Albright was the first woman to serve as secretary of state, appointed by President Clinton in 1997. Despite a smooth Senate confirmation process, Albright did face some opposition within Clinton's own administration. According to Albright biographer Thomas Blood, several of Clinton's closest advisers were concerned that being a woman would hamper Albright's effectiveness when dealing with countries that were more traditional in their views of women. Albright received considerable support from women's groups, however, and enjoyed bipartisan support in the Senate. Furthermore, she was favored by First Lady Hillary Clinton, who encouraged her husband to nominate Albright to the position. After Albright's term, President George W. Bush appointed Condoleezza Rice to serve as secretary of state, and she had the distinction of being the first African American woman to serve in the position. By the time President Obama nominated Hillary Clinton, concerns about women's ability to successfully serve as secretary of state seemed to have evaporated. In fact, according to a poll conducted by the *Washington Post* and ABC News, by the end of her term in 2013, Clinton's approval ratings were at an impressive 67 percent.

The importance of having women in office goes beyond their mere numbers. While having more women in office better reflects the demographics of the American population, it is what women bring to office that matters most to supporters of a more diverse government. If one accepts that men and women have differing experiences and perceptions because of their gender, then it makes sense that those differences would be reflected in the priorities and actions of people in public office. Thus, a government consisting predominately of men may reflect a more narrow view of government priorities than a government that has more diversity. Senator Nelson seems to note this in his recognition of Secretary Clinton's work on women's issues while in the State Department.

"When our Secretary of State confronts major national security challenges, her support has been pivotal—from the support she gave the President in the raid that took out bin Laden, to the drawdown of U.S. troops in Iraq and Afghanistan. She has been at the forefront of some of the toughest decisions of our time."

She has done so by empowering and appointing one of her personal friends, Melanne Verveer, to be the Global Ambassador for Women's Affairs. That position has taken Ambassador Verveer all over the globe. . . .

When our Secretary of State confronts major national security challenges, her support has been pivotal—from the support she gave the President in the raid that took out bin Laden, to the drawdown of U.S. troops in Iraq and Afghanistan. She has been at the forefront of some of the toughest decisions of our time.

The Secretary has also been steadfast in persuading the international community to enact crippling sanctions on Iran to isolate and to punish the regime for its pursuit of nuclear weapons.

I might say on a personal note, a Floridian has been missing for almost 6 years who was suddenly swept up and disappeared on the Iranian tourist island of Kish in the Persian Gulf. The Secretary has kept very vigilant in continuing to search for any piece of evidence of Bob Levinson and to ultimately bring him home. I thank the Secretary not only for Floridians such as myself, but for his wife, Christine Levinson, and seven children who want their father home. That quest continues unrelentingly by many people. I wanted to say thank you to Secretary Clinton for the efforts she has lent to this effort.

She has been one of the driving forces behind NATO's no-fly zone over Libya in order to prevent Qadhafi from massacring his own people. Through deft diplomacy, she has slowly opened Burma to the outside world. She is encouraging them to free political prisoners, hold parliamentary elections, and finally permit foreign investment. It is happening before our eyes.

Of course, she has taken special interest in the poorest nation in the Western Hemisphere, an island nation right off of the east coast of the United States, also less than an hour-and-a half flight from Miami; that is, the island of Haiti.

The island nation of Haiti—which is the island that Christopher Columbus was expected to have landed on, Hispaniola—now encompasses Haiti and the Dominican Republic. She has made Haiti one of the top foreign policy priorities, helping the impoverished island build back better after the devastating earthquake that killed over one-quarter of a million people. In no small measure has her husband President Clinton been a part of that attempt at restoration of Haiti from that devastating earthquake.

Last week, during Secretary Clinton's final appearance before the Senate Foreign Relations committee, she said: "Every time that blue and white airplane carrying the words 'United States of America' touches down in some far-off capital, I feel again the honor it is to represent the world's indispensable nation."

Madam Secretary, you have truly honored us with your indispensable leadership. On behalf of all our Senate colleagues, we thank you for your extraordinary service to this country.

Source: Statements by Senators Tom Harkin (D-IA) and Bill Nelson (D-FL), "Tributes to Secretary of State Hillary Clinton," *Congressional Record,* U.S. Senate, January 29, 2013, S354 and S342.

Debating Contraceptive Coverage in the Affordable Care Act

Remarks of Representatives Darrell Issa and Carolyn Maloney at Hearings of the House Committee on Oversight and Government Reform

February 16, 2012

Dialogue between Committee Chair Darrell E. Issa and Representative Carolyn Maloney

Statement of Representative Darrell E. Issa

One of President Obama's top goals for his presidency was to reform the nation's health care system. Although the health care industry in the United States is complex, the administration worked with members of Congress and leaders in the medical and insurance industries to develop comprehensive health care legislation. When the Patient Protection and Affordable Care Act was passed in 2010, it included requirements that preventative care procedures such as mammograms and colonoscopies be covered without an insurance co-pay. The law allowed additional preventative procedures to be added by the Department of Health and Human Services; included in the list of additional coverage was contraception. This required all employee insurance policies to provide contraception without co-pay. The provision of contraception created a great deal of controversy, especially for employers with a religious affiliation whose religions oppose the use of contraception. Opponents framed the issue as the government violating employers' religious liberties.

Today's hearing is a solemn one. It involves freedom of conscience. Ultimately, without the first pillar of our freedoms, the freedoms that we did not give up to our government, the American democracy and the experiment that has lasted over 200 years falls for no purpose. The architects of our Constitution believed our country would be a place that would accommodate all religions.

In fact, they could not agree on religion more than anything else.

Our Founding Fathers came from different religions, and they did not trust that one religious order would not circumvent another, for, in fact, many came from a country in which they were of one religion and had to change to another on a government edict.

Many looked at establishment of religion as all it is about, but ultimately our Founding Fathers, including Thomas Jefferson, including George Washington and others, all understood that, in fact, their conscience was their guide, and their conscience came overwhelmingly from their religious convictions, and therefore time and time again they made it clear that a man's conscience, particularly if it flowed from his faith, had a special role in our freedoms. . . .

Many will frame today not as First Amendment, but about the particular issue that comes before us related to the Obama health care plan. This is not about that. In fact, if it is about that, we should be over in the Energy and Commerce Committee or some committee dealing with health or other issues. This committee wants to fully vet with the most knowledgeable of both clergy and lay people that we could find the real questions of where does faith begin, and where does it end; where does government's ability to influence decisions made by people of faith begin, and where does it end. These basic questions go to the heart of the Constitution. . . .

I expect that we will hear from people who have spent their entire life pondering these very questions of faith and conscience. I expect we will meet in the second panel particularly from people who must execute both faith and often education and other responsibilities that have fallen to church and churchlike groups since our founding.

I take this as very solemn. I know that all of us on the panel do. The tone today is about learning and listening, and I certainly hope all of us who came here, including the students who are in the audience today, recognize how important this juncture in our democracy is.

Statement of Representative Carolyn Maloney

What I want to know is where are the women? When I look at this panel, I don't see one single woman representing the tens of millions of women across the country who want and need insurance coverage for basic preventive health care services, including family planning. Where are the women?

Mr. Chairman, I was deeply disturbed that you rejected our request to hear from a woman, a third-year student at Georgetown Law School named Sandra Fluke. She hoped to tell this committee about a classmate of hers who was diagnosed with a syndrome that causes ovarian cysts. Her doctor prescribed a pill to treat this disease, but her student insurance did not cover it. Over several months, she paid out hundreds of dollars in out-of-pocket costs until she could no longer afford her medication, and she eventually ended up losing her ovary. Your staff told us you personally rejected Ms. Fluke's testimony, saying, "The hearing is not about reproductive rights and contraception."

Of course this hearing is about rights, contraception and birth control. It is about the fact that women want to have access to basic health services, family planning through their health insurance plan. But some would prevent them from having it by using lawsuits and ballot initiatives in dozens of States to roll back the fundamental rights of women to a time when the government thought what happened in the bedroom was their business and contraceptives were illegal. Tens of millions of us who are following these hearings lived through those times, and I can tell you with great certainty we will not be forced back to that dark and primitive era.

Of the 10 witnesses who testified at this hearing, only 2 were women, both of whom spoke against the contraception coverage required by the Affordable Care Act. Representative Maloney raised the question "Where are the women?" to underscore that the people most affected by this provision—women—were largely excluded from a congressional hearing on the topic. She explains that her choice of witness, Georgetown law student Sandra Fluke, was prevented from testifying at the hearing and that the hearing was less about religious liberty than it was about suppressing women's reproductive rights. Fluke ultimately testified in front of an ad hoc committee of Democrats on her medical need for contraception and her support for its coverage. Her testimony gained national attention when conservative talk show host Rush Limbaugh made disparaging comments about her on February 29, 2012, calling her a slut and a prostitute who wanted taxpayers to pay for her sex life. Although Limbaugh ultimately apologized for his comments, the ensuing backlash, including the many advertisers who dropped their contracts with his show, may have ultimately assisted advocates for contraception coverage.

This is why last week the administration announced a common sense accommodation. Churches do not have to provide insurance coverage for contraceptives. They do not have to approve them. They do not have to prescribe them, dispense them or use them. But women will have the right to access them. Women who work at nonprofit religious entities like hospitals and universities will be able to obtain coverage directly from their insurance companies; not from religious organizations, but from independent insurance companies. Medical and health experts support this policy, economists support it, and a host of Catholic groups that were conspicuously not invited to testify today.

The vast majority of women, including women of faith, use some form of birth control at some point in their lives, whether to plan the number or spacing of their children or to address significant medical conditions. With all due respect to religious leaders, though you have every right to follow your conscience and honor the dictates of your faith, no one should have the power to impose their faith on others, to bend them to your will, simply because they happen to work for you. That in itself is an assault on the fundamental freedoms enshrined in our Constitution. . . .

I . . . urge you once again to let Ms. Fluke testify. Let one woman speak for the panel right now on this all-male panel. She is here in the audience today. She is steps away. Even if you think you will disagree with everything she says, don't we owe it to the tens of millions of American women whose lives will be affected to let just one, just one woman speak on their behalf today on this panel as requested by the Democratic minority?

Response by Representative Darrell E. Issa

This House takes very seriously the committee rules. It is a tradition, but not a rule, of the committee that the minority have a witness. It is a tradition that the minority have one witness. Just yesterday, the minority asked for and received two witnesses, one on each panel.

They were both qualified, one being a U.S. Senator. . . .

The second, today, we received, not 3 days in advance or 2 days or even a full day in advance as is the committee's requirement, but yesterday beginning at 1:30. . . .

The initial request by the minority was for two witnesses, the one who has been mentioned, and Barry Lynn. Barry

Because the Republican Party was the majority party in the House of Representatives, every House standing committee had a Republican majority and a Republican chair. Committee chairs exercise a great deal of influence in setting hearing topics and approving the witnesses who will testify. Although the minority party is generally granted the selection of at least one witness, the chair has the discretion to determine the proposed witness's qualifications and can ultimately approve or reject that witness. Chairman Issa explained that the selection of Sandra Fluke had not followed traditional protocols for a minority party witness and furthermore that she did not meet his criteria of a qualified witness, especially given the hearing's topic of religious liberty. Representatives Maloney and Eleanor Holmes Norton both left the hearing in protest of Issa's comments.

Lynn is a well-known . . . ordained minister, who has spoken on the issues of religious freedom; has entered into both civil and, in fact, legal proceedings for many, many years; is well regarded and well known, even if I disagree.

When asked about the two witness request, I asked, what are their qualifications? Additionally, I recognized immediately Barry Lynn as the executive director of Americans United for Separation of Church and State. He was, in fact, both because of his religious background and because of his position and because of his longstanding on that issue, he was fully qualified, and I accepted him.

During the intervening time outlined here, there was a retraction when we said there would only be one, and instead the minority chose the witness we had not found to be appropriate or qualified. Now, "appropriate and qualified" is a decision I have to make. I asked our staff what is her background, what has she done? They did the usual that we do when we are not provided the 3 days and the forms to go with it. They did a Google search. They looked and found that she was, in fact, and is a college student, who appears to have become energized over this issue and participated in approximately a 45-minute press conference, which is video available. . . .

I cannot and will not arbitrarily take a majority or minority witness if they do not have the appropriate credentials, both for a hearing at the full committee of the U.S. House of Representatives and if we cannot vet them in a timely fashion.

Source: *Lines Crossed: Separation of Church and State; Has the Obama Administration Trampled on Freedom of Religion and Freedom of Conscience?* U.S. House of Representatives, Committee on Oversight and Government Reform, February 16, 2012. Serial No. 112–122 (Washington, DC: U.S. Government Printing Office, 2012). Available at http://oversight.house.gov/wp-content/uploads/2012/06/02-16-12-Full-Committee-Hearing-Transcript.pdf.

A Mississippi Ballot Initiative to Change the Definition of Personhood

Voters' Guide to Arguments for and against Mississippi's Initiative No. 26

Summer 2011

Unlike the federal government, some state governments have mechanisms for citizens to participate directly in the legislative process by allowing them to vote on policy proposals. In some states, citizens with enough signatures on a petition can bring an unpopular state law to a popular vote in an attempt to overturn it, called a popular referendum. In the case of an initiative, citizens who have enough petition signatures are able to put a proposed law or constitutional amendment directly on the ballot. In 2011, Mississippi voters were given the option to vote on an initiative that would change the state constitution. Initiative 26 would mandate that the term "person" be defined to include all humans from the moment of their conception. Thus, all the rights and privileges of people living in the state would begin at the moment a man's sperm and a woman's egg meet. This brochure was developed to inform voters of Initiative 26 so they could make a more informed decision. Personhood amendments have been considered in numerous states, but so far all of these efforts have failed.

Initiative #26

Be it Enacted by the People of the State of Mississippi: SECTION 1. Article III of the constitution of the state of Mississippi is hearby amended BY THE ADDITION OF A NEW SECTION TO READ: SECTION 33. Person defined. As used in this Article III of the state constitution, "The term 'person' or 'persons' shall include every human being from the moment of fertilization, cloning or the functional equivalent thereof."

BALLOT TITLE:

Should the term "person" be defined to include every human being from the moment of fertilization, cloning, or the equivalent thereof?

BALLOT SUMMARY:

Initiative #26 would amend the Mississippi Constitution to define the word "person" or "persons," as those terms are used in Article III of the state constitution, to include every human being from the moment of fertilization, cloning, or the functional equivalent thereof.

Yes: Pro Argument by Brad Prewitt, Executive Director of the Yes on 26 Campaign Coalition

The Mississippi Personhood Amendment recognizes in our law that each individual human being has an 'unalienable' right to life from its biological beginning until natural death. When does life begin? Dr. Fritz Baumgartner of UCLA School of Medicine states: "Every human embryologist worldwide states that the life of the new individual human being begins at fertilization." The Bible tells us that God created humans "in his own image," thereby making human life sacred. Finally, the Constitution and the Declaration both ensure the fundamental right to life to all persons, without which all other rights are meaningless.

However, current Mississippi law does not protect an unborn child from being destroyed by his or her mother's choice or as part of a scientific experiment, because the unborn child is not legally classified as a "person." In Roe v. Wade the Supreme Court noted that if the "personhood (of the preborn) is established, the (abortion rights) case . . . collapses, for the fetus' right to life is then guaranteed specifically" in the Constitution. But, for the thirty eight years since Roe, the legal rights of personhood have been denied both to babies formed inside the womb and to those outside the womb by way of "cloning" and embryonic stem cell experimentation.

By voting "Yes on 26" we can amend our State Constitution and be the first in the nation to protect every human being from the very beginning of life, whether that life begins by natural or artificial means. By recognizing the personhood of our tiniest brothers and sisters, we will ensure that the preborn receive equal protection under the law regardless of their size, location, developmental stage or method of reproduction.

Since 1973 when the Supreme Court in *Roe v. Wade* invalidated state laws that made abortion illegal, opponents of legalized abortion have attempted to weaken access to abortion through restrictive state laws. These laws, such as mandatory waiting periods or required ultrasounds, do not prohibit abortion, but they do make receiving an abortion more difficult by adding expense and time to the process. Personhood USA is a Colorado-based organization that is taking antiabortion efforts in a slightly different direction. Rather than directly addressing access to abortion, the organization is attempting to get voters in a state to pass a constitutional amendment or law that defines "personhood" as beginning with fertilization of an ovum by a sperm. In this case, a zygote would have the same rights as a living, breathing human, allowing the willful killing of a zygote to fall under a state's homicide laws. With this definition in place, abortion would essentially become murder and thus illegal. Mississippi's Initiative 26 failed, but efforts are already under way to place it on the 2014 ballot.

No: Con Argument by Lynn Evans, Public Health Advocate

Sometimes an idea that seems promising has disastrous consequences. This is true for the Personhood Amendment.

In the 33 years since the first in vitro baby, hundreds of Mississippi couples who just wanted a baby of their own have thanked medical science for in vitro fertilization [IVF]. The treatment requires "harvesting" the mother's eggs, fertilizing the eggs outside the womb, and implanting the best one or two zygotes back into the womb. There, with luck, they will develop into healthy babies.

Since more than two eggs are harvested for IVF but only the best two candidates are usually implanted, what happens to the other fertilized eggs if they are defined as people? Can they be frozen, as is usually done? If frozen fertilized embryos are people, can they inherit property?

Medicine defines a pregnancy as an implanted egg. If a fertilized egg in a petri dish were to be defined as a person by passage of the Personhood Amendment, it is very likely that IVF would no longer be an option in Mississippi—especially for couples at risk for having a baby with a life-threatening genetic defect who now can choose IVF and have a healthy baby.

"Effective treatment of severe preeclampsia, molar gestation, and early ectopic pregnancies would be jeopardized by passage of the Personhood Amendment, threatening women's lives."

Not only would Mississippi couples who just want a baby be denied the option of IVF, certain forms of birth control—like IUDs—would be suddenly illegal, and miscarriages could become suspect.

Effective treatment of severe preeclampsia, molar gestation, and early ectopic pregnancies would be jeopardized by passage of the Personhood Amendment, threatening women's lives. New stem cell treatments for patients with Parkinson's disease, Lou Gehrig's disease, and cancers like leukemia and choriocarcinoma are also at risk.

If it were your friend or family member who needed the best treatment available, would you deny it to them?

Vote NO on the Personhood Amendment.

Source: Mississippi Secretary of State, *Initiative #26—Definition of a Person: Should the Term 'Person' Be Defined to Include Every Human Being from the Moment of Fertilization, Cloning or the Equivalent Thereof?* [Brochure on constitutional amendment], Summer 2011. Available at http://www.sos.ms.gov/elections/initiatives/Definition%20of%20Person-PW%20Revised.pdf.

Senator Leahy Urges Reauthorization of the Violence Against Women Act

Statements of Senator Pat Leahy
May 16 and December 20, 2012

Statement of Senator Patrick Leahy, Violence Against Women Reauthorization Act of 2012, May 16, 2012

Mr. President, last month, the Senate came together and passed the Leahy-Crapo Violence Against Women Reauthorization Act of 2012. Our legislation takes some much needed steps to help the most vulnerable victims of domestic and sexual violence, and it was passed with significant bipartisan support.

The Leahy-Crapo Violence Against Women Act was an example of what we accomplish when we put politics aside and work to find real solutions to real problems facing real Americans.

Few laws have had a greater impact on the lives of women in this country than the Violence Against Women Act (VAWA). By shining a light on the insidious crimes of domestic and sexual violence, this law's initial passage nearly 20 years ago sent a powerful message that violence against women would no longer be tolerated. The days of dismissing these crimes with a joke or a shrug were over. The resources, training and law enforcement tools provided by VAWA transformed the criminal justice and community-based response to abuse. It gave support and protection to the victims who for generations had been blamed, humiliated and ignored.

With each reauthorization of this landmark law, Congress has repeatedly shown its bipartisan commitment to ending domestic and sexual violence by building on the protections in the initial legislation and expanding the reach of VAWA to meet the remaining unmet needs of victims.

The bill that I introduced with Senator Crapo, and which passed the Senate with an overwhelming bipartisan majority just last month, is based on the successful tradition of preserving and enhancing protections. It is based on months of work with survivors, advocates, and law enforcement officers from all across the country and from across the political spectrum. We purposely avoided proposals that were extreme or divisive and selected only those proposals that law enforcement and survivors and the professionals who work with crime

Despite its history of strong bipartisan support, in October of 2011 the Violence Against Women Act (VAWA) expired, and by the end of the 112th Congress (2011–2012), Congress had yet to reauthorize the law. Congress will often pass laws that include an end date, at which time Congress has to revisit the law and pass it again to keep the law in effect. This reauthorization process allows members of Congress to reconsider the provisions of the law and make any changes they think are necessary. In 2012 both chambers of Congress considered bills that would reauthorize the VAWA, but the House and Senate versions were markedly different from one another. Like its predecessors, the Senate's version of the bill had support from both Republican and Democratic senators. Its sponsors were Democrat Patrick Leahy and Republican Mike Crapo, and it passed the Senate on a 68 to 31 vote, with 15 Republicans voting for the bill and the remaining 31 Republicans voting against it. The House version also passed but with a much slimmer margin of victory (222 to 205) and much more along party lines.

victims every day told us were essential. That is why the provisions in the Senate bill have such widespread support. More than 1,000 Federal, state, and local organizations have endorsed it, including service providers, law enforcement, religious organizations and many, many more.

The inclusive, open process of drafting this legislation is also why the Senate bill always had strong bipartisan support. It was a bipartisan effort from the beginning with eight Republican Senators cosponsoring the bill and seven more joining Democratic and Independent Senators in voting to pass the bill. We were able to move to the bill without a filibuster, to consider amendments, which were rejected, and to pass the bill with almost 70 votes. We adopted a bill of which the Senate can be proud, because it serves the interests of the American people while improving support and protection for victims of domestic violence and sexual assault.

I am alarmed the other body—the House—has chosen a different path. Instead of building on the broad bipartisan support for the Senate-passed Violence Against Women Reauthorization Act, Republican members of the House Judiciary Committee last week took up a bill, H.R. 4970, that they crafted in back rooms without the input of those who dedicate their lives to helping victims. This afternoon the House Republican leadership brought that same bill to the floor, with only minor modifications that do little to respond to the urgent concerns of victims, and is forcing an up or down vote while blocking any attempts to modify the legislation in response to the concerns raised by victims and service providers around the country.

Their legislation not only fails to include the critical improvements in the Senate bill that would increase protections for Native-American women, gay and lesbian victims, battered immigrant women, and victims on college campuses or victims in subsidized housing, it actually rolls back existing protections leaving many victims more vulnerable to sexual and domestic abuse.

Among the most troubling provisions are those that drastically undercut important, longstanding protections that are vital to the safety and protection of battered immigrant victims.

As a result of this misguided effort, the House bill is strongly opposed by many of the leading organizations that know these issues best, including the National Network to End Domestic Violence, the National Coalition Against Domestic Violence, the National Alliance to End Sexual Violence, the American

The bill introduced by Senator Leahy and passed by the Senate maintained the provisions of the previous version of the VAWA but added some protections to groups of people who had not previously been covered by the law but who have a higher incidence of sexual assault than the national average. For instance, provisions for lesbian, gay, bisexual, and transgendered (LGBT) persons were specifically addressed in the Senate bill, as were women on college campuses. Native American women were also included, with the law allowing non–Native American suspects of sexual assault to fall under the jurisdiction of tribal law enforcement and courts when the crime took place on an Indian reservation. The House version of the bill omitted these sections. Leahy and supporters of the Senate bill accused the House Republican majority of politicizing the reauthorization process because of their more conservative stance on issues such as LGBT rights. Furthermore, there was concern among House Republicans that giving jurisdiction to tribal law enforcement agencies and courts over sexual assault cases when the suspect was not Native American would lead to biased decisions against the suspect. Unfortunately for Native American women, without this change to VAWA the jurisdictional boundaries between state and tribal law enforcement agencies has often left these women without legal recourse when they were victims of violence at the hands of a non–Native American.

Bar Association, the YWCA, the Leadership Conference on Civil and Human Rights and many, many more.

The thousands of local advocates and service providers around the country that make up the National Network to End Domestic Violence warned in a letter to the House Judiciary Committee that H.R. 4970 would weaken, rather than enhance, protections for victims of domestic violence. . . .

House Republicans are headed down the wrong path. In fact, when the Senate rejected their alternative to our bipartisan bill last month by a strong bipartisan vote of only 37 in favor and 62 opposed, I had hoped that would end the partisanship and the gamesmanship and we would be able to move forward together to reauthorize the Violence Against Women Act. I was encouraged to see the lead sponsor of the Republican alternative, the distinguished senior Senator from Texas, do just that and join with us to support the bipartisan Senate bill upon final passage. . . .

Despite all this, House Republicans seem determined to destroy this bipartisan effort. As evidenced by the vote they are forcing today, they are intent on proceeding with their bill to roll back victim protections and insistent that it be done without the opportunity to consider the better, Senate-passed bill or, for that matter, any other amendments to their ill-conceived effort to undercut the Violence Against Women Act.

The House Republican bill not only fails to protect more victims, but actually weakens existing protections. I fear that it puts more lives at risk. . . .

Never before, in either Republican or Democratic administrations, Republican- or Democrat-controlled Houses or Senates, has the Violence Against Women Act been used to increase the dangers to women and so consciously disregard the unmet needs of our most vulnerable victims. Never before.

Last week the White House Advisor on Violence Against Women noted that the House Republican bill "adds burdensome, counter-productive requirements that compromise the ability of service providers to reach victims, fails to adequately protect Tribal victims, lacks important protection and services for LGBT victims, weakens resources for victims living in subsidized housing, and eliminates important improvements to address dating violence and sexual assault on college campuses." She is right.

"Never before, in either Republican or Democratic administrations, Republican- or Democrat-controlled Houses or Senates, has the Violence Against Women Act been used to increase the dangers to women and so consciously disregard the unmet needs of our most vulnerable victims. Never before."

Statement of Senator Patrick Leahy, Violence Against Women Reauthorization Act, December 20, 2012

Mr. President, I have been saying for weeks and months that we are overdue to pass into law the Leahy-Crapo

Violence Against Women Reauthorization Act, which the Senate approved in April with 68 bipartisan votes.

On January 3, 2013, the 112th Congress was brought to a close without the VAWA being reauthorized. Supporters of the 2012 Senate bill insisted that the bill would be reintroduced early in the 113th Congress, and indeed on January 22, 2013, S. 47 was introduced, a bill very similar to the Senate bill passed in 2012. On February 12, 2013, the bill passed the Senate with a vote of 78 to 22, an even bigger margin than in 2012. Sixteen days later the House of Representatives also passed the bill, by a vote of 286 to 138; 87 Republicans joined all 199 Democrats to pass the bill. This vote was the subject of some political intrigue. Although a majority of House Republicans opposed S. 47, it was clear to Speaker of the House John Boehner that the bill would pass, given the Republicans who were planning to vote with Democrats on the bill. As Speaker, it was in Boehner's authority to not bring the bill up for a vote, and in fact the unwritten Hastert Rule in the House states that the Speaker will only allow a vote if the outcome will be consistent with the majority party's views. In this case Boehner decided to buck tradition and put the bill on the House calendar, knowing that he would face criticism from his own party for doing so.

I am disappointed that the House still has not picked up this bi-partisan effort and that we are not getting the job done this year. I want everyone to know that I will be back next year, and we will get it done.

Just yesterday we were reminded again why this legislation is so important. In Colorado, a man just released from jail on domestic violence charges shot his way into a house, murdering his ex-girlfriend, and her sister, and her sister's husband, before killing himself. We have seen enough horrific violence. It is past time to act. . . .

For several weeks, I have been advocating a compromise on a key provision aimed at addressing the epidemic of domestic violence against native women. I want to compliment my partner on this bill, Senator Crapo, who has been working hard to try to bridge the divide and address concerns with the provision in our bill that gives limited jurisdiction to tribal courts to make sure that no perpetrators of domestic violence are immune from prosecution. Senator Crapo has pushed hard and has indicated a willingness to compromise significantly, as have I.

Sadly, others have continued to draw lines which would ultimately deny assistance to some of the most vulnerable victims. That is unacceptable.

I appreciate that there have at last been some renewed discussions about this bill in the House of Representatives but that is not enough. The only way to reauthorize VAWA this year is for the House to take up and pass the Senate-passed bill. If the House Republican leadership refuses to do that in the final days of this Congress, it is a shame. . . .

We have seen enough violence. If we cannot get the Leahy-Crapo bill over the finish line this year, we will come back next year, and we will get it done. I look forward to other Senators joining us as we continue this vital effort.

Source: "Violence Against Women Reauthorization Act," U.S. Senate, Statements by Senator Patrick Leahy, *Congressional Record,* May 16, 2012, S3226, and December 20, 2012, S8296.

Conclusion

When looking at the progress that has been made in women's rights, the accomplishments are impressive. Women in the United States went from not being able to own property in the middle of the 1800s to now comprising just under half the civilian labor force in the country. Women and girls cannot be prohibited from pursuing whatever education they want simply due to their sex, and they earn more college degrees than do men. Women who run for political office are just as likely to win their elections as men who are running in similar situations. Women in the United States are certainly better situated than they were when they obtained the right to vote in 1920, and for many women, these advances are easy to take for granted.

In fact, it is easy to ask whether we still even need feminism when so much has been accomplished. As early as 1998, *Time* magazine ran a cover asking "Is Feminism Dead?" asserting that the United States had moved into an era of postfeminism, in which the women's movement of the 1960s and 1970s was no longer needed. Perhaps indicative of this is the fact that a majority of Americans hold views that are consistent with feminist ideals, such as men's and women's equality, although they do not identify themselves as feminists. This acceptance of feminist ideals, while shunning the label of feminist, is one measure of how much has been accomplished by the feminist movement; these ideals are now mainstream and reflect the status quo for most people, even if these same people don't equate those ideals with feminism. However, as with most political and social movements, feminism has changed over time, and the problems identified by different groups of feminists still leave room for new issues and calls for rights to come up in the political arena. Thus, the future of women's rights in the United States may very well come down to what problems future feminists identify and to what extent they can translate their perception of these problems into public policy and mainstream culture.

For instance, when *Time* asked the iconic question of whether feminism was dead, many feminists were outraged, but the fact is that feminism had undergone a change by the late 1990s. Younger feminists built on the successes of their mothers and grandmothers but also identified problems that had not yet been addressed by

175

the earlier feminist movement. For instance, these later third-wave feminists recognized that the rights secured for women in the 1960s and 1970s, or the second wave of feminism, did not take into account differences among women but instead treated women as a monolithic group. This was especially the case in regard to work and educational opportunities. For the most part, the women who benefitted most from these policies were educated white women, that is, the types of women largely involved in the women's movement. The reality is that a woman's race, ethnicity, socioeconomic status, and sexuality will shape her experiences and opportunities, and the intersections of these various traits create different social spaces for different groups of women. This in essence will affect a woman's ability to take advantage of the rights she has been given.

For example, women who can afford higher education benefit the most from a law such as Title IX, but Title IX is only marginally beneficial to a woman who drops out of high school or doesn't have the resources to continue her education after graduation. In the 10 years between 2000 and 2010, the costs for higher education increased by 42 percent. This has a larger effect on people from middle and lower socioeconomic classes, who are less likely to attend higher education than more affluent people. Thus, while access to education is much less dependent on a person's sex today than it was 40 years ago, there are still divisions across groups of people that feminists attempt to address. In part this is because these other differences may overlap to some degree with gender.

Similarly, in cases decided since *Roe v. Wade,* the Supreme Court has allowed states to create barriers to obtaining an abortion while still not permitting the outright ban of the procedure. These barriers, such as 24-hour waiting periods and mandatory ultrasounds, have a disproportionate effect on women who lack financial resources. Wealthier women may not like the metaphorical hoops they have to jump through in order to get an abortion, but taking off another day from work or having to pay for an additional medical procedure before paying for the abortion will not present the types of difficulties that would be faced by women who are poor. Women who live in urban areas are also at an advantage, since very few rural areas in the United States have clinics that perform abortions. In Mississippi, for instance, there is only one abortion clinic still in practice for the entire state. Women in areas far from this clinic still have the right to an abortion but are simply unable to act upon that right as easily as other women. In both of these examples, the rights to an equal education or to an abortion are there for all women, but not all women can exercise the right in the same way. While third-wave feminists identified the consequences of factors such as race and socioeconomic status on women's ability to exercise their rights, this problem is arguably much harder to address through public policy than were the problems tackled by second-wave feminists.

As with the shift from second-wave to third-wave feminism, if the understanding of feminism continues to change, presumably there will continue to be discussions of women's rights that are shaped by these new conceptualizations of the term. For instance, in March 2013, Facebook's chief operating officer Sheryl Sandberg generated both anger and accolades with her book *Lean In: Women, Work, and the Will to Lead* in which she claims that women are in part responsible for the gender gaps in pay and position because they hold themselves back. While she does not deny that there are societal pressures on women to not be pushy or bossy, she says that women ought to be more assertive in order to achieve their goals and gain higher positions. Sandberg asserts that she is a feminist, but unlike the feminists of the second and third waves, she lays at least part of the blame for women's continued lag behind men at the feet of women themselves. It is difficult to know whether this model of feminism will take hold, but obviously if it were to become a more mainstream conceptualization of feminism, the discourse over women's rights would change substantially.

In general, rights in the United States have expanded over time, not only for women but also for many groups that have faced and may still face oppression. Change, however, is not often easy or quick, and as can be seen by looking at women's rights, the process can even take the occasional step back. It is important to note that when progress has occurred, it has ultimately been the result of citizens actively pursuing change. For true activism to take place, women and men must first pay attention to the actions of their government and then act on their beliefs. Activism is clearly present on many college campuses, as more universities sponsor women's centers or academic programs in women's studies. These often nationwide programs encourage activism on behalf of women, such as drawing attention to disparities in women's and men's pay on Equal Pay Day, encouraging positive body image on Love Your Body Day, or increasing awareness of violence against women through programs such as Take Back the Night and the Clothesline Project. Men can be active in any of these programs, but there are organizations and events specifically for male feminists, such as Walk a Mile in Her Shoes in which men raise awareness of sexual violence by walking a mile in high heels. Changing the perceptions and minds of both the public and governmental officials takes effort, and this need for activism will continue as Americans pursue a world in which men and women are valued equally.

Chronology

1848

Elizabeth Cady Stanton and Lucretia Mott organize the first women's convention in Seneca Falls, New York, from which the Declaration of Sentiments and Resolution emerges.

1869

The National Women's Suffrage Association is formed by Susan B. Anthony and Elizabeth Cady Stanton.

1872

The Supreme Court opinion for *Bradwell v. State of Illinois* articulates that it is legitimate for the government to prevent women from holding certain jobs because of their inherently weaker natures.

1873

The Comstock Act was passed by Congress, making it illegal to possess, disseminate, or publish any information considered obscene, including information about birth control and abortion.

1893

Colorado becomes the first state to recognize women's right to vote.

1908

In *Muller v. Oregon,* the U.S. Supreme Court upholds state laws designed to protect women by limiting the number of hours they may work in a day.

1916

Margaret Sanger opens the first birth control clinic in the United States in Brooklyn, New York.

1920

Congress creates the Women's Bureau in the U.S. Department of Labor to protect the interests of women in the workforce.

In anticipation of the Nineteenth Amendment's ratification, the League of Women Voters is created to educate women voters and to encourage participation in elections.

On August 18, the right of women to vote is officially recognized when the Nineteenth Amendment to the U.S. Constitution is ratified.

1921

Congress passes the Sheppard-Towner Maternity and Infancy Protection Act to provide support for the health care needs of women and children.

Margaret Sanger creates the American Birth Control League, the predecessor to the contemporary Planned Parenthood Federation.

1923

The Equal Rights Amendment is first introduced in Congress.

1961

President John F. Kennedy creates the Commission on the Status of Women to study and make recommendations about women in the workforce.

1963

In response to a recommendation by the Commission on the Status of Women, Congress passes the Equal Pay Act.

1964

The Civil Rights Act of 1964, one of the most comprehensive civil rights laws in the country's history, is passed by Congress.

1965

In *Griswold v. Connecticut,* the Supreme Court rules that laws prohibiting the sale of contraception to married couples are an unconstitutional violation of the right to privacy.

President Lyndon B. Johnson signs Executive Order 11246 requiring that affirmative action policies be implemented by the federal government regarding race, color, religion, and national origin. Sex was not included in the policy until 1967.

1967

President Lyndon B. Johnson signs Executive Order 11375, amending Executive Order 11246 by adding sex to the list of classifications that must be considered in employment decisions by the federal government.

1972

Congress passes the Equal Rights Amendment, although the amendment will ultimately fail to be ratified by the states.

The Patsy Takemoto Mink Equal Opportunity in Education Act, better known as Title IX, is passed by Congress to prohibit sex discrimination in education.

1973

The landmark Supreme Court case *Roe v. Wade* overturns state laws that make abortion illegal.

1975

In *Taylor v. Louisiana,* the Supreme Court rules that states cannot exclude women from a pool of potential jurors due simply to their sex.

1976

Member of Congress Henry Hyde introduces an amendment, referred to as the Hyde Amendment, to limit federal funding of abortion services through programs such as Medicaid.

1978

Congress passes the Pregnancy Discrimination Act to prohibit employers from discriminating against women on the basis of pregnancy or potential for pregnancy.

1981

Sandra Day O'Connor becomes the first woman appointed to the U.S. Supreme Court after her nomination by President Ronald Reagan and her confirmation by the Senate.

1984

The Supreme Court rules in *Grove City College v. Bell* that any educational institution that receives federal funds in any form, including student financial aid, is bound to the anti–sex discrimination provisions of Title IX.

On July 12, Geraldine Ferraro is nominated by Democratic presidential candidate Walter Mondale to be his vice presidential running mate.

The New York State Court of Appeals rules in *People v. Liberta* that a state law exempting married women from the definition of rape when the perpetrator is her husband is unconstitutional.

1989

In *Webster v. Reproductive Health Services,* the Supreme Court upholds parts of a Missouri law that allows restrictions to be placed on the use of state funds for abortion purposes.

1991

The Supreme Court rules in *United Auto Workers v. Johnson Controls* that employers who exclude female employees from working certain jobs because of potential risks to unborn children are guilty of illegal sex discrimination.

The National Breast Cancer Coalition is formed to lobby Congress for funding and other initiatives to help eliminate breast cancer.

Law professor Anita Hill testifies before the Senate Judiciary Committee in October, asserting that she had been the victim of sexual harassment by Supreme Court nominee Clarence Thomas.

1992

In *Planned Parenthood of Southeastern Pennsylvania v. Casey,* the Supreme Court upholds a Pennsylvania law that establishes requirements for a woman to obtain an abortion, such as a waiting period and parental consent for minors.

1993

On February 5 President Bill Clinton signs the Family and Medical Leave Act, which allows most employees to take unpaid leave to care for a family member without fear of losing their jobs.

1994

Congress passes the Violence Against Women Act, a law broadly supported by both Democrats and Republicans in Congress.

1996

Due to its policy of male-only admission, Virginia Military Institute is found to be in violation of the Equal Protection Clause of the Fourteenth Amendment to the Constitution in the Supreme Court case *United States v. Virginia.*

On October 13, Congress passes the Drug-Induced Rape Prevention and Punishment Act to help combat the use of date rape drugs to commit sexual assault.

1999

In *Neal v. Board of Trustees of the California State Universities,* the Ninth Circuit Court of Appeals rules that it is legal for a university to remedy discrimination against women in sports opportunities by decreasing the number of men's sports offered.

2000

Congress combines its reauthorization of the Violence Against Women Act with the Victims of Trafficking and Violence Protection Act, passed to combat the crime of human trafficking.

2003

President George W. Bush signs the Partial-Birth Abortion Ban into law to prohibit particular late-term abortions.

2005

Congress reauthorizes the Violence Against Women Act.

2007

In *Ledbetter v. Goodyear Tire and Rubber Company,* the Supreme Court rules against Lilly Ledbetter's claim of sex discrimination because of the length of time between the act of discrimination and her filing a complaint with the Equal Employment Opportunity Commission.

2009

Congress passes the Lilly Ledbetter Fair Pay Act, broadening the amount of time women have to make claims of sex discrimination against their employers.

2011

The Department of Health and Human Services issues guidelines for reproductive health coverage under the Affordable Care Act, which includes insurance coverage of contraception with no co-pay.

Congress fails to reauthorize the Violence Against Women Act, and the law is allowed to expire for the first time since 1994.

Voters in the state of Mississippi vote against a constitutional amendment that would define legal personhood as beginning at the moment of conception.

2012

Congress fails to pass the Paycheck Fairness Act, a bill supported by President Barack Obama to give additional protections against sex discrimination to women than provided for in the Lilly Ledbetter Fair Pay Act of 2009.

2013

Congress overcomes partisan conflict and reauthorizes the Violence Against Women Act.

Glossary

abortion: In popular usage, abortion refers to a medical procedure that intentionally brings an end to a pregnancy. This can be accomplished in one of several ways, depending on the length of the pregnancy. Early in a pregnancy a combination of hormone drugs can induce an abortion, and later in a pregnancy there are several surgical procedures in which the embryo or fetus is removed from a woman's uterus.

amici: Abbreviation of the Latin phrase "amicus curiae," which literally means "friend of the court." In judicial terminology, the term is used for information or concerns that are formally submitted to the U.S. Supreme Court by individuals or groups with an interest in a case.

bona fide occupational qualification (BFOQ): An exception to the prohibition against sex discrimination found in Title VII of the Civil Rights Act of 1964. The law allows a person's sex to be considered in employment decisions when sex is relevant to a particular job.

circuit court of appeals: One of 12 regional courts in the federal judiciary that can review the decisions of federal district courts. The decisions of courts of appeal apply only to the states in its region, or circuit, but can be further reviewed by the U.S. Supreme Court and applied more broadly to the country.

civil rights: The rights of citizens to be treated equally. Civil rights are protected in the U.S. Constitution by the Thirteenth and Fourteenth Amendments and also by numerous federal and state laws that prohibit discrimination due to certain personal characteristics, such as sex, race, color, national origin, religion, disability, and age. Some states add sexual orientation to this list.

congressional hearing: The method by which congressional committees receive information from the public about issues or bills being considered by the committee. Witnesses testify by invitation and are often experts in an area or have some direct experience with an issue being considered.

Congressional Record: The published record of all activities that take place in the full House of Representatives and the Senate, including votes, debates, and statements.

contraception: Another term for birth control, which is the intentional attempt to prevent pregnancy through various devices such as condoms, drugs, surgeries for sterilization, and sexual practices.

date rape: Sometimes referred to more broadly as acquaintance rape, the term usually indicates that a person was raped by someone she or he knows socially but is not limited to people who are actually on a date. The term grew in usage with the prevalence of so-called date rape drugs being used to commit sexual assault.

district court: A federal trial court that can hear both civil and criminal cases. These 94 courts comprise the lowest level of the federal court system and are the origination for most cases in the federal judiciary. There is at least 1 federal district court in every state.

domestic violence: A method of controlling a person with whom one has an intimate relationship through physical, emotional, and/or psychological abuse. Domestic violence can be committed by a family member, a spouse, or a partner. Although people of both sexes can be victims of domestic abuse, it is more common for women to be the victims of male abusers.

Equal Employment Opportunity Commission (EEOC): The federal agency that enforces antidiscrimination laws. Created by Congress in the Civil Rights Act of 1964, the EEOC investigates claims of employment discrimination due to race, color, national origin, sex, religion, age, and disability and may file a lawsuit if the claims are substantiated.

Equal Rights Amendment: A proposed amendment to the U.S. Constitution that would make it unconstitutional to deny people equal rights on account of their sex. Although written and first introduced to Congress in 1923, the Equal Rights Amendment was not approved by Congress until 1972. The amendment failed when too few states ratified it.

eugenics: A process of manipulating reproduction to encourage, discourage, or prevent certain types of people from having children. Eugenics in the United States was historically directed at African Americans, felons, and mentally disabled people and was accomplished by encouraging or requiring the use of birth control, abortion, or sterilization.

feminism: The movement that advocates for economic, political, and social equality between women and men. Feminism often combines the belief in equality with activism to promote policies and societal practices that can bring about this equality in practice.

Fifteenth Amendment: An 1870 amendment to the U.S. Constitution that prohibits discrimination in voting rights due to race, color, or previous condition of servitude. Women's suffrage organizations had hoped to add sex discrimination to the list of prohibited discrimination to obtain the right to vote, but the amendment applied only to men.

Fourteenth Amendment: An amendment to the U.S. Constitution ratified in 1968 that defines American citizenship and grants certain rights to all citizens, including the rights to due process under the law and equal protection under the law. These rights are referred to as the Due Process Clause and the Equal Protection Clause and serve as a basis for citizens' civil rights.

gender: The social roles, traits, and behaviors that are associated with the different sex categories. While sex differences between males and females are physiological, the gender differences of masculinity and femininity are considered learned, or socially constructed, behaviors.

human trafficking: The illegal trade and exploitation of human beings for financial purposes. This can include forced labor, such as in factories or as domestic workers, or can take place as sex slavery in which people, usually women, are forced into prostitution.

intimate partner violence: Similar to domestic violence, this is violence that occurs between intimate partners, such as a spouse or current or former partner. Women are significantly more likely to be victims of violence at the hand of an intimate partner, including battering, sexual assault, stalking, and emotional and psychological forms of abuse.

mammogram: An X-ray procedure that can alert physicians to the presence of cancer in a person's breast and give physicians a better indication of location and size of the cancer. Mammograms have resulted in earlier detection of breast cancer and better outcomes for treatment.

National Organization for Women: A women's rights organization created in 1966 to help achieve equality for women. Feminist in outlook, members engage in political activism and lobby government officials on issues such as equal education and workplace opportunities, reproductive rights, violence against women, and racism.

National Right to Life: An antiabortion rights organization created in 1968 to promote laws and policies that prohibit or discourage abortions. The organization is also active on other issues considered detrimental to human life, such as human cloning, assisted suicide, and stem cell research.

Nineteenth Amendment: The 1920 amendment to the U.S. Constitution that granted women the right to vote.

opinion of the court: Refers to the explanation provided by a federal court for a decision it makes on a case, generally at the circuit court or Supreme Court levels. The majority opinion is the primary explanation for the court's decision, although nonbinding concurrent and dissenting opinions can also be prepared if there is some disagreement on the court.

personhood: This is the concept that defines when a living human being is entitled to rights, such as those rights associated with citizenship of a country or with simply being human. In the United States, opponents of abortion have attempted to legally define personhood as beginning at conception as a political means to ban the practice of abortion.

Planned Parenthood Federation of America: A health care provider operating more than 750 clinics in the United States that focuses primarily on women's health and their reproductive health needs. Although Planned Parenthood provides a breadth of health services, because some clinics offer abortion services the organization has come under political attack from abortion opponents.

second-wave feminism: A term used to describe the feminist movement from the 1960s through the 1980s. This movement focused primarily on women's equality in the areas of employment rights, education, and reproductive rights.

sexual harassment: A form of sex discrimination that generally takes place in the workplace or in educational institutions and involves either the request of sexual favors in exchange for some advantage, called quid pro quo harassment, or the creation of an environment that is intimidating to a person of a particular sex, called hostile work environment.

sexual violence: A term that encompasses many sexual acts that are attempted or completed against a person and are against that person's will, including rape, molestation, sexual assault, exhibitionism, stalking, and threats of these acts.

social construction: The idea that certain aspects of humanity and its perceptions of reality are dependent on the society in which people live. As applied to gender differences, this theory leads to the conclusion that masculinity and femininity are learned behaviors, influenced by society, rather than based on the physiological differences between males and females.

suffrage: This term refers to the right of people to vote in political elections. In the United States, suffrage has been expanded to include almost all citizens 18 years of age and older.

Susan G. Komen Foundation: An organization founded in 1982 to advocate for people with breast cancer by raising funds for research, providing education on the disease, and lobbying the government to provide different breast cancer programs. It is the largest breast cancer advocacy group in the United States.

third-wave feminism: A term used to describe the movement for women's rights from the early 1990s into the 2000s. This movement encompasses a broader range of issues and people than was included in the second wave of feminism, including the perspectives of women from various races, cultures, and sexualities.

viability of a fetus: The point in a pregnancy at which a fetus is able to live outside its mother's uterus. The point of viability has become politically relevant as opponents of abortion have attempted to limit women's access to abortion after the point of viability. This is not an easy point to determine, however, because technological advances have lowered the average age of viability.

women's movement: A general term referring to the efforts of women to gain equality in the United States. There have been two main eras of the women's movement: the early movement from the mid-1800s until the early 1900s that focused on political rights and the movement of the 1960s and 1970s that focused on employment, education, and reproductive rights issues.

Bibliography

Beauvoir, Simone de. 1953. *The Second Sex*. Translated by H. M. Parshley. New York: Knopf.

Black, M. C., et al. 2011. *The National Intimate Partner and Sexual Violence Survey: 2010 Summary Report*. Atlanta, GA: National Center for Injury Prevention and Control, Centers for Disease Control and Prevention, http://www.cdc.gov/ViolencePrevention/pdf/NISVS_Report2010-a.pdf.

Bradwell v. State of Illinois, 83 US 130 (1872).

Brownback, Sen. [KS], et al. 2000. *Congressional Record* 146 (October 11): S10164–S10188.

Center for American Women and Politics. 2013. "Women in Elective Office 2013." Eagleton Institute of Politics, Rutgers University, Newark, NJ, http://www.cawp.rutgers.edu/fast_facts/levels_of_office/documents/elective.pdf.

Centers for Disease Control and Prevention. 2008. *Surveillance for Violent Deaths: National Violent Death Reporting System, 16 States, 2005*. Morbidity and Mortality Weekly Report 57 (SS-3), http://www.cdc.gov/mmwr/pdf/ss/ss5703.pdf.

Centers for Disease Control and Prevention. 2012. "Reproductive Health: Data and Statistics." Centers for Disease Control and Prevention, http://www.cdc.gov/reproductivehealth/data_stats/#abortion.

Clinton, William J. 1993. "Statement on Signing the Family and Medical Leave Act." *Weekly Compilation of Presidential Documents*, February 5.

Dewey, John. 1885. "Education and the Health of Women." *Science* 6 (151): 341–342.

Elshtain, Jean Bethke. 1981. *Public Man, Private Woman: Women in Social and Political Thought*. Princeton, NJ: Princeton University Press.

"Executive Order No. 11246." *Federal Register* 30 (September 24, 1965): 12319.

"Executive Order No. 11375." *Federal Register* 32 (October 13, 1967): 14303.

Friedan, Betty. 1963. *The Feminine Mystique*. New York: Norton.

Griswold v. Connecticut, 381 US 479 (1965).

Grove City Collect v. Bell, 465 US 555 (1984).

Harkin, Rep. [IA], and Rep. Nelson [FL]. 2013. "Tribute to Secretary of State Hillary Clinton." *Congressional Record* 159 (January 29): S354, S342.

Hyde, Rep. [IL]. 1976. "Amendment Offered by Mr. Hyde." *Congressional Record* (June 24): H20410.

Kennedy, John F. 1963. "Remarks Upon Signing the Equal Pay Act." *Weekly Compilation of Presidential Documents.* June 10.

Leahy, Sen. [VT]. 2012. "Violence Against Women Reauthorization Act of 2012." *Congressional Record* 158. May 16: S3226. http://www.gpo.gov/fdsys/pkg/CREC-2012-05-16/pdf/CREC-2012-05-16.pdf.

Leahy, Sen. [VT]. 2012. "Violence Against Women Reauthorization Act." *Congressional Record* 158 (December 20): S8296. http://www.gpo.gov/fdsys/pkg/CREC-2012-12-20/html/CREC-2012-12-20-pt1-PgS8295.htm.

Maloney, Rep., and Rep. McCarthy [NY]. 2011. "Honoring Geraldine Ferraro." *Congressional Record* 157 (April 5): H2298. http://www.gpo.gov/fdsys/pkg/CREC-2011-04-05/html/CREC-2011-04-05-pt1-PgH2298-2.htm.

McCullum, Rep. [FL], et al. 1996. "Drug-Induced Rape Prevention and Punishment Act of 1996." *Congressional Record* 142 (September 25): H11122–H11126.

Mississippi Secretary of State. 2011. "Initiative #26—Definition of a Person: Should the Term 'Person' Be Defined to Include Every Human Being from Moment of Fertilization, Cloning, or the Equivalent Thereof?" http://www.sos.ms.gov/initiatives/Definition%20of%20Person-PW%20Revised.pdf.

Muller v. Oregon, 208 US 412 (1908).

Neal v. Board of Trustees of the California State University, 198 F.3d 763 (9th Cir. 1999).

Obama, Barack. 2012. "President Obama's Remarks on Wage Equality." *Daily Composition of Presidential Documents,* June 4.

Olson, Kathryn. 2012. "America's Girls Need Sports." Women's Media Center, http://www.womensmediacenter.com/feature/entry/americas-girls-need-sports.

People v. Liberta, 64 N.Y.2d 152 (1984).

Planned Parenthood of Southeastern Pennsylvania v. Casey, 505 US 833 (1992).

Rich, Adrienne. 1995. "Claiming an Education." Presented at Douglass College Convocation, September 6, 1977. In Adrienne Rich, *On Lies, Secrets, and Silence,* 231–235. New York: Norton.

Roe v. Wade, 410 US 113 (1973).

Sandberg, Sheryl. 2013. *Lean In: Women, Work, and the Will to Lead.* New York: Knopf.

Sanger, Margaret. 1920. *Woman and the New Race.* New York: Brentano's.

Smith, Rep. [VA], et al. 1964. "Amendment Offered by Mr. Smith of Virginia." *Congressional Record* 110 (February 8): H2577.

Stanton, Elizabeth Cady. 1848. "Declaration of Sentiments and Resolutions." America.gov Archive, http://www.america.gov/st/pubs-english/2005/May/20050531160341liameruoy0.2459375.html.

Stanton, Elizabeth Cady, and Sojourner Truth. 1867. Statements from the "Proceedings of the First Anniversary of the American Equal Rights Association, Church of the Puritans, New York, May 9 and 10." Library of Congress, American Memory, http://memory.loc.gov/cgi-bin/query/r?ammem/rbnawsa:@field(DOCID+@lit(rbnawsan3542)).

Taylor v. Louisiana, 419 US 522 (1975).

"Testimony of Anita F. Hill, Professor of Law, University of Oklahoma, Norman, OK." *Nomination of Judge Clarence Thomas to be Associate Justice of the Supreme Court of the United States: Hearings before the Committee on the Judiciary, United States*

Senate, One Hundred Second Congress, First Session. October 11–13, 1991. http://www.loc.gov/law/find/nominations/thomas/hearing-pt4.pdf.

Truman, Jennifer L., and Michael Planty. 2012. *Criminal Victimization, 2011.* U.S. Department of Justice, Office of Justice Programs, Bureau of Justice Statistics, http://www.bjs.gov/content/pub/pdf/cv11.pdf.

United Automobile Workers v. Johnson Controls, 499 US 187 (1991).

United States v. Virginia, 518 US 515 (1996).

U.S. Congress, House Committee on Education and Labor. 2007. *Justice Denied? The Implications of the Supreme Court's Decision in Ledbetter v. Goodyear Employment Discrimination Decision.* 110th Cong., 1st Sess., June 12. U.S. Government Printing Office, http://www.gpo.gov/fdsys/pkg/CHRG-110hhrg35806/pdf/CHRG-110hhrg35806.pdf.

U.S. Congress, House Committee on Interstate and Foreign Commerce. 1920. *Public Protection of Maternity and Infancy.* 66th Cong., 3rd Sess., December 20, 21, 22, 23, 28, and 29.

U.S. Congress, House Committee on Labor and Senate Committee on Education and Labor. 1920. *Equal Pay Act.* 66th Cong., 2nd Sess., March 4.

U.S. Congress, House Committee on Oversight and Government Reform. 2012. *Lines Crossed: Separation of Church and State; Has the Obama Administration Trampled on Freedom of Religion and Freedom of Consciences?* 112th Cong., 2nd sess., February 16.

U.S. Congress, House Committee on Rules. 1917. *Creating a Committee on Woman Suffrage in the House of Representatives.* 65th Cong., 1st Sess. May 19.

U.S. Congress, House Special Subcommittee on Education of the Committee on Education and Labor. 1970. *Discrimination against Women.* 91st Cong., 2nd Sess., June 17.

U.S. Congress, House Subcommittee on the Constitution of the Committee on the Judiciary. 2003. *Partial-Birth Abortion Ban Act of 2003.* 108th Cong., 1st Sess., March 25.

U.S. Congress, House Subcommittee on Crime and Criminal Justice of the Committee on the Judiciary. 1992. *Violence against Women.* 102nd Cong., 2nd Sess., February 6.

U.S. Congress, Senate Committee on the Judiciary. 1981. *Nomination of Sandra Day O'Connor of Arizona to Serve as an Associate Justice of the Supreme Court of the United States.* 97th Cong., 1st Sess., September 9–11.

U.S. Congress, Senate Committee on the Judiciary. 1993. *The Response to Rape: Detours on the Road to Equal Justice.* 103rd Cong., 1st Sess., May 1993.

U.S. Congress, Senate Subcommittee on Aging of the Committee on Labor and Human Resources. *Why Are We Losing the War on Breast Cancer?* 102nd Cong., 1st Sess., June 20.

U.S. Congress, Senate Subcommittee of the Committee on the Judiciary. 1932. *Birth Control.* 72 Cong., 1st Sess., May 12–20.

U.S. Congress, Senate Subcommittee on Constitutional Amendments of the Committee on the Judiciary. 1970. *The Equal Rights Amendment.* 91st Cong., 2nd Sess., May 5–7.

U.S. Congress, Senate Subcommittee on Employment and Workplace Safety of the Committee on Health, Education, Labor, and Pensions. 2007. *Too Much, Too Long? Domestic Violence in the Workplace.* 110th Cong., 1st Sess., April 17.

U.S. Department of Education. 2012. "Fast Facts: Degrees Conferred by Sex and Race." National Center for Education Statistics, http://nces.ed.gov/fastfacts/display.asp?id=72.

U.S. Department of Labor. 2012. "Civilian Labor Force Participation Rates by Age, Sex, Race, and Ethnicity." Bureau of Labor Statistics, www.bls.gov/emp/ep_table_303.htm.

U.S. Department of Labor. 2013. "Unemployment by Sex and Age, December 2012." Bureau of Labor Statistics, www.bls.gov/oped/ted/2013/ted_20130108.htm.

U.S. Department of State. 2012. *Trafficking in Persons Report, 2012.* http://www.state.gov/documents/organization/192587.pdf.

Webster v. Reproductive Health Services, 492 US 490 (1989).

White House, Office of the Press Secretary. 2011. "The White House and National Science Foundation Announce New Workplace Flexibility Policies to Support America's Scientists and Their Families." http://www.whitehouse.gov/the-press-office/2011/09/26/white-house-and-national-science-foundation-announce-new-workplace-flexi.

Index

About the Author

Aimee D. Shouse is professor and chair of the Department of Women's Studies at Western Illinois University. She received her PhD in political science from Vanderbilt University (1996). Shouse is the author of *Presidents from Nixon through Carter, 1969–1981: Presenting the Issues in Pro and Con Primary Documents* (Greenwood, 2002) and coedited, with Richard J. Hardy, Janna Deitz, and Johngo Lee, *The Presidential Contest 2008: Essential Readings and Voter Information* (Kendall Hunt Publishing, 2007).